Under the Skin

MW00779601

Under the Skin considers the motivation behind why people pierce, tattoo, cosmetically enhance, or otherwise modify their body, from a psychoanalytic perspective. It discusses how the therapist can understand and help individuals for whom the manipulation of the body is felt to be psychically necessary, regardless of whether the process of modification causes pain.

In this book, psychoanalyst Alessandra Lemma draws on her work in the consulting room, as well as films, fiction, art and clinical research, to suggest that the motivation for extensively modifying the surface of the body, and being excessively preoccupied with its appearance, comes from the person's internal world – under their skin. Topics covered include:

- body image disturbance
- appearance anxiety
- body dysmorphic disorder
- the psychological function of cosmetic surgery, tattooing, piercing and scarification.

Under the Skin provides a detailed study of the challenges posed by our embodied nature through an exploration of the unconscious phantasies that underlie the need for body modification, making it essential reading for all clinicians working with those who are preoccupied with their appearance and modify their bodies including psychotherapists, counsellors, psychiatrists and psychologists.

Alessandra Lemma is a psychoanalyst and a clinical and counselling psychologist. She is a Member of the British Psychoanalytic Society, a Senior Member of the British Association of Psychotherapists, and Associate Fellow of the British Psychological Society. She is the Trust-wide Head of Psychology at the Tavistock and Portman NHS Foundation Trust and Honorary Professor of Psychological Therapies at the School of Health and Human Sciences, Essex University. She has published widely on psychotherapy and psychoanalysis.

Under the Skin

A psychoanalytic study of body modification

Alessandra Lemma

Routledge
Taylor & Francis Group

LONDON AND NEW YORK

First published 2010
by Routledge
27 Church Road, Hove, East Sussex BN3 2FA

Simultaneously published in the USA and Canada
by Routledge
711 Third Avenue, New York, NY 10017

Routledge is an imprint of the Taylor & Francis Group, an Informa business

Typeset in Times by Garfield Morgan, Swansea, West Glamorgan
Paperback cover design by Andy Ward

British Library Cataloguing in Publication Data
A catalogue record for this book is available from the British Library

Library of Congress Cataloging-in-Publication Data
Lemma, Alessandra.
   Under the skin : a psychoanalytic study of body modification / Alessandra
Lemma.
        p. cm.
   Includes bibliographical references and index.
   ISBN 978-0-415-48569-2 (hardback) – ISBN 978-0-415-48570-8 (pbk.)
1. Tattooing–Psychological aspects. 2. Body piercing–Psychological aspects.
3. Permanent makeup–Psychological aspects. 4. Psychoanalysis. I. Title.
   GT2345.L46 2010
   391.6'5–dc22

                                                                2009033331

ISBN: 978-0-415-48569-2 (hbk)
ISBN: 978-0-415-48570-8 (pbk)

To Jeremy and Matteo

THE NEW LIBRARY OF PSYCHOANALYSIS

General Editor: Alessandra Lemma

The New Library of Psychoanalysis was launched in 1987 in association with the Institute of Psychoanalysis, London. It took over from the International Psychoanalytical Library which published many of the early translations of the works of Freud and the writings of most of the leading British and Continental psychoanalysts.

The purpose of the New Library of Psychoanalysis is to facilitate a greater and more widespread appreciation of psychoanalysis and to provide a forum for increasing mutual understanding between psychoanalysts and those working in other disciplines such as the social sciences, medicine, philosophy, history, linguistics, literature and the arts. It aims to represent different trends both in British psychoanalysis and in psychoanalysis generally. The New Library of Psychoanalysis is well placed to make available to the English-speaking world psychoanalytic writings from other European countries and to increase the interchange of ideas between British and American psychoanalysts. Through the *Teaching Series*, the New Library of Psychoanalysis now also publishes books that provide comprehensive, yet accessible, overviews of selected subject areas aimed at those studying psychoanalysis and related fields such as the social sciences, philosophy, literature and the arts.

The Institute, together with the British Psychoanalytical Society, runs a low-fee psychoanalytic clinic, organizes lectures and scientific events concerned with psychoanalysis and publishes the *International Journal of Psychoanalysis*. It runs the a training course in psychoanalysis which leads to membership of the International Psychoanalytical Association – the body which preserves internationally agreed standards of training, of professional entry, and of professional ethics and practice for psychoanalysis as initiated and developed by Sigmund Freud. Distinguished members of the Institute have included Michael Balint, Wilfred Bion, Ronald Fairbairn, Anna Freud, Ernest Jones, Melanie Klein, John Rickman and Donald Winnicott.

Previous general editors have included David Tuckett, who played a very active role in the establishment of the New Library. He was followed as general editor by Elizabeth Bott Spillius, who was in turn followed by Susan Budd and then by Dana Birksted-Breen.

Current members of the Advisory Board include Liz Allison, Giovanna di Ceglie, Rosemary Davies and Richard Rusbridger.

Previous Members of the Advisory Board include Christopher Bollas, Ronald Britton, Catalina Bronstein, Donald Campbell, Sara Flanders, Stephen grosz, John Keene, Eglé Laufer, Alessandra Lemma, Juliet Mitchell, Michael Parsons, Rosine Jozef Perelberg, Mary Target and David Taylor.

ALSO IN THIS SERIES

Impasse and Interpretation Herbert Rosenfeld
Psychoanalysis and Discourse Patrick Mahony
The Suppressed Madness of Sane Men Marion Milner
The Riddle of Freud Estelle Roith
Thinking, Feeling, and Being Ignacio Matte Blanco
The Theatre of the Dream Salomon Resnik
Melanie Klein Today: Volume 1, Mainly Theory Edited by Elizabeth Bott Spillius
Melanie Klein Today: Volume 2, Mainly Practice Edited by Elizabeth Bott Spillius
Psychic Equilibrium and Psychic Change: Selected Papers of Betty Joseph Edited by Michael Feldman and Elizabeth Bott Spillius
About Children and Children-No-Longer: Collected Papers 1942–80 Paula Heimann. Edited by Margret Tonnesmann
The Freud–Klein Controversies 1941–45 Edited by Pearl King and Riccardo Steiner
Dream, Phantasy and Art Hanna Segal
Psychic Experience and Problems of Technique Harold Stewart

Clinical Lectures on Klein & Bion Edited by Robin Anderson
From Fetus to Child Alessandra Piontelli
A Psychoanalytic Theory of Infantile Experience: Conceptual and Clinical Reflections E Gaddini. Edited by Adam Limentani
The Dream Discourse Today Edited and introduced by Sara Flanders
The Gender Conundrum: Contemporary Psychoanalytic Perspectives on Feminity and Masculinity Edited and introduced by Dana Breen
Psychic Retreats John Steiner
The Taming of Solitude: Separation Anxiety in Psychoanalysis Jean-Michel Quinodoz
Unconscious Logic: An Introduction to Matte-Blanco's Bi-logic and its Uses Eric Rayner
Understanding Mental Objects Meir Perlow
Life, Sex and Death: Selected Writings of William Gillespie Edited and introduced by Michael Sinason
What Do Psychoanalysts Want?: The Problem of Aims in Psychoanalytic Therapy Joseph Sandler and Anna Ursula Dreher
Michael Balint: Object Relations, Pure and Applied Harold Stewart
Hope: A Shield in the Economy of Borderline States Anna Potamianou
Psychoanalysis, Literature & War: Papers 1972–1995 Hanna Segal
Emotional Vertigo: Between Anxiety and Pleasure Danielle Quinodoz
Early Freud and Late Freud Ilse Grubrich-Simitis
A History of Child Psychoanalysis Claudine and Pierre Geissmann
Belief and Imagination: Explorations in Psychoanalysis Ronald Britton
A Mind of One's Own: A Psychoanalytic View of Self and Object Robert A Caper
Psychoanalytic Understanding of Violence and Suicide Edited by Rosine Jozef Perelberg
On Bearing Unbearable States of Mind Ruth Riesenberg-Malcolm
Psychoanalysis on the Move: The Work of Joseph Sandler Edited by Peter Fonagy, Arnold M. Cooper and Robert S. Wallerstein
The Dead Mother: The Work of André Green Edited by Gregorio Kohon
The Fabric of Affect in the Psychoanalytic Discourse André Green
The Bi-Personal Field: Experiences of Child Analysis Antonino Ferro
The Dove that Returns, the Dove that Vanishes: Paradox and Creativity in Psychoanalysis Michael Parsons
Ordinary People, Extra-ordinary Protections: A Post Kleinian Approach to the Treatment of Primitive Mental States Judith Mitrani
The Violence of Interpretation: From Pictogram to Statement Piera Aulagnier
The Importance of Fathers: A Psychoanalytic Re-Evaluation Judith Trowell and Alicia Etchegoyen
Dreams That Turn Over a Page: Paradoxical Dreams in Psychoanalysis Jean-Michel Quinodoz
The Couch and the Silver Screen: Psychoanalytic Reflections on European Cinema Andrea Sabbadini
In Pursuit of Psychic Change: The Betty Joseph Workshop Edited by Edith Hargreaves and Arturo Varchevker
The Quiet Revolution in American Psychoanalysis: Selected Papers of Arnold M. Cooper Arnold M. Cooper, Edited and Introduced by Elizabeth L. Auchincloss
Seeds of Illness and Seeds of Recovery: The genesis of suffering and the role of psychoanalysis Antonino Ferro
The Work of Psychic Figurability: Mental States Without Representation César Botella and Sára Botella
Key Ideas for a Contemporary Psychoanalysis: Misrecognition and Recognition of the Unconscious André Green
The Telescoping of Generations: Listening to the Narcissistic Links Between Generations Haydée Faimberg
Glacial Times: A Journey through the World of Madness Salomon Resnik
This Art of Psychoanalysis: Dreaming Undreamt Dreams and Interrupted Cries Thomas H Ogden
Psychoanalysis and Religion in the 21st Century: Competitors or Collaborators? David M. Black
Recovery of the Lost Good Object Eric Brenman
The Many Voices of Psychoanalysis Roger Kennedy
Feeling the Words: Neuropsychoanalytic Understanding of Memory and the Unconscious Mauro Mancia
Constructions and the Analytic Field: History, Scenes and Destiny Domenico Chianese

Projected Shadows: Psychoanalytic Reflections on the Representation of Loss in European Cinema
Edited by Andrea Sabbadini
Encounters with Melanie Klein: Selected Papers of Elizabeth Spillius Elizabeth Spillius
Yesterday, Today and Tomorrow Hanna Segal
*Psychoanalysis Comparable and Incomparable: The Evolution of a Method to Describe and Compare
Psychoanalytic Approaches* David Tuckett, Roberto Basile, Dana Birksted-Breen, Tomas Böhm, Paul
Denis, Antonino Ferro, Helmut Hinz, Arne Jemstedt, Paola Mariotti and Johan Schubert
Time, Space and Phantasy Rosine Jozef Perelberg
Rediscovering Psychoanalysis: Thinking and Dreaming, Learning and Forgetting Thomas H. Ogden
Mind Works: Techniques and Creativity in Psychoanalysis Antonino Ferro
Doubt Conviction and the Analytic Process: Selected Papers of Michael Feldman Michael Feldman
Melanie Klein in Berlin: Her First Psychoanalyses of Children Claudia Frank
The Psychotic Wavelength: A Psychoanalytic Perspective for Psychiatry
Richard Lucas
Betweenity: A Discussion of the Concept of Borderline Judy Gammelgaard
The Intimate Room: Theory and Technique of the Analytic Field Giuseppe Civitarese
Bion Today Edited by Chris Mawson
Secret Passages: The Theory and Technique of Interpsychic Relations Stefano Bolognini
*Intersubjective Processes and the Unconscious: An Integration of Freudian, Kleinian and Bionian
Perspectives* Lawrence J. Brown
Seeing and Being Seen: Emerging from a Psychic Retreat John Steiner
Avoiding Emotions, Living Emotions Antonio Ferro
Projective Identification: The Fate of a Concept Edited by Elizabeth Spillius and Edna
O'Shaughnessy
Creative Readings: Essays on Seminal Analytic Works Thomas Ogden
The Maternal Lineage Edited by Paola Mariotti
Donald Winnicott Today Edited by Jan Abram
Symbiosis and Ambiguity: A Psychoanalytic Study Edited by John Churcher, José Bleger and
Leopoldo Bleger
Psychotic Temptation Liliane Abensour
The Theory and Technique of Psychoanalytic Supervision: The Sao Paulo Clinical Seminars Antonino
Ferro

TITLES IN THE NEW LIBRARY OF PSYCHOANALYSIS TEACHING SERIES

Reading Freud: A Chronological Exploration of Freud's Writings Jean-Michel Quinodoz
Listening to Hanna Segal: Her Contribution to Psychoanalysis Jean-Michel Quinodoz
Reading French Psychoanalysis Edited by Dana Birksted-Breen, Sara Flanders and Alain Gibeault
Reading Winnicott Lesley Caldwell and Angela Joyce
Initiating Psychoanalysis: Perspectives Bernard Reith, Sven Lagerlöf, Penelope Crick, Mette Møller
and Elisabeth Skale
Infant Observation Frances Salo
Reading Anna Freud Nick Midgley

TITLES IN THE NEW LIBRARY OF PSYCHOANALYSIS 'BEYOND THE COUCH' SERIES

Under the Skin: A Psychoanalytic Study of Body Modification Alessandra Lemma
Engaging with Climate Change: Psychoanalytic and Interdisciplinary Perspectives Edited by Sally
Weintrobe
Research on the Couch: Single Case Studies, Subjectivity, and Psychoanalytic Knowledge R.D.
Hinshelwood

Contents

Acknowledgements   viii

Introduction: the body as canvas   1

1   As you desire me   25

2   The symptom of ugliness   42

3   Mirrors   56

4   Being seen or being watched   74

5   Occupied territories and foreign parts: reclaiming the body   92

6   Copies without originals: envy and the maternal body   112

7   The botoxing of experience   129

8   Ink, holes and scars   148

Conclusion: an order of pure decision   172

Notes   178
References   186
Index   200

Acknowledgements

This book has been in my mind for many years, but I suspect that it might have stayed there had it not been for the stimulating discussions about the body and its modification that I was privileged to have with my colleague Richard Graham, with whom I co-chaired the Body Image Disturbances Workshop at the Tavistock and Portman National Health Service (NHS) Foundation Trust. I am deeply indebted to him and to all the other workshop members, particularly Roberta Mondadori, Maria Rhode, Margot Waddell and Gianna Williams.

I would also like to thank Susan Levy, Linda Young and Heather Wood for their invaluable editorial suggestions on an earlier draft of this book and for their generous support and encouragement, which made all the difference. The many discussions we had about this book helped me to formulate my ideas more clearly. Jean Matheson and Helen Ruszczynski provided valuable help with typing and chasing references.

I have researched this book widely and have taken in a lot of ideas from a great many sources. I have endeavoured to acknowledge them all. Some core ideas have been very formative in my thinking about the body and are so embedded in my overall arguments that I may not have always clearly referenced the works. While I take full responsibility for the views expressed here, I nevertheless want to acknowledge a few sources that have especially shaped my thinking about the body, most notably the ideas developed by Didier Anzieu, Esther Bick, Dana Birksted-Breen, Don Campbell, Peter Fonagy, Julia Kristeva, Moses and Egle Laufer, and Mary Target.

I also want to thank all my patients who have helped me to begin to understand what it means to be-in-a-body.

Last but by no means least, I want to thank my husband, Jeremy, and my son, Matteo, who both generously and lovingly accepted my preoccupation with this book over many months.

Introduction
The body as canvas

We all have a story to tell but we don't always choose to do so. The story we cannot avoid telling is the one that our body inevitably narrates.

Danny's traumatic early life was etched in ink – across his arms, his neck and his face. He sat opposite me, in the little room in which we would meet for two years, in a young offenders' institution, and I struggled to look at him. On his left cheek he had the tattoo of a skull, with a pierced ring running through its nose. I felt assaulted by his appearance. Yet, behind this armour of ink, I grew to know a terrified young man who was serving a sentence for manslaughter. He was only fifteen at the time.

Danny, the son of parents who were both addicted to drugs, was exposed from the very start of his life to disturbing and violent experiences. Soon after his birth, his father left without trace and he then lived with his mother and siblings in invariably squalid conditions. His mother made ends meet through prostitution. It was not long before Danny was recruited into a circle of drugs, sex and violence. His body knew no boundary: he had been sexually and physically abused. His body knew no mind: he had little capacity to reflect on his experience. He used his body destructively because no other mind had ever availed itself to attend to just how angry and frightened he felt.

When Danny hit puberty, he rapidly grew in stature and strength, and was transformed into a large, imposing young man. The many violent phantasies he had harboured towards his mother in particular were now no longer contained by the physical limitations of his small, pre-pubescent body. After a heated row, he pushed his mother down a flight of stairs and she died.

Around the age of thirteen, Danny told me, he became very preoccupied with covering his body with tattoos and piercings. By the time he was arrested, at least 50 per cent of his body was covered in ink. Modifying the surface of his body had become a kind of addiction: he sought out the process of transformation as much as the visual outcome. Each tattoo or piercing was his personal stamp on his body. Our explorations of his compulsion to mark his body helped me to understand that for Danny this had been the only way he could feel that his body belonged to him. It was an attempt to reclaim it and so reclaim a sense of himself as separate. With each tattoo he wanted to erase the hated other that he experienced so concretely to be located in his body. This could be achieved only through an actual, painful intrusion into the skin. By turning his body into a canvas, with the word 'HATE' tattooed across his knuckles, he also vividly communicated to others that they would be best advised to leave him alone.

Danny was the first young person I ever worked with. He powerfully brought home to me the psychic importance of the body and of how internal fragmentation and hatred can be managed through changing the body's appearance.

All the modifications I will be discussing in this book are to the surface of the body, and many are to the surface of the skin specifically. Yet the narratives I have been privileged to listen to, inside and outside of the consulting room, suggest that the motivations for extensively modifying the surface of the body, and/or for being excessively preoccupied with its appearance, are to be found in the person's internal world – *under the skin*, as it were.

I have come to understand that the more compulsive and extreme forms of body modification reflect a difficulty in integrating this most basic fact of life: we cannot give birth to ourselves. This 'truth' is felt nowhere more acutely than in our bodies. The body is testament to our interrelatedness. The shared corporeality of the mother and baby, from which we all have to emerge, is the physical prototype of psychic dependency. The emergence out of this shared physical space is never absolute because the body is indelibly inscribed with the imprint of the (m)other. When the fact of our dependency on others cannot be integrated into our sense of who we are – perhaps because, as was the case for Danny, his mother and others had actually intruded into his body – the subjective experience of the body is invariably compromised.

How we experience being-in-a-body is not solely dependent on whether our body has been somehow intruded into. It also depends on whether we feel our body to be desirable. The too-desiring or the not-desiring-enough mother inscribes the body and profoundly shapes the development of the body self. I place particular emphasis on the early relationship to the mother because the trajectory from the shared corporeality of mother and baby, through the vicissitudes of her relationship to his body, and then through to feeling desirable yet separate, is an especially perilous one for the patients I will be discussing.

Feeling beautiful or ugly is fundamentally object-related. This will seem obvious enough to a psychotherapist, but this relational perspective is not available to the individuals I will be describing. Yet, the hatred of the body that is so palpable in these patients variously reflects the identification of the body with a hated and/or felt-to-be hateful object. Inevitably, therefore, in these patients one encounters marked difficulties with separation from the primary object of desire, most commonly the mother. The individual who believes that he can give birth to himself, or that he can somehow reclaim his body through altering its surface and shape, does so in order to sever his tie to the object, or to create a phantasised ideal self who will be loved after all.

Of course, we *all* struggle to manage two basic facts: we are beings-in-a-body and we are the subject of the other's gaze. These facts present ongoing challenges requiring us, throughout the lifespan, to integrate the meaning of our corporeality into our sense of who we are. In this book I am concerned with how for some people the challenges presented by these two 'facts' are managed internally, primarily through the external manipulation of the surface of the body, for example, through cosmetic procedures, tattoos, piercings and scarification. Some of these patients present with marked body dysmorphia and are overly preoccupied with an imagined or very minor flaw in their appearance (see Chapter 4). Several of the patients I discuss, however, would not fulfil diagnostic criteria for Body Dysmorphic Disorder (BDD), and yet they also played out their unconscious conflicts on the body's surface, and found solutions to psychic pain through the modification of the body. Although some of the patients I discuss were very preoccupied with their desirability, and the body modification was an attempt to find a more desirable physical form (Chapters 1, 2, 4 and 7), others modified the body to reappropriate it, or to visually attack the other with its refigured, and sometimes disfigured, form (Chapters 5, 6, 7 and 8).

My primary aim in this book is to share ideas about how we can under-stand individuals for whom the manipulation of the body is felt to be psychically necessary even if in the process they may inflict considerable violence against their physical selves. It is the *compelling* nature of the pull towards modifying the body, whether in actuality, or as a comforting phan-tasy in one's mind, that distinguishes these patients. I am not referring here to individuals who modify their bodies during an acute psychotic episode. The patients I will be describing in this book were not floridly psychotic, but from an analytic point of view we would understand their decision to alter their bodies as being guided by the ascendance of a psychotic process in the mind.

A recurring question in the literature – and perhaps this might be more appropriately termed a tension – is between those who view body modifi-cations as 'figurations' and those who regard them as 'disfigurations' (Brain 1978). The extent to which the decision to modify one's body, sometimes in very extreme ways, can be understood as self-affirming rather than self-destructive divides those who have written on this subject (e.g. Davis 1995; Pitts 2003; Sanders and Vail 2008).

Some of the more sociological literature on the body is skewed in the direction of explanations that situate body modification practices, for example, as attempts to reclaim the body from a hostile or alienating contemporary culture (e.g. Pitts 2003), or those who see it as an expression of spirituality (e.g. Musafar 1996). Some of this literature is written by people who are personally immersed in the practices under discussion (e.g. DeMello 2000) resulting in texts that are very rich, but not unbiased.

Typically, these accounts do not consider the existence of an unconscious mind, or the actual violence perpetrated against the body in the name of fashion or spiritual enlightenment. To ascribe individual, and often unconscious, meaning to these practices is not the same as judging them. Moreover, it is neither helpful nor possible to generalise about the meaning and functions of these practices because the motivations underpinning the decision to modify the body are complex and diverse: superficially similar methods of body modification may have diverse ends. But one thing binds them together: given that the body develops within our early relationships with other people (see Chapter 3), its modification invariably expresses something about the quality of internalised relationships, and impacts on both internal and external relationships.

Indeed, there are developmental stages when body modification practices can acquire particular meaning and salience as ways of articulating a separate identity, or as a form of protest against parental authority, such as tattooing or piercing in adolescence. One might even go as far as to say that for many young people they provide a 'helpful' medium for working through particular conflicts, as long as the behaviour does not become too compelling. These are meaningful routes for giving expression to conflicts over the ownership of the body that, to an extent, have become normalised through popular culture. In particular contexts, they can therefore be understood to reflect a more transient phase while also lending themselves to being deployed as ways of working out internal conflicts. But they do not necessarily represent a more enduring, central, organising function in the person's psychic economy.

There is a difference between body modifications that are attempts to decorate the body or to 'figurate' it (Brain 1978), and those body modi- fications that may be said to be in the name of beauty or social affiliation, but that instead are underpinned by a more despairing and/or violent state of mind towards the self and the object. Someone who has one or two tattoos done along with their peers during adolescence is in quite a different state of mind from someone who visits the tattoo parlour once a month and devotes hours to the self-care rituals that tattoos require in the short term. The difference is not simply quantitative, or necessarily particular to the method chosen for altering the body, though the degree of harm perpetrated against the body is an important dimension. Neither is it distinguished by the underlying unconscious phantasy. For example, the phantasy of being one's own creator is central to some individuals who seek out cosmetic surgery, as I will go on to elaborate, but this is a phantasy that we have probably all harboured at one point or another. Rather, the difference lies in how *compelling* and *necessary* the pursuit of body modification becomes for the individual, and hence how compelling the underlying phantasy has become, such that without the enactment of the phantasy, the individual's sense of self fragments.

Understanding the dominant unconscious phantasy underpinning the pursuit of body modification is central to helping these patients. Several of the chapters (Chapter 2 onwards) are devoted to exploring specific phantasies. I will describe three unconscious phantasies – there are probably others – that I have observed in the patients I have seen. These phantasies are felt to be necessary to the psychic equilibrium of individuals for whom body modification has acquired a more compelling quality, namely the *reclaiming phantasy* (Chapters 4, 5 and 8), the *self-made phantasy* (Chapters 4, 6, 7 and 8) and the *perfect match phantasy* (Chapters 1, 4 and 7).

In the *reclaiming phantasy*, I am suggesting that the body modification serves the function of rescuing the self from an alien presence felt to now reside within the body. This phantasy therefore concerns the *expulsion* from the body of an object felt to be alien or polluting. In the *perfect match phantasy*, the body modification serves the function of creating a perfect, ideal body that will guarantee the other's love and desire. Whereas the perfect match phantasy concerns the *fusion* of an idealised self with an idealised object, the *self-made phantasy* expresses an *envious attack* on the object. Here the object's independence is intolerable and a profound grievance towards the object fuels the envy. The self retreats into believing that it can create itself, thereby circumventing the object, and hence any experience of dependency.

All these phantasies reveal how the body provides both the content of phantasy (Bronstein 2009) and becomes the canvas on which these phantasies are then enacted.[1] These phantasies are attempts to describe, and to formulate, my current understanding of the psychic function of body modification, hence they are provisional hypotheses, not 'facts' – though I am aware that hypotheses can all too readily lead to reification of processes that are, in reality, far more fluid and nuanced. Moreover, these phantasies are not mutually exclusive: at any given point in time in an individual's experience, the function of body modification may shift and will be underpinned by different phantasies.

My own approach to this area concurs to some degree with that adopted by Favazza (1996) in relation to what he refers to as 'ritual self-mutilation': drawing on his study of various body modification practices cross-culturally, he concludes that they serve a therapeutic function, and that in those individuals who are mentally unwell it represents an attempt at self-healing. I, too, understand the manipulation of the body as representing in some cases an attempt at a kind of 'cure'. Just as some people self-medicate through drugs or alcohol, some do so through modifying their body. For some people body modification can feel very compelling and, like an addict, they undergo numerous procedures such as cosmetic procedures or tattoos, in an attempt to cure psychic pain.

A body of my own

Babies need a (m)other to help them to meaningfully bring together their otherwise disorganised sensory experience. Out of this early fragmentation a psychic/libidinal map of the body will emerge. Crucially, this map is not only organised by biology, but also by the highly idiosyncratic meanings and phantasies about the body held by parents, the family and the wider cultural system. The body is thus not just a physical reality: the way we experience it is inevitably defined by our earliest fears and desires because the body also reflects unconscious introjective and projective processes.

The importance of the early gazing relationship, and of the skin-to-skin contact, between mother and baby cannot be emphasised enough (see Chapters 2 and 3). Touch and vision are inseparable, a single axis underpinning the earliest physical experiences. At their best, looking and touching can confer the gift of love. But when these are absent, or in short supply, or when looking and touching are laced with hatred, possessiveness or envy, then the body self may feel neglected, shamed or intruded upon. These early physical and sensory experiences with others are inscribed somatically and lay the foundations for the development of the body self, and hence of the self.

Where there are difficulties in the earliest gaze–touch relationship with the object of desire, it can prove impossible to feel at home in one's own body, or indeed to feel that the body *is* one's own. Difficulties may then become manifest particularly during adolescence as the body presents itself forcefully to the mind under the pressure of puberty. In these cases the body that is felt to be the cause of the internal unease or turmoil becomes the canvas on which the psychic distress is externalised and worked on (Laufer and Laufer 1984; Bronstein 2009). When the early visual and tactile relationship has not led to the satisfactory cathexis of the body self, this represents an important area of developmental deficit that creates particular vulnerabilities in the integration of the body self into the person's sense of who they are (Krueger 1989, 2004).

Of course, the role of the father is vitally important too. In the majority of the cases I discuss, the father was absent and the mother all too present, even if for some she was felt to be emotionally unavailable. This underlines the devastating psychic impact of an absent father and the use that may then be made of the body to hold the self together and to resist the regressive pull back into a fused, symbiotic relationship with the mother (Fonagy and Target 1999; Campbell 2008).

Bodies-for-one and bodies-for-two (and more)

The body can be open and receptive to the other or it can shut down, keeping the other out. It may be adorned and groomed or it may be neglected and attacked, transformed beyond recognition in the pursuit of a body one can call one's own. It may be felt to be the site for meeting or for rejection. It may provide reassurance that one is loved or confirmation of one's fundamental undesirability. The body, in other words, is the most pliable medium at our disposal for displaying or communicating our internal states of mind. Our relationship to our body is probably the most concrete marker we have of how we feel about ourselves and about others.

Frank (1991), a sociologist, has identified different categorisations for understanding the social body that are very helpful for conceptualising the felt experience of the body and how the body is used interpersonally. He distinguishes the *monadic body* that is closed in on itself and focused on 'consumption'. By contrast, the *communicative or dyadic body* exists in reciprocal relations with others. Its aim is to communicate to others what it feels – be it pain or joy. Frank suggests that:

> the [communicative] body has the potential for more diffuse realisations. Diffusion is no longer the threat of dissolution but the various possibilities of pleasure and expression.
>
> (1991: 89)

The fluidity of the body that Frank evokes in his notion of the dyadic body is also well captured by Schilder (1950):

> The image of the body thus shows characteristic features of our whole life. There is a continual change from crystallized rather closed entities to states of dissolution to a stream of less stabilized experience and from there a return to better forms and closed entity. It is therefore the continuous building up of a shape which is immediately dissolved and built up again.
>
> (Schilder 1950: 209–210)

This fluidity is core to the dyadic body. It makes it possible to be in one's body, but the body is also open and receptive to the other with all the attendant risks this may involve.

By contrast, the monadic body is the body we retreat back into when intimacy and, more specifically, when dependency on the other is felt to be challenging to the integrity of the self. The monadic body, as I will be using the term in this book, building on Frank's distinction, is a body for one, hermetically sealed off from the perils of intimacy. The compelling pursuit of body modification typically expresses a retreat into the monadic body where this state can itself become idealised and can become a 'psychic retreat' (Steiner 1993). The individual inhabits a closed bodily, sensory world that keeps others out, and that interferes with the capacity to distinguish symbol from symbolised. Work with these patients poignantly highlights the terrible price they pay for remaining trapped in a non-verbal bodily universe. Part of their problem is that they cannot find the words to describe their experience and so construct a narrative about it, which would free them from the concreteness of existence within the confines of a body-for-one, and help them instead to inhabit a body-for-two – a communicative, dyadic body (Ogden 1989; Mancia 1994; McDougall 1995; Lombardi 2002; Ferrari 2004).

The body on the couch

Because words are essential tools for the practice of psychotherapy, it is possible to overlook the importance of the physical, and more specifically, of the visual in our work and so ignore the two bodies in the consulting room. My own work in this area, as I am sure will be the case for any clinician who has a special interest in somatic presentations, has sensitised me to the patient's experience of his body, and also to my own bodily responses, as a potential source of countertransference. More specifically, and perhaps this is more pertinent when working with patients who are preoccupied with, and held together by, their physical appearance, the visual relationship between patient and therapist has struck me as deserving more attention than we normally accord it, with a few notable exceptions (Wright 1991; Steiner 2004, 2006; Peringer 2006; Kilborne 2007).

Although words can have a containing function, for some patients, the visual relationship matters more – at least until some inroads have been made in understanding their use of the body and their experience of the gazing relationship. In this respect the use of the couch with patients whose anxieties are so concretely experienced in the body, and for whom physical appearance is a central preoccupation, requires careful consideration. In my experience, for some of these patients, the use of the couch is unhelpful (at least to begin with), not because it provokes a malignant regression (though it may do that too), but primarily because it bypasses the visual field and the conflicts that are encapsulated through the meeting of the two gazes. The invitation to lie on the couch may indeed be welcomed by some of these patients because they want to avert the mutual gaze of therapist and patient, out of fear of what it might do to them (for example, they may feel shamed as the therapist looks at them), or out of fear of what their gaze might expose to the therapist (for example, it may reveal their hatred). Conversely, some patients seek out the visual relationship to intimidate or humiliate the therapist. But here, too, I have wondered whether the use of the couch is primarily protective for the therapist rather than necessarily helpful for this kind of patient.[2]

Work with these individuals requires a particular attunement to the body self and to the bodily countertransference so that it becomes possible to construct 'a language to enable corporeity to speak' (Lombardi 2002: 370). It is, of course, vital not to shame the patient by exposing prematurely, through the verbal medium, what the body silently, yet forcefully, expresses. Fonagy and Target (2007) have helpfully articulated how the analytic process itself:

> subjectively in part is a physical experience that is described meta- phorically as close, holding, containing. . . . These terms all indicate a physical sense of what it means to enter a psychologically trusting relationship. The experience of analytic intimacy would not have meaning without the backdrop of physical sensation evoked by the action language of metaphor.
>
> (Fonagy and Target 2007: 431)

Sometimes we need to hold in our body and in our mind the patient's projections until meaning can emerge.

Understanding the patient's experience of being-in-a-body, and being-in- a-body in relation to the therapist's physicality too, is important in every therapy, but it is clearly even more so when the patient's presentation has a strong somatic component. These patients present their bodily as well as psychical experiences such that our attention needs to be focused on the patient's lived experience of the body as much as on their spoken narrative. Body modification is a language of action and it resists representation through language. Yet it is a potentially rich language. The tattoo, for example, like a dream image, symbolises and displaces psychic meanings (Grumet 1983).

Because these patients have a characteristically underdeveloped capacity to reflect on what they feel – many don't even know *what* they feel to begin with – the work is slow and requires a gentle introduction to the notion of a mind. Although work in the transference is vitally important, I have found that these patients, to begin with, need gentle encouragement to simply elaborate interpersonal narratives. Working with dreams is especially help- ful in this respect and it becomes important to note not only their defensive aspects, but also the way the dreams reveal the patient's progressive attempts to represent experience (Bolognini 2008).

In practice very few of these patients report dreams spontaneously. When I started to explicitly convey that I was interested in their dreams, and when we began by exploring them outside of the transference (that is, I 'minded' the transference, but it was not the primary focus of my interventions at this early stage), I found that the dreams provided helpful bridges into the notion of an unconscious mind without exposing the patient to the more threatening immediacy of the transference. Once this notion was more established, it became possible to start focused work in the transference.

Understanding the patient's experience of his *body-self* is fundamental to understanding psychic structure. That the body is the starting point of mental functioning was core to Freud's (1923) own understanding of the development of the ego. As he famously put it, the ego is 'first and foremost a body-ego; it is not merely a surface entity but it is itself the projection of a surface' (Freud 1923: 26), that is, the most primitive form of self-representation is first and foremost a body representation, deriving from proprioception and the experiences of pain and pleasure. In a later footnote inserted in 1927, Freud added:

> The ego is ultimately derived from bodily sensations, chiefly from those springing from the surface of the body. It may thus be regarded as a mental projection of the surface of the body, besides . . . representing the superficies of the mental apparatus.
>
> (Freud 1923: 26)

For Freud the ego was thus represented as a psychical map, a projection of the surface of the body. More specifically, the ego was seen to be a mental representation of the individual's libidinised relationship to his body. Throughout life, ego structure and identity are founded to a significant degree on the sensations and awareness of the body (Freud 1923; Hägglund and Piha 1980; Schilder 1950). One important implication of this is that the ego derives its functioning from body models (Lichtenberg 1978), such that the earliest experiences of taking into the mouth (i.e. introjecting) and of spitting out (i.e. projecting) could be said to form the foundation of all experience (Abraham 1924; Fenichel 1945). Freud thus cemented the view, later developed by others, that the body-self is the container and foundation for the sense of self (Winnicott 1966, 1972; Mahler and Furer 1968; Haag 1985; Krueger 1989; Sandler 1994; Bloom 2006).

For Freud the drives always had their source in the body. He defined the drive as 'the psychical representative of the stimuli originating from within the organism and reaching the mind' (Freud 1915: 122). He added that the drive is a 'measure of the demand made upon the mind for work in consequence of its connection with the body' (1915: 122). If we think of his definition of the instinct, it is this reference to 'work' that explains the transformations that take place, changing the contents of its initial expression. Green (1998) underlines that this highlights a double process: the first one is the transformation of the stimuli born in the body and reaching the mind, changing themselves from somatic excitations to psychic representatives; the second is the work imposed on the mind in aiming to change the situation of frustration in communicating his representations to the other.

(Green 1998: 655)

Freud thus emphasised the importance of both the drive and of the object, but the importance of the object was to be especially highlighted by his successors. As far as the drive is concerned, however, his thorough description weaves together the notions of development as rooted in the body, excitation reaching the psyche, and the measure of the demand for work imposed on the psyche due to its link with the body.

Henry Rey later spelled out the clinical implications of Freud's profound insights about the body: 'in every analysis one has to arrive at the body-self if one wants to achieve deep and enduring change' (Rey 1994: 267). Understanding the vicissitudes of the development of the body-self in the context of the earliest relationship with the 'object of desire' is core to helping patients who modify their bodies because of the quality of the identifications that ensue and that are then enacted the transference.

Comparatively few contemporary British publications concern themselves with the mind-body question and, consequently, a fundamental aspect of the patient's experience is sometimes overlooked.[3] There are some notable exceptions to this, such as the landmark work on the body in adolescence by Moses and Egle Laufer (1984), the work of Peter Fonagy and Mary Target (2007) on the embodied self, and recent papers by Catalina Bronstein (2009) and Sarah Flanders (2009) on the use of the body in adolescence. By contrast, French analysts, especially those involved in the Paris Psychosomatic School (e.g. Marty 1980; Aisenstein 2006), Italian analysts (e.g. Gaddini 1987; Lombardi 2002, 2009; Ferrari 2004), and a good number of North American analysts from the 1950s onwards (e.g. Hoffer 1949, 1950; Kestenberg et al. 1971; Lichtenberg 1975, 1978; Anderson 2008; Bucci 2008) have all tackled the mind-body question more vigorously and they appear more attuned to the body in the therapeutic situation.

The importance of keeping in mind the patient's body-self, because this is central to understanding psychic structure, cannot be overemphasised. Moreover the body *is* living memory and our unconscious phantasies are expressed through the body (Resnik 2005). In the consulting room what we can sometimes observe through the work with some of these patients is what I have come to think of as the *Cartesian psychic retreat*, that is, the way in which the patient defensively maintains a mind-body dualism in which the mind is 'the self' and the body is 'other' – as 'other' it can be dispensed with, improved, modified or triumphed over. Ostensibly overly invested in the body's appearance, the unconscious aim is nevertheless to bypass the implications of reality that are rooted in the body. The function of the retreat is to protect the self from awareness of the unconscious meaning of an embodied self.

Working with these patients presents particular countertransference hazards, not least because our embodied nature poses numerous challenges. It is probably fair to say that a degree of preoccupation with the body and its appearance is present in all of us. We all modify our bodies, too, every time we select what to wear in the morning or put make-up on, or we may fantasise about modifying it. Indeed, as we listen to patients' experience of their ageing or felt-to-be flawed bodies, and they discuss the cosmetic fixes that are available, we may identify with the seduction of such solutions. We must not delude ourselves: buying an anti-wrinkle cream is on a continuum with having Botox injections, not in an altogether different dimension.[4] The fact that we would not opt for Botox is not the point here. It is important that we understand and recognise these seductions in ourselves, and know something about our own experience of being-in-a-body and of being, inevitably, the object of the other's gaze.

The body in society

In our advanced technological culture, body images appear to be infinitely mutable.[5] This is deeply seductive. So-called 'progress' fuels the phantasy that we can exist, to borrow Ewald's (1993) telling phrase, in an 'order of pure decision'. In this kind of external world the challenge is no longer felt to be about how to manage lack of freedom, but how to manage 'no freedom *from* choice' (Goodall 2000: 150). In the internal world, psychoanalysis allows us to understand that the real challenge is how to stand up to the seductions of identification with a narcissistic, omnipotent object, as I hope subsequent chapters will illustrate.

It is probably fair to say that, in vulnerable individuals, the use of the body to manage psychic pain is unhelpfully reinforced by such sociocultural processes. The widespread availability and popularisation of cosmetic surgery and procedures is a good example. In the twenty-first century, your toes can be shortened and collagen can be injected into the sole of the foot with the sole aim of slipping comfortably into, and tolerating, Jimmy Choo heels. In New York some parents reward their daughters' college graduation with breast implants. In China, in the island of Hainan, patients can check into a dedicated plastic surgery hospital called the 'Dreaming Girls Fantasy' for extensive cosmetic reworking. In Beijing women from all over China compete in a plastic surgery competition. The winner of the 2004 competition had had four surgical procedures, the first runner up, ten (Kuczynski 2006).

The total overhaul of one's appearance has become commonplace in women's magazines and has inspired a vast array of makeover shows that form part of reality TV (RTV). With its emphasis on metamorphosis, makeover RTV is the modern day equivalent of the archaic fairytale – a version of Cinderella for the twenty-first century (Fraser 2007). I will briefly focus on these shows because they aptly illustrate how a particular type of television format, which is culturally very popular and mainstream, encourages and provides a platform for the enactment of unconscious conflicts for some individuals. In Chapter 1 I will describe some work with participants for these kinds of shows.

In these shows two key contradictory, yet deeply seductive, messages are conveyed (Fraser 2007; Gailey 2007). Cosmetic surgery and procedures are portrayed as legitimate self-management practices, not unlike brushing one's teeth. At the same time, however, the narratives are framed as aspirational: the participants are reclaiming their so-called true self, or empowering themselves and taking charge of their destiny. It is the combination of these two factors that makes these shows so compelling. In other words, they normalise what is felt by the participants and the viewers alike as being beyond their wildest dreams and present it as a legitimate path for self-development and self-cure.

Sometimes the only trace of the unarticulated psychic pain that has been cut out of the 'old face' to reveal the 'new face' is visible on the bewildered face of the partner who, as he uncomfortably smiles for the camera, appears unsure as to whether to be pleased or deeply concerned about the implications of the change in his partner (most of these programmes involve female participants). One wonders how *he* is now left feeling, still stuck, as it were, with his actual face and the reality of his life.

In *Extreme Makeover* – a popular American show – a range of interventions are suggested to improve the participant's appearance: for example, cosmetic dentistry, rhinoplasty, breast augmentation and liposuction. The participants often explicitly request to remould their bodies according to individual parts of celebrities (e.g. Angelina Jolie's lips). The programme thus 'makes over reality' by creating a part-object universe: we enter the domain of bits of people (e.g. someone else's lips), which can now be appropriated. By encouraging this, the makeover show promises the appearance of autonomy over one's bodily representation. Importantly, such shows have moved beyond the simpler questions of identity vis-à-vis consumption. As Fraser (2007) shrewdly observes, 'No longer is it enough to *have* the items *to be like* the ideal, now the aim is *to become it*' (Fraser 2007: 189, italics in original). In this sense *Extreme Makeover* provides the ready-made means to actualise the self-made phantasy, that is, you can give birth to yourself while denying any dependence on the other. Importantly, it does so within the normalising framework of popular TV, masking the reality of the human distress that, in my experience of assessing potential participants (see Chapter 2), all too often lies behind the conscious wish to participate in these shows.

The beauty industry feeds off, and into, these kinds of shows, supporting the monadic body, focused in on itself. Like the drug dealer who preys on the vulnerability of the addict, the beauty industry panders to our anxieties about our bodies and ageing, persuading us that these are problems we can solve, rather than facts of life we have to somehow come to terms with. Socio-cultural influences inevitably shape our responses to these more internal processes:

> Part of the strength of consumer culture comes from its ability to harness and channel genuine bodily needs and desires, albeit that it presents them within a form which makes their realisations dubious – the desire for health, longevity and sexual fulfilment, youth and beauty represent a reified entrapment of transhistorical human longing within distorted forms.
>
> (Featherstone 2000: 193)

Society thus provides a context for living out one's personal distress in ways that distance the person from psychic pain, legitimising shortcuts to what would otherwise require long and painful psychic work (see Chapters 2 and 7).

There is undoubtedly something appealingly simple about concentrating on the shape of a nose, or the wrinkles on one's face, as the solution to problems that the person may find impossible to put into words, let alone solve. It is hard to avoid concluding that we have come to think of our bodies as something like an accessory that can be traded in for a better version when required (Kuczynski 2006). The cosmetic solutions are as quick as they are evanescent in their longer-term effects. The manic state of mind that can be generated by the relentless, and paradoxical, media pressure to look beautiful so that we can stand out above the rest while at the same time promising that beauty is available to all (if only you buy the right, and costly, products, which by definition are not accessible to all), acts against the knowledge of the evanescence of the media's 'promise'.

These socio-cultural trends reveal how self-identity has itself become a global product. Specifically, as Giddens (1991: 5) has articulated, it is far more 'deliberative', and we are witnessing an ongoing 're-ordering of identity narratives' in which a concern with the body is central (Giddens 1991; Featherstone 2000). The narcissistic cultivation of bodily appearance is a response to these social realities, but it is also, as I have been emphasising, an expression of a need to construct and control what the body unconsciously represents: it can be experienced as terrifying, out of control, or even disgusting because of our developmental histories. More broadly, as a species, we clearly have difficulty managing our embodied nature. It is therefore unsurprising to find defensive structures at a group level to manage core ontological anxieties rooted in the body. In an external climate of seemingly infinite possibilities for self-creation, the potential for perverse solutions to psychic conflicts is thus facilitated by cultural processes.

Cross-cultural perspectives on body modification

We live in what has been aptly termed a 'scopic' economy (Rumsey and Harcourt 2005) that relies on being scoped by others and in which some physical attributes are perceived to be more attractive and are more valued than others.[6] In all cultures the body always mediates relationships with others. Preference for attractive individuals, irrespective of age, has been reliably established (Jackson 2002). Moreover preference for attractive faces has been shown to start early: six-month-old babies prefer mathematically averaged prototypical faces in the same way that adults do (Rubenstein et al. 1999).[7]

We are inevitably shaped by the body ideals and values prevailing in a given culture. Schilder (1950) noted that the body will be projected into the world and the world will be introjected into the body – these projective processes will thus be coloured by the culture of the individual and the messages about the body that are prevalent in that culture.

In discussing cross-cultural practices, as ever, there is the danger of 'exoticising' particular body practices that are prevalent in non-Western cultures. However, I hope that as the book unfolds, it will become clear that the Western body modification practices I discuss are no more or less unusual.[8] Indeed, cross-cultural studies reveal that the propensity not only to alter, but also to distort, or disfigure, the given body is *universal* (Brain 1978; Sanders and Vail 2008).

As long as we remain preoccupied with questions of identity, we will continue to manipulate our bodies and to 'customise' them to lend form and meaning to our personal and social identities. Body modification marks the body, inscribes it, and so constructs it within psychical, cultural and even political fields. This is not a recent phenomenon. The anthropological evidence strongly suggests that there has never been a time when specularity (i.e. that we are an image for the other) was not at least in part constitutive of human subjectivity. As Lacan put it: 'We are beings who are looked at in the spectacle of the world' (Lacan 1977: 75). The pursuit of so-called beauty is thus the inevitable symptom of human subjectivity (Pacteau 1994).

Ever since the inception of cave drawing, it has been through images that we see and are seen. We have always used artefacts to remould the given body. In Southern Africa archaeologists have found tubes of red ochre that were used 40,000 years ago for decorating the face and body (Kuczynski 2006). Archaeological evidence suggests that tattooing, for example, was probably practised among peoples living in the late Stone Age. Carved figures from European sites dated 6000 years BC show facial and body markings thought to represent tattoos (Sanders and Vail 2008).

Non-Western body modification practices are primarily symbolic state-ments in which the bodily decorations and alterations convey messages about the group's beliefs and values. Traditionally, these modifications have been invested with the power to assure immortality and with protective qualities in the afterlife. In Fiji, women who died without tattoos were believed to be beaten by the spirits of other women and served as food for the gods (Hambly 1925). Manicai, a green copper ore, and Engelina, a dark red lead ore, were both ground into powder and used as eye shadow by the Egyptians. These cosmetics have been found packed into graves so that the deceased could wear eye shadow in the next life. Seemingly, not even death can free us from the anticipation of the other's look.

In many traditional cultures, tattoos and scarifications have been invested with prophylactic or therapeutic functions. The Bagwa of Cameroon, for example, use scarification as a form of preventative medicine: a four-pointed star on the right side near the liver was supposed to protect the person from hepatitic infection. The attribution of healing powers to body modification is very much apparent in those individuals in the Western world who pursue these practices as attempts at self-cure (Favazza 1996). The malleability of the body lends itself to it being used as a canvas on which a more desirable form can be drawn or where a felt-to-be soiled or damaged body can be wiped clean and redrawn.

Although the anthropological literature is very informative, identifying possible continuities in the functions served by body modification practices between traditional and Western cultures, this should not be taken to mean that their meanings are equivalent. Primitive body modification practices are elaborately involved in ritual and social institutions. Their meanings are collectively shared across the generations, not only in some select subgroups. It is indeed debatable as to whether cultural meanings and identities can be appropriated by one culture without somehow distorting their meaning and use within the cultural group in which they originated (Pritchard 2000).

Relocated from their tribal origins, these body practices lose their fundamental social function of communicating information about group values, traditions and philosophy and can acquire highly idiosyncratic meanings that cannot be simply interpreted through an understanding of social customs. Rather, they require deciphering in light of the person's individual history. As we adopt these traditional practices in the West, outside of their original context, their meaning becomes more individua-lised, less collective, and hence the scope for the behaviour to become an expression of, and a response to, individual distress increases. Although I therefore consider that there are important continuities across cultures and historical periods in the use made of the body in relation to questions of identity, their meanings and functions cannot be exactly superimposed. Indeed Western beauty rituals such as plastic surgery have become 'props to disintegrating personalities, concealing not only lines and wrinkles but inner distress' (Brain 1978: 188), rather than being primary signals of shared values in a given community that bind people together.

The manipulation of the body as a way of communicating important information about our identity, values and affiliations appears evident across cultures. Body modification practices signal to others meanings that are especially important to us personally and as representatives of a given group. Particular subcultures will inform these choices, and the exigencies of affiliation to the subculture will inevitably interact with the individual meaning that the bodily manipulation holds for that given individual. For example, an adolescent's decision to tattoo may well signal a wish to belong to, and to be recognised as belonging to, a gang, but the meaning for the young person of inscribing the body may also reflect a particular state of mind that cannot be solely accounted for by an explanation that foregrounds the group or social function. In some instances the group function is subordinate to more pressing internal needs that are less conspicuous.

Postmodern bodies: the impact of the media

A former editor of *Cosmopolitan*, discussing the technique of digital airbrushing in fashion magazines, remarked: 'Truth is, nobody has any idea what anybody really looks like' (quoted in Bordo 2003: 272). And yet, the images of slender, pre-pubescent bodies, or of flawless, unlined skin, invade our minds. They seem to be 'real' and so incite many to model themselves on what is effectively only a digitally enhanced image. Unsurprisingly, body dissatisfaction is widespread: both men and women report it and it is by no means restricted to Western cultures or to particular age groups. (For an overview of this area, see Orbach, 2009). Indeed the diet and cosmetic industry has now turned its attention to the male body. Nowadays, the athletic, muscular male body has become an aesthetic requirement that has sensitised men to the tyranny of the specular image. These changes can be discerned, for example, in the trend since the late 1970s in the design of male action toy figures, which are now much more muscular (Pope et al. 2000).

Women consistently report greater dissatisfaction with their bodies than men from adolescence onwards, but the prevalence of dissatisfaction in men is increasing, with recent estimates ranging from 50 to 70 per cent (Feingold and Mazzella 1998). There are suggestions of inverse trends between the genders whereby dissatisfaction for girls increases as they progress into puberty whereas for boys levels of satisfaction increase (Smolak 2004). Overall, research strongly supports what has been termed a 'normative discontent' (Rodin et al. 1985) with our bodies – a bodily discomfort that is seemingly felt by both men and women.

The relentless emphasis on beauty in the media has been blamed for this trend. Studies researching the impact of the media on body dissatisfaction point overall to reduced satisfaction following exposure to idealised media images, and indicate that both men and women use media images as benchmarks for self-comparison even though they are contemporaneously critical of what they perceive as 'unrealistic' ideals (Grogan 2008). Bordo (2003) argues that the postmodern body is sustained by

> fantasies of re-arranging, transforming and correcting, limitless improvement and change. Defying the historicity, the mortality and, indeed, the materiality of the body. In place of that materiality we have cultural plastic.
>
> (Bordo 2003: xvi–xvii)

Her focus is particularly on the female body. Along with many other distinguished feminist authors, she argues that women are controlled through their bodies. But men also feel this tyranny.

Of particular concern is the increase in body dissatisfaction in pre-pubertal children. The influence of the media seems likely to play a part here. When Thompson et al. (1999) give the example of a two year old who, when asked whether she wanted hair like her mother when she grew up, replied, 'Want hair like Barbie', we are reminded that no one is immune from the relentless impact of the ready-made images of so-called beauty to which we appear to become enslaved at ever younger ages. Magazines, soaps and reality TV all converge on the image of the body beautiful and how to get it. All these media tend to promote often rigid and unreachable ideals of attractiveness. They hold up mirrors that reflect back to us a body that is defective or wrong in some way (Bordo 2003). Yet, they create the illusion that perfection is attainable, swiftly glossing over the fact that the images we are bombarded with have themselves been manicured, danger-ously blurring the boundary between fiction and reality.

The media's ethical conscience has been moved in the last few years, resulting in a commitment by some (but by no means all) not to use very thin models in fashion shows and shoots so as to stop glamorising personal distress (the 'heroin chic' look) by dressing it up in Armani. But these are lone efforts in an industry whose own machinery still rests on the propagation of the illusion that thin bodies or stretched, immobile faces *will* make us feel better.

There have always been tensions over whether the media mirrors or creates attitudes that, in turn, impinge on how we feel about our bodies. Although the media and culture do play a part in the subjective experience of one's body relative to the cultural norms, it is oversimplistic to think that this provides a convincing account of why people go on to develop body image disturbances and need to modify the body.

Several feminist authors (e.g. Orbach 1978, 2009; Bordo 2003) have put forward compelling arguments to support the view that body image disturbances are culturally normative and not manifestations of individual pathology. Yet awareness of and mere exposure to societal pressures is an insufficient explanation for these kinds of disturbances since people clearly vary in the extent to which they buy into the beauty spin and become enslaved to it, and only a minority go on to develop levels of clinically significant disturbances (Thompson and Van Den Berg 2002). In saying this I do not want to set up an antagonistic relationship between a socio-cultural/feminist analysis of body image disturbance and a psychoanalytic one. Attempts to establish what is primary or productive in the development of these difficulties are unlikely to yield any simple answer.

Thinking about the body

The body does not develop in a vacuum: the body, as we have seen, is a social body, it is a *gendered* body, and there is no such thing as a 'natural' body (or indeed a normative relationship to the body). As a result, when thinking, and writing, about this subject from the standpoint of an *individual's* unconscious experience of the body, these socio-cultural realities create inevitable tensions. I do not think that these are resolvable in any simple manner, if at all, but I would nevertheless like to say a few words about my conceptual starting point.

An intrapsychic and interpersonal focus provides the basis for this study. I hope it will be clear by now that I consider that these realms of experience exist in a dialectical relationship with the external world. We cannot think about the body outside of the cultural, social and political discourses that frame all of our lives, and that exert more or less pressure on us, in particular on our pursuit of a desirable appearance.

When we speak about the body we are inevitably also always speaking about a *gendered* body. The experience of being-in-a-female body will differ from the experience of being-in-a-male body, and this, in turn, will be coloured by the prevailing cultural projections into the respective female or male body. This is a vitally important dimension of an individual's experience of being-in-a-body, and one that has been eloquently articulated by many authors (see, for example, Cixous 1976; Grosz 1990; Frosh 1994). But this is one dimension that I will not be able to do justice to in this book (except, to an extent, in Chapters 1 and 6) because my primary aim is to explore what I consider to be the underlying anxieties resulting from our embodied nature irrespective of gender. To varying degrees, and in different ways, the body is problematic for us all and sometimes it becomes the site for enacting conflicts and for figuring psychic pain. As I have been suggesting, it is probably beyond question that socio-cultural pressures exert an influence on how we perceive and experience our bodies. But the more difficult truth is that, irrespective of these external pressures, the body

– be it a female or a male one – is hard for us to integrate into our subjective experience of who we are because it is the most incontrovertible evidence of our ultimate dependency and helplessness: neither self-creation nor immortality are within our reach.

It is also important to underline that there is no such thing as a 'natural body' from which we can meaningfully and reliably measure some kind of deviation. The latter term is a misnomer that presupposes the existence of a body untinged by the environment. But all bodies, to varying degrees, are modified and hence constructed. This is why I will be using the term the '*given* body' instead. This underlines that at the moment of birth, the body one has is the body, at least in part, that one is given, and that is instantaneously 'modified', we might say, by the look(s), touch and projections that first meet the baby's body (see Chapter 3). The way the baby's body is approached physically and in the minds of those relating to the baby will be shaped, in turn, by the dominant meanings assigned to the body within a specific family, and within the given socio-cultural context into which the baby is born.

When considering the psychic function of body modification, we are also immediately confronted with the question of whether these practices are 'normal', or created by socio-cultural pressures, or whether they are best understood as another kind of self-harming behaviour – that is, an indicator of individual pathology. The extent to which body modification practices have entered the mainstream (with the exception of scarification, which remains less common in Western cultures except within particular communities), suggests, at the very least, a degree of caution in assuming pathology too readily. Moreover, the relegation of these practices to the domain of pathology – as something 'we' don't do – may itself be construed as a defensive manoeuvre to bypass a more personal connection with the meaning of the body in our own minds. After all, we all modify our bodies, if only through clothes, make-up or hair dye. A proportion of those reading this book will have pierced or tattooed parts of their body and availed themselves of cosmetic procedures, orthodontics, and even cosmetic surgery in a minority of cases.

Body modification, per se, is not the province of a group of people who are very different to the rest of 'us'. We are all dependent upon the gaze of the other, and as solicitous of it, and hence these practices most likely provide solutions to universal anxieties. A secondary thread in this book is therefore to keep in mind the way in which the body is problematic for all of us. For this reason, in the earlier chapters (Chapters 1–3), I discuss the development of the body self, and I emphasise the challenges posed by an embodied existence for us all. This provides the basis for then considering the more particular experiences of those individuals who find being-in-a-body especially challenging, often because of their early developmental experiences.

It is difficult to think, and to write, about the body, and its sometimes extreme and violent modification, without somehow implying that there is a normative relationship to the body from which a few individuals deviate. Even though many of the types of modification I discuss are not only commonplace, but also encouraged in many cultures (for example, cosmetic procedures), their pursuit does not have a uniform meaning for all those who avail themselves of these practices.

Moreover, it will be clear from the cases I will discuss that although these individuals may well feel that what they are doing is 'normal' because everyone else is doing it, they are actually often perpetrating violence against themselves and/or the other who has become unconsciously identified with the body. As I outlined earlier, I approach body modification as the actualisation, through the relationship to the body, of an internalised object relationship. It is the *quality* of this relationship that distinguishes the pathological use made of the body in some cases from the more everyday, but no less meaningful, use we all make of the body to define and express our identity.

In the cases I discuss, the modification of the body serves the primary function of managing unconscious anxieties and conflicts that cannot be reflected upon. The psychic adaptations that are secured, as it were, through the manipulation of the body are profoundly unstable and consequently lead the individual to despair and/or in search of more bodily changes that can become more extreme and more risky. In approaching the pathological use of the body I am therefore primarily concerned with the function it serves in a person's psychic economy, and whether the use made of the body is primarily in the service of relating to the other or of attacking the other.

Without this added dimension of understanding, we run the risk of ignoring the violence and sadism that may also be a part of the internal scenario for some individuals. The unconscious phantasies underpinning body modification are therefore important. What may be consciously felt to be an 'empowering' tattoo in a particular social context may yet be predicated on an unconscious attack on the object that ultimately keeps the individual locked in an aggrieved relationship with the object.

When working with adolescents, for example, for whom many conflicts are expressed and explored through the manipulation of the body, it is readily apparent that tattoos and piercings are an important social currency that is, nevertheless, also potentially pregnant with individual psychological meaning. There is some evidence that tattoos in adolescence are a marker for other risk-taking behaviour such as drug use, sexual activity, increased risk of eating disorders and of suicide and greater body image dissatisfaction (Farrow et al. 1991; Armstrong et al. 1996; Houghton et al. 1996; Armstrong and Pace-Murphy 1997; Carroll et al. 2002; Brooks et al. 2003; Sarwer 2006; Sarwer et al. 2006). This intimates at the considerable psychic unrest that may be present in some young people who are modifying their bodies.

The body and its modification has become a socially sanctioned site for the expression of internal conflicts. A psychoanalytic perspective allows for the generation of hypotheses about individual, and typically unconscious, meaning(s), as well as making it possible to discern possible patterns across groups of patients. As ever, the analytic focus needs to rest squarely on the communicative significance of these behaviours in each individual case, viewed in their due developmental context. This then allows us to discern their function in the psychic economy of a given individual, at a particular point in his development *and*, of course, in a particular culture.

A few words about the sources for this book

When working with adolescents, you cannot escape the body in the consulting room. It was my work with young offenders that first alerted me to the clinical importance of keeping the body in mind, and that informs the subject matter of this book: the psychic function of body modification. Although my ideas have been shaped by my work with adolescents who have presented with a range of body image disturbances, they are equally applicable to adults and the majority of the cases I describe concern psychoanalytic work with adult patients.

I have arrived at my own current understanding by drawing on several sources: adolescent and adult patients seen in prisons and in public service mental health settings as a clinical psychologist and psychotherapist, and in private practice as a psychoanalyst. A number of the cases therefore refer to once to three times weekly psychotherapeutic work, and only a few refer to intensive four to five times weekly work. My experience of working with young people who use tattoos and other forms of modifications to the surface of the skin was gained primarily in young offender institutions early on in my career and then later as part of my work with young people in mental health settings.

In thinking about body modification in a broader context beyond that of the consulting room I have also drawn on my longstanding experience of undertaking psychological assessments of participants applying to take part on reality TV programmes, some of which involved makeover and transformation shows. Finally, I have also been informed by five detailed interviews I carried out in a more naturalistic setting involving people who had elected to undertake tattoos and/or piercings, but who were not involved with mental health services. I am very grateful for their time and willingness to help me understand the meaning of their choices.

I have purposefully chosen not only to base this book on clinical work, but also to draw on my experience beyond the consulting room, because the body is at the interface of the individual and the social. I was keen to explore the subjective experience of the body outside the more restricted domain of those who seek help or who have been referred for professional help, to see if the themes my patients were struggling with resonated with people living their lives without therapeutic intervention, but who nevertheless had also chosen to modify their bodies.

It will be apparent on reading this book that I draw on a range of theoretical frameworks. Although my own approach is firmly rooted in a predominantly British object relational model, in order to understand my patients I have found it necessary to turn to aspects of French psychoanalysis in particular, most notably the work of Lacan and Kristeva. In these texts notions such as desire, and of the importance of the visual order, are more richly elaborated. Inevitably, this shifting between frameworks glosses over the conceptual clashes that exist. I have tried to signpost this wherever possible, mostly in end-notes, but it is beyond the remit of this book to enter into detailed metapsychological discussions. Neither do I enter into detailed discussions of Lacanian theory or aim to provide a comprehensive review of his ideas: I have selected only those ideas that are pertinent to the dynamics I am trying to understand, especially in relation to the field of vision.

I am very indebted, too, to the work of several artists and filmmakers whose visual representations, sometimes through the use of their own bodies, have broadened my understanding of the dynamics I continue to grapple with. In particular I have drawn on the cinematic works by David Cronenberg and the body art of Orlan and Stelarc to illustrate universal anxieties related to our embodied nature. The exploration of artistic works is relevant and valid because phantasies, as the setting of desire (or its perversion), are to be found in public forms of phantasy such as novels, art and films (Cowie 1984). However, I am not approaching these works in order to analyse the artists themselves, but rather as illustrations of the themes covered in this book. Having said this, where relevant, I do refer to published interviews with the artists that shed some light on the themes I am exploring.

In order to preserve the confidentiality of patients and others whom I have interviewed, I have changed biographical information and other details. Permission was obtained from those I interviewed to use excerpts of our interviews.

The ideas I present in this book are evolving and I hope will serve to stimulate further revisions and/or elaborations by others who share an interest in this area.

A word on terminology

For the purposes of clarity I have chosen to use the masculine pronoun unless otherwise specified. I opted for this partly because body modification and the pursuit of beauty have been traditionally viewed as a predominantly female problem. In choosing the masculine pronoun I thus want to counterbalance this view and emphasise that the themes developed in this book carry equal emotional salience for both genders.

I have chosen to use the term 'cosmetic surgery' as opposed to 'plastic surgery' to underline the use of surgery on perfectly healthy bodies.

Finally, I am using the term 'other' to refer to an actual other and 'object' to refer to the internalised representation of a person. I use the term (m)other to indicate that it is typically the mother I am referring to as the primary caregiver (but that clearly this is not always necessarily so), and that it is this early experience that colours our later experiences.

Chapter 1

As you desire me

If I make the lashes dark
And the eyes more bright
And the lips more scarlet,
Or ask if all be right
From mirror to mirror
No vanity's displayed:
I'm looking for the face I had
Before the world was made
                    (Yeats 1865)

I am looking for the face I had . . . What exactly are we looking for? Yeats hints that it is *the face I had before the world was made*, that is, the face of a person who has not yet had to be an exteriority to itself (i.e. who has not yet assumed the position of observer to itself). It is the face of the 'I' who has not yet had to be separate and had to depend on the other's look. It is the face unblemished by reality, by what we have to bear in ourselves, and with others, as we develop. It is also, he says, the face I *had* – not just past, lost, but also that the self once *possessed*. Indeed what has to be relinquished – what is lost – and what we all keep trying to recreate, more or less compulsively, is the omnipotent state of mind in which one believes one is what one has (e.g. I have a small nose and hence I am 'good'/lovable) (Lemoine-Luccioni 1983), and in which what one has, is of one's own creation, that is, we are the artist *and* the canvas. This excess of narcissism conceals from us what actually defines us: an insufficiency, a lack. It is a state of mind that is inimical to the vicissitudes of desire, and therefore to relating with others because, in its more extreme form, its hallmark is the delusion that the other does not exist.

   I am looking for the face I had . . . The past tense that Yeats deploys here is evocative: it speaks to a quality of being that is lost and that we yearn to recapture in the mirror. It evokes a longing for time to stand still. And yet we are what we become and that is always evolving, subject to internal and external forces we are never completely in charge of. Nowhere are the inexorable changes we must all undergo more enduring and visible than through our changing bodies as we develop: the transition from the visceral togetherness of life inside the womb to adaptation outside the womb, or from the comforts of a child's carefree body to the assault of a pubertal body that runs faster than our mind can walk, or from a potent adult body to the gradual undoing of this body whose integrity breaks down into a series of malfunctioning parts with every passing moment.

How we integrate the biological changes that steadfastly and resolutely lead us towards death would be challenge enough, but our experience of our body is fundamentally shaped by the quality of our relationships with others and, more particularly, whether through our earliest exchanges with others we internalise an image of ourselves as lovable and desirable.

The object of desire

The face I had is the face that has not yet met the other's desire. We both yearn to be the object of desire and fear, or even hate, its inevitable ties. The existence of the other's desire, which is expressed and experienced most concretely through the earliest gaze–touch relationship with the 'object of desire' (Britton 1998), can be, for some people, an experience of being enslaved to, or consumed by, the other.

I am choosing the term *object of desire* as opposed to 'primary object' or 'significant other' to underline the sensory, sensual, bodily components of this earliest relationship and how critical it is to the establishment of a desiring and desirable body-self. This provides the foundation for the expectation that the self will be desirable and loved, and that it can desire and love.

In order to approach the experiential realm of being-in-a-body, it is essential to think about desire. The body, desire and sexuality were at the heart of Freud's account of development, but they appear to have lost currency in much contemporary analytic literature, and consequently analytic theory and practice are all the poorer for it (Fonagy 2006).

I am concerned here with 'desire' in relation to two related processes. First, in order to feel desirable we are dependent on the other's libidinal cathexis of our body self, most crucially in early development, that is, we are dependent on the other's desire for us. Second, and related to the latter, I consider it vital developmentally to have the experience of being able to arouse in the other – in the object of desire – an acknowledgement of the *necessity* of the self to the other as proof of the self's desirability. This, I am suggesting, is an experience that is originally mediated by the felt-to-be desirability of the body self in early development, and of the body self's perceived ability to both elicit and to satisfy the other's desire. I am not suggesting that the (m)other should make the child feel he is 'necessary' in a way that impinges on his development as a person in his own right. Rather, what is important is to have the experience that it is possible for the self to satisfy the other's desire in an unconditional manner. Of course, these moments are temporary and illusory in one sense – a child cannot fulfil, and should not fulfil, the whole of the (m)other's desire. But feeling, at least some of the time, that we are the ideal for the other is as important developmentally as learning to bear one's limitations and imperfections.

In this respect Lacan's incisive analysis of the dialectic of desire is profound, as he draws attention to the way in which it is not sufficient to be an object of love or of need; what is required, as he puts it, is 'to stand as the *cause* of desire' (Lacan 1977: 81, my italics). Lacan does not root this in the body, but I want to suggest that this 'requirement' is felt acutely at the level of the body self and can be discerned in our attempts to mould the body according to a physical form that we imagine will guarantee us a privileged, exclusive access, and control over the other. In order to more fully grasp the dialectics of desire we need to turn to the visual relationship between self and other.

The field of vision

Throughout life the body remains an exposed site. No matter how much we cover it up, conceal it, even change it, the body never escapes from the imprint of the other through the other's gaze. Sartre, (1943) argued that 'the look' (le regard) is the domain of domination and mastery. It both provides access to its object without requiring contact with the object, but it also, of course, allows the object to have mastery over us. In all these ways the body thus always bears the trace of the other. This fundamental psychic truth has to be somehow integrated into our image of ourselves. Facing the reality of the body thus involves a paradox: it means simultaneously taking ownership of the body, its desires and limitations, and integrating the fact that the body is the site where we meet the other, where we negotiate the meaning of sameness and difference, of dependency and separation.

Sartre (1943) captured very well the interpersonal tension we all have to manage in his discussion of 'the look'. He described two different kinds of looking: there is the me-who-looks (the voyeur), but this me-who-looks is inevitably also the me-who-is-on-view (the spectacle). The tables turn round – always. *The face I had* belongs to a self that omnipotently assumes that its own look is the point in relation to which the world is ordered. The realisation that the self assumes its coherence in relation to the other's perspective is deeply threatening, not least because this other perspective is inaccessible to us in so far as we cannot control in any absolute way the other's thoughts, feelings or perceptions. Being cognisant of our own specularity leads to the discovery that our foundations lie outside of oneself or, as Sartre (1943) put it, that we 'exist for the other'. This 'existing for the other' implies a state of dependency that, I am suggesting, is experienced first and foremost in the body.

Lacan's field of vision introduces the central role of desire.[1] For Lacan, however, desire is a linguistic process, detached from any taint of bodily excitation. In this respect Julia Kristeva's (1995) views – which are an elaboration of Lacan's – retain what I consider to be an essential connection with the body, through her emphasis on the pre-symbolic dimension of experience.[2] She is referring here to the space in which meaning is semiotic, that is, below the surface of the speaking being (e.g. bodily energies, rhythm).[3] Much of her work has concerned itself with the mind/body dichotomy, showing how bodily energies permeate our signifying practices, and hence how body and mind can never be separated. We will return to her ideas in more depth in Chapter 5. For now, however, it is helpful to stay with Lacan, despite the above caveat, because some of his ideas are nevertheless very pertinent to this discussion.

Lacan (1977) proposes that the other's gaze, through which the voyeur becomes the spectacle for the other, strips him of his sense of illusory mastery. Lacan thus points out that at the core of human being is an exhibitionistic impulse: in order for us to see ourselves we must be seen. He compares this visual mediation to photography:

> in the scopic field, the gaze is outside, I am looked at, that is to say, I am a picture. . . . what determines me, at the most profound level, in the visible, is the gaze that is outside. It is through the gaze that I enter life and it is from the gaze that I receive its effects . . . the gaze is the instrument through which light is embodied and through which. . . . I am *photographed*.
>
> (Lacan 1977: 106)

The problem with being a photograph for the other is that it can feel as if we become a still, imprisoned in someone else's moment over which we have no control. No matter how we present ourselves, we cannot ultimately control what the other sees. This is so because the other's perception of us is embedded in the shifting matrix of their own unconscious feelings, memories and phantasies, and it is filtered through projective mechanisms that make us either desirable, 'bad' or invisible to the other (Silverman 1996).

However desirable we feel, we will probably all nevertheless traverse moments in our lives when we feel dogged by an experience of insufficiency,[4] of not being desirable *enough*. This subjective experience is rooted first and foremost in the body, and it is in our body that we continue to feel it most viscerally throughout life. We all have to find ways of managing this unsettling experience in ourselves, more or less successfully. We do so sometimes directly through the manipulation of the body, for example, trying to make ourselves look attractive. This universal, core experience of insufficiency is predicated on an important, if painful, fact of life that shatters our omnipotent strivings: we cannot fulfil the mother's desire in any absolute sense (Freud 1924; Lacan 1977; Kristeva 1982). Indeed, when this phantasy is actualised (as when a child is 'used' by the mother to satisfy her desire), the functioning of the mind is compromised.

We are then faced with a central paradox: we cannot fulfil the mother's desire, yet we bear the imprint of her desire (or lack of) on our body. Throughout life it is the experience of feeling desired by the other that softens the blow to our omnipotence, that gives us respite from an otherwise relentless confrontation with our insufficiency. We replace the lost, early omnipotence through recreating it in the moment we feel desired, when we can feel ourselves to be the ideal for the other as they desire us. We thus search for an ideal image of ourselves in the other. The urgency with which we may seek this is powerfully expressed in Pirandello's play *As You Desire Me* (1930). In a moving exchange between its main protagonist, L'Ignota, whose identity is in question, and Bruno, the husband, whose wife she may or may not be, she implores him to 'look' at her:

> Look at me, Bruno, look at me. I have been here for four months. . . .
> Look at me. . . . Let me see myself in your eyes. Look at me, look at
> me! I've created myself in that image, the image I see gazing back at me
> in your eyes. That is now me – as you desire me.
>
> (Pirandello 2005: 47–48)

It can be difficult to reconcile oneself to the fact that it is ultimately only through the other that we can discover and/or rediscover an image of ourselves as ideal. This realisation inevitably confronts the self with the separate existence of the other such that the very person who can bestow on us an image of ourselves as ideal, is the same person who can withdraw it. The inevitable dependency that this discloses may be felt to be deeply threatening for some people. Moreover, if what the (m)other-as-mirror reflects back to us is a blank, or if the image is laced with envy or hatred, then the integrity of the self may be challenged.

Although an idealised image of the body – the body we want to have – is likely to be partly shaped by broad cultural standards, the individual meanings ascribed to the body by significant others play an important role (see Chapters 2 and 3). If we think about idealisation, we need to also consider identificatory processes. Through idealisation, the person invests an other with the power to make the self perfect, which immediately places the self in an identificatory relation to the other. In *On Narcissism* Freud (1914) reminded us that: 'What man projects before him as his ideal is the substitute for the lost narcissism of his childhood' (Freud 1914: 94). The vicissitudes of identification are such that the fate of the idealised other can be uncertain depending on the self's capacity to grant the other its separateness and autonomy. A healthy identification is inspired, as it were, by the perceived ideal form of the other, but it is not equated with it. Rather it involves 'forming an imaginary alignment' (Silverman 1996: 71) in our minds, acknowledging its source (the object of identification), and then making it our own.

> A young woman with profound anxiety about her appearance came for her session one day dressed in exactly the same dress I had worn the previous week. Some years later, when the therapy was ending, and she had made considerable progress, she reflected on this phase of the therapy and observed, laughing: 'Now I would never do that and yet I feel that I do dress a bit like you'. It was her capacity to draw a clear distinction between 'a bit like you' and her early projection of herself into my body such that she had to 'be me', that evidenced the change that had taken place.

If the other is perceived to possess the wholeness or unity of which the self feels deprived, then envy may be mobilised. This particular dynamic has been present in a number of cases of women who have undergone cosmetic surgery where the pursuit of surgery was an enactment of the wish to appropriate the maternal, creative body – what I call the *self-made phantasy* – and so circumvent any dependency on the object of desire (see Chapters 6 and 7). Envy may also be mobilised if the (m)other's own felt insufficiency is projected into the baby's body self.

Even when all is proceeding relatively well in development, narcissistic fragility is inscribed in the body self: the experience of shame is rooted in the body. This is why we are all susceptible, to varying degrees, to the lure of changing the surface of the body, if only through clothes or make up, to make ourselves feel better or to ensure our appeal to the other. The more we are deprived of the experience of being the ideal for the other at least some of the time – and most crucially if this deprivation occurs in the early months – the more difficult it becomes to live in an 'ordinary' (i.e. a body rooted in the reality of its inevitable limitations) body. Idealisation then becomes more urgent, more rigid and uncompromising. Being beautiful can then become a dominant, unyielding organising feature in the internal world – a kind of psychic retreat (Steiner 1993) which is fuelled by the *perfect match phantasy*, that is, the phantasy that through beautifying the surface of the body, the self and the object will be tied together in a mutually admiring gaze. One of the important functions of the good-enough mother, we might say, is to help her baby to live in an ordinary body that *sometimes* can do extraordinary things. Too little libidinal investment by the mother and the body self feels neglected and unloved; too much and it may feel colonised and usurped by the mother's needs and projections.

The colour of desire

Je fais souvent ce rêve etrange et penetrant
D'une femme inconnue et que j'aime et qui m'aime
Et qui n'est chaque fois ni tout a fait la meme
Ni tout a fait une autre, et m'aime et me comprend.

('I often have this strange, affecting dream of an unknown woman, who loves me and whom I love, and who each time is neither quite the same nor quite other, and she loves me and understands me').

Paul Verlaine's (1962) words have always moved me because they speak so directly to the phantasy of finding the mother we have not yet encountered (Olivier 1989), that is, a phantasised mother who will surely love us. Verlaine poignantly captures the notion of repetition in mental life: he understands that this is not the mother we know, and yet she is profoundly connected with the original object of desire. My work with individuals for whom the body has become a problematic site, or the only felt to be possible site for the transformation of the self, has led me to speculate about some possible gender differences, not in the use made of the body, but in the unconscious function of body modification.

The early physical exchanges between mother and baby are vitally important for the establishment of attachment (see Chapters 2 and 3), but they are also central to shaping our experience of ourselves as desirable. This experience is, first and foremost, a bodily experience. For the rest of our lives, our bodies mediate desire. The quality of parental love and of the libidinal cathexis of the body in early life will partly determine how comfortable we feel in our body. Indeed as Schilder (1950) grasped in his landmark, timeless study on the body image, the body is profoundly shaped by the desires (or lack of) that are projected into it by others.[5]

The impact on the self of the (m)other's gaze and touch is one of the primary trajectories through which subjectivity is routed. Through her gaze and her touch the mother invests her baby's body self with her libido. I want to suggest that, for both genders, the too-desiring or the not-desiring-enough mother of early childhood can compromise the development of the body self. Desire lies at the heart of the earliest relationship, which is why I have been emphasising that the baby relates to an object of desire. In turn, he needs to secure his own position as the object of desire for the mother,[6] and hence he has to manage *her* desire. As Stimmel (2004) reminds us through her reading of the story of the Oedipus myth that foregrounds Jocasta's experience, the mother is faced with the need to separate from her child. Maternal longings and desire have to give way to the necessity of separation and loss. Yet, Stimmel (2004: 1176) contends, that 'a mother's wishes for reunion with her child are not inherently pathological, only potentially so'. Indeed, depending on how desiring she is, and on the quality of her desire, the mother plays a very significant role in helping the child to feel more or less loved, more or less desirable. Whether she knows it or not, Freud was clear that it is the mother who sets off all the baby's bodily sensations and intense pleasures – she is the 'first seducer':

> A child's intercourse with anyone responsible for his care affords him an unending source of sexual excitation and satisfaction from his erotogenic zones. This is so especially since the person who is in charge of him, who, after all, is as a rule his mother, herself regards him with feelings that are derived from her own sexual life. . . . A mother would probably be horrified if she were made aware that all the marks of affection were rousing the children's sexual instinct and preparing for its future intensity . . . moreover if the mother understood more of the high importance of the part played by instincts in mental life as a whole . . . she would spare herself any self-reproaches even after her enlightenment. She is only fulfilling her task in teaching the child to love.
>
> (Freud 1940: 185)

In his mother's arms the baby thus experiences the earliest 'psychic blueprint (and perhaps a corporeal imprint?) of sexual and love relationships to come' (McDougall 1995: 10).

Of course, the baby does not yet possess the means to understand, or to act upon, the inevitable sexual messages emitted by the mother (Laplanche 1989) as she takes care of his bodily hygiene. As Freud (1940) suggests, she inevitably establishes certain parts of his body as erotogenic zones. But the mother's own unconscious mediates her physical gestures and relationship to the baby's body:

> Without negating the conscious motivation of the mother's solicitude, her unconscious fantasies are also at work here. In other words, the mother's sexuality is always something in excess of the satisfaction of the infant's need – *an excess* which cannot be accommodated within an infantile psychosomatic structure that is still predominantly situated at the level of need.
>
> (Pacteau 1994: 115; my italics)

The problem posed by this 'excess' of the mother's sexuality is interestingly developed in Lacan's (1982) reading of *Hamlet* as he locates Hamlet's problem as his mother's (Gertrude) desire, placing Gertrude as the 'Other of demand' (Lacan 1982).

Too much desire and the child will recoil, feeling his body to be colonised by the mother's 'demand'. But the absence of a mother's desire can be just as problematic. A mother's inhibitions as she handles the baby's body will also be indelibly inscribed in the body. The legacy of not being desired is as insidious as the pressure to meet the mother's demand. This may lead to a need to alter the given body in search for a bodily form that will elicit desire. The good-enough mother's task is therefore a challenging one: she has to strike the right level of libidinal investment in the child's body so that the baby feels desired, but not intruded upon.

Importantly, at the intersection of the first stirrings of desire, the little boy and the little girl have an asymmetrical experience in relation to the mother. The little boy is, at birth, exposed to the opposite sex. In this sense desire may flow more easily in the dyad, which is not to say that this is a less complicated path, since for him the challenge lies in how to extricate himself from his Oedipal entanglement. By contrast the little girl, who is not an Oedipal object for her mother, may feel that she simply cannot get enough positive investment in her bodily self,[7] that she cannot elicit the mother's desire enough, if at all, to shore up her quota of desirability. Instead she has to wait for her turn when, and if, her relationship with her father is more accessible to her. Whereas for men the risk lies in feeling imprisoned by the mother's desire, for the little girl, she may feel that from the start she yearns for another sort of body, the sort of body that elicits the mother's desire (Olivier 1989).

If I were called upon to speculate on gender differences in relation to the underlying experiences of male and female body modifiers I would venture to suggest that in male body modifiers the experience of the mother was more often a stifling one. The body modification serves the function of rescuing the body from the maternal takeover by concretely marking it as separate. I am thus suggesting that the male body modifier perhaps more often carries the burden of excessive and intrusive desire.

In the female body modifier, the experience tends to be more frequently that her body was simply not desired (enough) by the mother and hence she feels compelled to modify it so as to get the 'right' body that will elicit her desire, or she attacks her body, under the guise of making it more beautiful, as a way of signalling her bodily grievance to her mother (i.e. 'You have not given me enough'). Here, I am thus suggesting, that for the woman the body carries the burden of an absence, of a deficit of desire.

Of course, in practice, these distinctions are never so rigid. Moreover, I can think of female patients who share the goal of the male body modifier and vice versa. I am therefore only tentatively suggesting here that there may be interesting trends that distinguish the majority of male and female body modifiers – a hypothesis requiring further investigation.

The body then never ceases to signal the relationship to the mother. The psychic impact of an excess of desire or too little desire may be felt by some very concretely at the level of the body self. Problems arise when the object of desire uncannily merges with the maternal figure of demand or with a more absent, rejecting maternal figure. When body modification is felt to provide a solution to internal conflicts, we invariably find that the object of desire partakes of the insistent, nagging character of demand, becoming an impossible-to-satisfy internal object in neurosis, and a more terrifying one in psychosis.

In search of the mother's desire: the perfect match phantasy

As I mentioned earlier, the search for an ideal, desirable image of ourselves in the other's eyes can acquire a frantic, manic quality. If Frankenstein's creature had been born in the twenty-first century he might have been tempted to heal his deep narcissistic wounds by taking part in a reality TV makeover show. With its emphasis on metamorphosis and transformation RTV takes on the function of the archaic fairy godmother who can make the *impossible* happen. This is why such shows have widespread appeal: stories of this kind promise us (the viewer) change too.

If these shows promise to realise the 'impossible', we might well wonder who or what is felt to be *impossible*? As I have been suggesting, this impossible thing is the satisfaction of the mother's desire. I am wary of generalisations, but I would like nevertheless to share some observations from work – other than my clinical work – that have led me to speculate about one possible pathway to the use of body modification as the solution to psychic problems. I will use this example specifically to illustrate the enactment of the *perfect match phantasy*. Here the body modification serves the function of creating a perfect, ideal body that will guarantee the mother's love and desire. The subjective experience is of a painful, humiliating insufficiency and this narcissistic wound cures itself by manic flight into changing the body's surface. The perfect match phantasy therefore concerns the *fusion* of an idealised self (very concretely felt to be an idealised body) with an idealised object/body.

Over many years, in my capacity in advising television production companies, and in assessing contestants for RTV shows, I have assessed over two hundred people. I would like to focus here on my detailed assessment of sixteen young girls, aged sixteen years upwards[8], who had elected to take part in a RTV show that involved a number of interventions to improve their overall presentation, several of which were directly aimed at altering the body (without, however, using any surgery).[9]

I assessed each girl for approximately two hours and made notes during the interviews such that I have a reliable record of what they told me. Of the sixteen girls, thirteen had overtly difficult relationships with their mothers. Eight of these had 'absent' mothers: two mothers had died during early childhood (one shortly after giving birth), two mothers had left the home and not taken the daughter with them, and four had physically present mothers who were, however, absent emotionally (typically depressed).

On meeting these girls it was quickly apparent that they did not inhabit their bodies comfortably – the distinguishing feature being that they seemed more like a caricature of a person. They were either reacting against any hint of femininity, and so presented as masculine both in their physical posture and attire (one young girl arrived in mechanic's overalls) and in their exploits ('I can down a pint quicker than any bloke I know', said one), or they presented as overly sexualised and recounted stories of quite extensive promiscuity, wearing the one-night-stand as an emblem of their adeptness at avoiding any semblance of intimacy and dependency.

Behind the carefully constructed tough veneer (which was concretely expressed through the presentation of their bodily self: tattoos, piercings, choice of clothing, posture) these girls nevertheless revealed considerable fragility. Two of them were in fact excluded from taking part in the programme. The others were well enough (psychiatrically speaking, that is) to take part, yet determined to play out their search for the mother's loving gaze on the screen.

As their stories unfolded, two recurring themes emerged. The first concerned the mostly conscious fantasy of how being seen on TV would enhance popularity, mostly among their peers. Only one girl was explicit in her wish to pursue a career in TV and viewed the programme as a way of securing this. Interestingly, this was not a strong motivation in the other girls.

The second and, I think, by far more powerful motivation concerned the wish to 'prove' their desirability. For the two girls I have chosen to focus on here by way of illustration, I understood this to reflect the mostly unconscious phantasy of finding a desirable physical form that was anticipated to guarantee the mother's loving gaze.

One girl, Ms E., whose mother had abandoned her at a very young age, and who presented as very masculine, put it thus when I asked her why she was keen to take part in the programme:

well . . . I don't know why I want to take part in this really . . . I guess I think it could be a good laugh . . . dressing up . . . I've never had a bra fitting [laughs]. You know, my dad never met anyone else . . . so I guess I had none of the girly stuff – shopping for clothes, make up, that kind of thing . . . like some of my friends had with their mothers.

After I asked her whether she had ever tried to find her mother, she replied:

I don't know where she is now. I don't want to know. I got a letter from her when I was ten and she asked me to send her a picture of me. She

said she wanted to see me and would come to visit. She never did. I don't
want her to find out where I am now. What's the point?

I observed that by appearing on TV she was, in a way, making it more likely
that her mother might see her. This made her pause for several minutes and
then she became tearful:

Damn [punches herself very hard on the leg]. I didn't want to cry!

I asked her why she thought she was now crying:

I hate thinking about her. It always upsets me . . . I guess I have thought at
times about why she left, why she did not take me with her. My dad's not
good at talking about these things and I think he prefers not to think
about the past. So I don't really know why she left. . . . When I was little I
used to think it was because of me . . . she was a really pretty woman . . .
a bit of a 'loose' woman, my dad said, but I don't know if that's right . . .
just as well she can't see me now [looks down at her stained overalls].

The quality of the exchange with Ms E. stood out and the interview was
especially moving; she was able to be quite reflective in the end and to think
with me about her longing for her mother to see her 'looking at my best'.
Although most of the other girls were not as accessible as she was, some of
their stories were similarly moving variations on this theme: a longing to be
looked at with admiring, loving eyes. One of the striking features was the
way in which all but one of the girls excitedly anticipated 'dressing up' with
a very childlike quality, imagining the nice clothes they would wear. As I
listened to them the image that was conjured in my mind was of them
diving into an idealised version of an opulent wardrobe/maternal body and
dressing up in mother's clothes. The two girls I am concentrating on here
highlighted the opportunity to wear clothes 'made of nice materials' or
'made of expensive stuff'. The clothes were anticipated to provide a kind of
second skin (Lemoine-Luccioni 1983; Anzieu 1989). Most interestingly, *all*
made spontaneous reference to the bra fitting sessions that were a staple
part of the show, giving voice, I thought, to a yearning for the touch and
libidinal cathexis of the bodily self by a mother who could 'support' the
development of their femininity.

The girl whose mother had abandoned her early on in life, Ms E., mentioned
that she hated her breasts and had read in a magazine that 'a good bra can
make a lot of difference'. I mused aloud that what might make a difference

was perhaps not just the bra itself, but the fact that someone would be taking an interest in her appearance. At first she dismissed what I said, but what followed in our exchange was striking. She spontaneously told me that as a little girl she used to stroke her body with her older cousin's silk slip that she surreptitiously took from her drawer whenever she visited her house. She then laughed, embarrassed, and said she was not sure why she had mentioned this to me. I found this especially moving, as if she was letting me know something of how deprived she had felt of mother's loving touch, and of how she now needed to provide this for herself. Ferenczi indeed noted how bodily self-stimulation could be understood as a substitute 'on one's own body for the lost object' (Ferenczi 1938: 23–24).

The second girl – Ms Y. – a bright but very brittle young girl, looked physically downtrodden. Her clothes were ripped, her hair was cropped short and her nails were bitten back. She described growing up in a very depressed family: her father had been long-term unemployed and her mother has seemingly never overcome the death of her own mother when Ms Y. was barely one year old. When I asked Ms Y. why she had applied to take part in the programme, she replied:

> Why not? Sounds like fun. Plus I will get to stay in a nice place, not the shit hole I live in.

I observed that she seemed to want to get away from something quite depressing:

> I like having fun. Better than being at home . . .

I said that home seemed to be the last place she wanted to be in:

> My mum is depressed, my dad's given up – it's not much fun.

I asked her to then tell me about her mother:

> I hate talking about her. . . . I saw a counsellor years ago because the school was worried about me and that's all she wanted to talk about . . . she's . . . I don't know . . . I can't think of anything to say about her. We barely talk to each other. Not that she talks to anyone really.

I observed that it seemed very difficult to even approach her mother in her own mind. At this point she relaxed a bit:

> I don't really know her. . . . She's always been there I guess, but not really – do you know what I mean. . . . She's never been like my best friend's mum. She's always out there, getting involved, taking X shopping, buying clothes and stuff. . . . My mum doesn't care about things like that.

I said that her best friend's mum seemed to be the kind of mum she wished she had. Ms Y's eyes lit up and a spark of life was injected into our exchange as if she was, in that moment, relating to an enlivening object:

> Yeah . . . I mean, my mum doesn't even care if I do this [the TV show]. She probably won't even watch it, but X's mum is really into this and she has really wanted me to do it. I see her everyday, like . . . it's a bit like a second family . . . .

I said she seemed to feel that it was hard to get her mother to even *look* at her. Ms Y. responded to this very concretely, but her answer is nevertheless striking:

> She's as blind as a bat! She can only really see out of one eye.

This was a powerful communication and reflected the way that Ms Y. related internally to a blind object – one that could not see her and help her, in turn, to see herself.

If the mother-mirror is absent or hostile in her relationship to the baby's body, the individual will later most likely search for the loving gaze in whatever mirrors are available. Encouraged by her 'surrogate' mother (her best friend's mother) Ms Y. could take comfort from the knowledge that at least one (m)other would be looking at her with admiring, supporting eyes. Being the object of the camera's gaze, and then the object of the audience's gaze, was compellingly tempting for several of the young girls I assessed. For them the TV programme promised to transform them into desirable and lovable girls whose mothers would surely not turn their eyes away from them.[10]

In Ms Y. there was, perhaps inevitably given the extent to which she had felt her mother had turned away from her into her own melancholic state, a more aggressive psychic backdrop to her desire to be admired, namely the wish to triumph over the mother. When I asked her what she thought her mother would think if she did manage to see the show, Ms Y. succinctly replied:

I hope it makes her realise what a slob she's become.

Where there has been an undercathexis of the bodily self by the mother, as was the case for Ms Y., there may be not just the yearning for an idealised mother who will look at the self with admiring, loving eyes, but also an accompanying sense of grievance about the felt deprivation and hence a need to attack the object. In some of the patients I have worked with, this grievance takes on a more pernicious quality in their minds. The body modification then becomes the means through which all ties to the object of desire are severed and the body self is omnipotently reinvented (what I call the self-made phantasy). We will return to these themes in later chapters.

Looking and being looked at

As we have seen, there is a fundamental asymmetry in vision: the unpalatable truth is that the other never looks at the self from the place from which we see ourselves. Put another way, the mother's gaze is not isomorphic with the child's own image. The body is so fundamental developmentally because it becomes the organising site of perspective, but it is also, simultaneously 'an object available to others from their perspectives – in other words, it is both subject and object' (Grosz 1990: 38).

In his work on beauty, Meltzer (1988) draws attention to another inherent paradox in human relations – another unpalatable asymmetry. He notes that as the baby apprehends the mother's beauty, he is simultaneously exposed to a knowledge withheld.[11] Meltzer's (1988) notion of 'aesthetic conflict' is helpful in understanding the experience of uncertainty in relation to the object of desire. Meltzer highlights a core, and according to him universal, conflict faced by the baby at the breast, looking at his mother. He refers to the aesthetic impact on the baby of the 'beautiful mother', which he considers to be the primal representation of the beauty of the world. He writes evocatively of 'aesthetic reciprocity' to capture the meeting of the mutually admiring gaze of both mother and baby. He specifies how this blissful experience simultaneously exposes the baby to the mother's 'enigmatic inside', that is, to what he cannot see or know. This is another way of describing how the present mother always contains the shadow of the absent mother – of the (m)other who is beyond our omnipotent control. At the core of each of us there exists a painful yearning to know the inside of the other who, by virtue of its separateness, can never be fully apprehended and possessed by the self. Proust beautifully captures this elusive nature of the other:

> I might caress her, pass my hand slowly over her, but, just as if I had
> been handling a stone which encloses the salt of immemorial oceans or
> the light of a star, I felt that I was touching no more than the sealed
> envelope of a person who inwardly reached to infinity.
>
> (Proust 1972: 248–249)

This is the challenge that we all face in coming to terms with otherness: as
the baby looks at the mother, searching for himself in her, he is confronted
with something that is hidden – 'sealed' away (and in some cases 'sealed-
off') – behind her appearance. Even when all is going well, looking and
being looked at thus exposes us to uncertainty.

The apprehension of beauty therefore makes a heavy demand on the
baby: it evokes the oceanic feeling of oneness – the fusion with the maternal
breast – while also exposing the baby to the reality of the object's separateness. Indeed Milner (1985) argued that the artistic form reactivates and
synthesises these two experiences. The appreciation of beauty is thus both
about an experience of symmetry (Matte Blanco 1975), while requiring an
ongoing dialectic with the awareness of otherness, or if we stay with Matte
Blanco's bi-logic frame of reference, we could say that it requires main-
taining awareness of asymmetrical relations that discriminate and recognise
difference (see Chapter 2).

From the outset, Meltzer (1988) thus suggests, we are all confronted with
a painful state of uncertainty. We find more or less adaptive ways of
reconciling ourselves to what we cannot see and can never know with any
certainty about those we are closest to and hence, too, about what they see
in us. If this experience is, however, reinforced in actuality by a mother who
holds up an opaque, one-way mirror, the task of bearing what Meltzer
(1988) refers to as her unknowable 'enigmatic interior' may expose the baby
to tormenting doubt about what it is that the mother sees in him. This
predicament, and its potentially tormenting quality, was well captured by
Sartre:

> The other looks at me and as such holds the secret of my being, he
> knows what I am. *Thus the profound meaning of my being is outside of
> me, imprisoned in an absence.*
>
> (Sartre 1943: 207, my italics)

We never grow out of the search for the (m)other's loving and desiring
gaze. In more or less compulsive ways we go on searching for it, sometimes
using the manipulation of the body to capture it, or to create the illusion
that this is possible. If we are lucky we find it, or refind it, at particular
points in our more intimate relationships, only to lose it again because that
is all it can be; we can never possess the other's desire, which would be
tantamount to being the other for oneself. We can enjoy the other's desire

for us, be inspired by it, but it can never be ours for the keeping. Regressive moments can be only brief – a temporary oasis from the painful recognition of the difference and separateness that nevertheless guarantees the survival of the self and of the other.

Chapter 2

The symptom of ugliness

I had admired the perfect form of my protégés. Their grace, beauty and delicate complexions but how I was terrified when I viewed myself in a transparent pool! At first I stared back, unable to believe that it was indeed I who was reflected in the mirror; and when I became fully convinced that I was in reality the monster that I am I was filled with the bitterest sensation of despair and mortification. Alas! I did not yet entirely know the staple effects of this miserable deformity.

(Shelley 1818: 116)

Frankenstein's mother

In June 1816, in the Swiss Alps, a young woman then aged only nineteen, developed the idea for a story that was set to become a classic – *Frankenstein*. The idea for the novel grew out of an exchange of ideas involving the poets Percy Shelley and Lord Byron, Byron's physician, John Polidor, and Mary Shelley. Casually, they speculated about the reanimation of a corpse – speculations that must have resonated deeply with Mary Shelley's own early experience of losing her mother. Byron went on to suggest that they each wrote a ghost story. And indeed this is what Mary Shelley set out to do – except that what she wrote was a story about the 'ghosts' in her own nursery (Fraiberg et al. 1975), that is, about her own unprocessed early experience with her parents. Indeed, familial fact and fantasy are the integral fabric of *Frankenstein*.

Frankenstein is the tale of a 'modern Prometheus' – Victor Frankenstein – as signalled by the novel's subtitle. Following the death of his mother, Frankenstein leaves home to attend university, where he becomes overly preoccupied with the possibility of creating a new being using the parts of deceased bodies that he collects through digging up graveyards. After he literally 'shocks' his new creation into life by passing an electric current through its body, he is confronted with the reality of his botched creature and he rejects it. The creature, abandoned by his creator, and rebuffed by all who meet him because of his unsightly physical appearance, sets out to pursue Frankenstein to call him to account. Frankenstein's refusal to even grant the creature a companion like himself provokes the creature to avenge himself by killing the people Frankenstein loves. In the end creature and creator pursue each other through icy waters where they both meet their death.

Victor Frankenstein's aim of bestowing animation to lifeless matter has led many to interpret the novel as reflecting the theme of the dangers of scientific ambition and its moral implications. Although there have also been numerous other, more psychological interpretations of the narrative, and some specifically psychoanalytic ones (see, for example, Gold 1985), I want to focus selectively here on the way in which the novel provides one of the most vivid portrayals of the potential destructiveness of parental projections into the baby's *body*.

Because of its emphasis on the visual – the creature at the outset is not in any sense bad, it is simply 'ugly' – *Frankenstein* poignantly illustrates the fate of the baby deprived of the mother's loving gaze. The creature is rejected by Frankenstein on account of his ugliness, and we might also say, that the creature is ugly *because* he has not been desired. Although the creature is depicted as 'hideous', in fact the novel vividly speaks to the intersubjective nature of perceptions of beauty and ugliness – a point we will return to later in this chapter. Moreover, the novel details how the other's projections, and the inevitable deprivation, as inscribed on the body, can then incite envy and violence in the one who is thus projected into.

The relationship between Frankenstein and his creation is as good a case study as any from which to start an exploration of the gazing relationship and its vicissitudes. I should add that although I want to stress here the gazing relationship, as I will explore in more detail in Chapter 3, looking and touching are inextricably linked. A look can be experienced as an actual loving 'touch', and the earliest exchanges between mother and baby are visual *and* tactile ones. Importantly, too, a hateful look can be experienced quite concretely as a physical assault as recognised in the popular expression 'if looks could kill'.

Frankenstein the novel has spawned numerous films, most of which cast the story in the horror genre and have as its centrepiece a hideous creature set on a path of destruction. Popular culture has adapted the story in simplified terms, but Shelley's narrative is far more nuanced, as touching as it is disturbing. The creature is more affecting than its screen image counterpart because he does not grunt or stumble; rather, he speaks with feeling. It is this that makes it possible to understand his destructiveness as we recognise that his envy and hatred are born of loss and rejection. Indeed, Mary Shelley lingers over the creature's painful degradation due to his ugliness before he is depicted as an enraged murderer and fiend.

It is striking that the narrative of Frankenstein's creature has been ignored in so many of the stage and film workings of the story. It is as if we (the audience) prefer the more frightening and emotionally less complex image of the creature stumbling through the fog, hands and arms stretched out ahead of him, looking for his next victim, than being faced with the pain he feels, or the hatred that results from feeling so ugly and unloved. The now classic impersonation of the creature by Boris Karloff is probably the most moving: the image of Karloff's outstretched arms evokes the uncoordinated gestures of a baby longing to be held, while the fog he travels through as he pursues Frankenstein conjures up an inner state of 'foggy', barely apprehended objects that provide no internal sustenance as he struggles to make sense of his experience. As the creature's longing to be desired by Frankenstein is thwarted, repeatedly, and he brushes up against the primacy of the visual order and others flee from him in fear or attack him, the longing outstretched arms are perverted into the chilling gesture that eventually leads to strangling – the arms that yearn for physical contact presage the arms that will kill.

Death is the final outcome of the narrative, but the creature's beginnings also bear the hallmark of dead and murderous internal objects. When the creature is born, Shelley conjures up a picture of horror:

> It was on a dreary night in November, that I beheld the accomplishment of my toil. With an anxiety that almost amounted to agony, I collected the instruments of life around me, that I might infuse a spark of being into the lifeless thing that lay at my feet. . . . The rain pattered dismally against the panes, and my candle was nearly burnt out, when, by the glimmer of the half-extinguished light, I saw the dull yellow eye of the creature open; it breathed hard, and a convulsive motion agitated its limbs. . . . His yellow skin scarcely covered the work of the muscles and arteries beneath; his hair was of a lustrous black, and flowing . . . but these luxuriances only formed a more horrid contrast with his watery eyes, that seemed almost the same colour as the dun white sockets in which they were set, his shrivelled complexion and straight black lips.
>
> (Shelley 1818: 58)

But the real horror is the look on Victor Frankenstein's face as he apprehends his creation, alive, for the first time. He looks and literally runs away, effectively abandoning the 'newborn' to die. Birth is a 'catastrophe' and the newborn is never touched, never held – he is simply the recipient of a look of disgust and horror:

> How can I describe my emotion at this catastrophe, or how to delineate the wretch whom with such infinite pains and care I had endeavoured to form? His limbs were in proportion and I had selected his features as

beautiful. Beautiful! Great God! . . . the beauty of the dream vanished
and breathless horror and disgust filled my heart.

(Shelley 1818: 318)

Frankenstein's narcissism is plain to see (Gold 1985; Kestner 1995), the
idealisation and inevitable denigration painful to witness as he rejects his
creation that is never anything more than an appendage that can be
dispensed with. Yet, the creature is so much an extension of his creator that
he appears as another self looking back at the self, leading to spiralling
paranoia and persecution most vividly evoked by their chase through icy
waters. The confusion, resulting from excessive projective identification,
between creator and creature probably accounts for why, in the popular
imagination, the name Frankenstein often evokes not the deeply troubled
young scientist, but his creation. Frankenstein's psychotic pursuit of the
creature across icy waters provides one of the most appropriately 'chilling'
illustrations of the destructiveness inherent in projective identification. In
the end both creator and creature become more and more intertwined, their
identities merging as they approach death, locked into each other. It is only
death that finally separates them.

Throughout the novel the creature remains without a name. By not
naming him, he is denied any kind of individuality or recognition because,
fundamentally, he belongs to Frankenstein. This highlights the central issue
of ownership of the body – whose body is it? This is indeed a recurring
theme in my work with patients who modify their bodies. Through these
patients we can observe how the modification of the body – from the more
everyday modification through the clothes we wear right through to piercings and scarifications – is an expression, at least in part, of an attempt to
mark the body as 'belonging to me', and so separate from the object.

Frankenstein brings the creature to life for his own narcissistic gratification only then to control him, at first promising him a companion as
hideous as himself so that he would not be so alone, and then denying him
even the request that he might be loved by an other, if not by the one who
gave him life. It is this final deprivation, and assertion of Frankenstein's
ownership of the creature's body, and so of his fate, that leads the creature
to avenge the betrayal, murdering both Frankenstein's best friend, Clerval,
and his new wife Elisabeth. I am suggesting that it is the creature's actual
emotional deprivation that fuels envious retaliation when provoked by the
love and desire Frankenstein has access to from his devoted companions
and that he feels for them.

As I mentioned earlier, *Frankenstein*'s elaboration of the subjective
experience of looking and being looked at is very germane to the subject
matter of this book. The creature longs to be recognised by his creator, but
the gaze of the other invariably confirms his ugliness and rejection.
Frankenstein rejects his newborn creation on account of his ugliness –

perceived as such because the creature is only a reflection of the 'hideous' feelings or parts of himself that he has projected into him. When the creature reveals himself to the blind Delacey he finally meets acceptance, if only because Delacey cannot in fact see him. But even this respite from the otherwise relentless cycle of rejection is dashed as the horrified eyes of Felix, Sophie and Agatha light upon him:

> For from that moment I declared everlasting war against the species, and more than all, against him who had formed me, and sent me forth to this insupportable misery.
>
> (Shelley 1818: 138)

Frankenstein's offence is not the creation of a monster, but his inability to love him. He *looks* at him and finds him repellent: the loving gaze that normally welcomes the baby to life outside the womb is precisely the juncture at which Frankenstein rejects his monster-baby. The creature, by virtue of his visible difference, transgresses our sense of what is beautiful and so reflects back, as a kind of mirror, the position of the one who excludes him (Botting 1995). It is in this very sense that the novel can be read as a cautionary tale about the deadly consequences of violent projections into the baby's body.

Through Frankenstein's frenzied final hours as he sews up the creature's body before he passes the current through it, we witness a violent process of projective identification into the creature's as yet 'unborn' body. The way the creature's body is put together out of decomposed tissues – the vestiges of former lives now dug out of their graves – provides a disturbing portrayal of the signs of an absence already inscribed on the body at birth. In Frankenstein's mind the creature's body is a composite figure of faded lives whose loss cannot be mourned because, I want to suggest, grievance lies at the heart of this particular loss.

In the novel, Frankenstein loses his mother at the age of seventeen, before he is set to go to university. This grief remains unresolved. He acknowledges that it takes a long time to offset 'that the brightness of the beloved eye can ever be extinguished' (Shelley 1818: 45). We are given the impression of a somewhat over-idealised relationship between Frankenstein and his mother. Yet, although the novel does not dwell on the cause of his mother's death, it is of note that she dies following a period of caring for Victor's adoptive sister, Elisabeth (whom he later marries and who is eventually killed by the creature), from whom she contracts scarlet fever. In the end, we might say, that it was Elisabeth who was in the mother's mind's eye, whom she physically nursed and devoted herself to, not Frankenstein. And it is because she cared for Elisabeth that the mother dies. Deprived of his mother's admiring gaze, Frankenstein sets off for university and becomes intent on circumventing the significance of the mother in reality, and in his mind, as he pursues feminine nature to her 'hiding places' to appropriate for himself the maternal role, allowing him to create a new species without the intervention of woman.[1]

The search for the mother's loving gaze and touch was a central theme in Mary Shelley's personal life and, I would like to suggest, that it was the primary driver for *Frankenstein*'s narrative. Mary Shelley's real-life losses and internal conflicts are barely concealed in the narrative structure and characterisation, though she never herself made a connection between her own suffering and the creature's plight. Shelley's own 1831 introduction to the novel highlights the 'hideous thoughts' that went into the writing of Frankenstein: the ghastly image that overwhelmed her in 1816 when 'forbidden and ugly materials' (Shelley 1831) had, like the creature itself, come alive in her mind. *Frankenstein* is a powerful metaphor for both cultural and personal crises, but it is the latter that concerns us here and that most likely speaks to Mary Shelley's own unconscious preoccupations: her phantasy of the baby as a monstrous agent of destruction *and* as the pitiful victim of maternal abandonment, which is primarily felt in the body because, in her own experience, what was rejected was the baby's bodily self.

Mary Shelley was the daughter of Mary Wollstonecraft and William Godwin.[2] Her mother died of a retained placenta eleven days after giving birth to Mary. Her father subsequently married his neighbour – Mary Clairmont – seemingly keen for a second wife to provide a surrogate mother for Mary. Although he gratefully remembered his parents, significantly Godwin never could bring himself to forgive his own mother for sending him away from home while still an infant to be nourished by a nurse. In Godwin one senses a man unlikely to have been able to provide much solace to a little girl grieving for the mother she never knew. Just as his own nourishment as a baby had been provided functionally by an outsider, he managed to find a replacement for the function of a mother for Mary, but was unable to provide her with a stepmother who would care for her emotionally. As several biographers have pointed out, Mrs Clairmont – the stepmother – was hardly the same as Mary's mother: she is described as vulgar, mundane, and preoccupied with the welfare of her own two children. Unsurprisingly, she failed to establish a good relationship with Mary Shelley.

Mary Shelley's position in her father's affections was further undermined when in 1803, before her sixth birthday, the new Mrs Godwin presented her husband with a son, Little William. This is likely to have been very painful for Mary Shelley, not only because he represented a rival for her father's all too scarce affection, but also because in the family's unconscious system resided an earlier 'Little William' – the son William Godwin had expected in 1797 when he and the then pregnant Mary Wollstonecraft, over-confident of the sex of the child she was carrying, had repeatedly promised themselves a 'little William' (Wardle 1966). The first 'little William', as it were, turned out to be Mary herself – the baby responsible for her mother's death and her father's grief. In the shadow of this early traumatic experience, Mary Shelley perhaps knew only too well the parental look of disappointment. Rejection and abandonment were inscribed in her body – a body that, like the creature's, could later never be enjoyed and feel like a source of life and hope. Perhaps it was this personal experience that spawned the idea for Frankenstein's workshop of 'filthy creation': once Frankenstein decides to create life, he frequents the vaults and charnel houses and studies the human body in all its forms of decay and decomposition.[3]

A relentless cycle of birth and death dominated Mary Shelley's life. Pregnant at sixteen, and almost constantly pregnant throughout the following five years, Mary Shelley's adult life was also punctuated by loss. She lost most of her babies soon after they were born. This experience may account for why birth is presented as a hideous thing in the novel. In February 1815 Mary's first child – a baby girl – was born illegitimate and premature. The journal entries chronicle breastfeeding and reading side-by-side followed by a desolate entry four days later when the baby died, unnamed: 'Find my baby dead . . . a miserable day.' Some days after the baby's death Mary Shelley also recorded a dream: 'Dreamed that my little baby came to life again, that it had only been cold and that we rubbed it before the fire and it lived.' By now, the dead baby had become an 'it' – like Frankenstein's own creation. The dream poignantly speaks to what must have been Mary Shelley's agony, and bears uncanny echoes of Frankenstein's pursuit of creating life out of death. It is of note that in the novel Frankenstein gives life to a creature who is never loved perhaps reflecting how the character of Frankenstein embodied a version of her own absent mother who was never present to look at her, touch her and love her.

Following the loss of her first baby, the journal entries illustrate Mary Shelley's need to find refuge in a gruelling reading programme at Percy Shelley's side, seeking solace in her mind, perhaps because the body was by then the site of such devastation and loss. Although she eventually married Percy Shelley in 1816, it was only after the suicide of his wife, Harriet. It was as if everything potentially alive – her babies, her new marriage – invariably followed in the wake of a traumatic loss.[4]

Mary Shelley's own 'Little William' – her third child – died in 1819, aged three. More than the others, this loss appears to have devastated her, perhaps because the little boy had become so identified in her mind with her father (after whom he was named) whose love and approval she continued to crave. These proved to be unrealistic expectations, given Godwin's evident difficulty in availing himself emotionally to his daughter. Following the death of Little William, Percy Shelley wrote to Godwin to ask him to soothe Mary 'on account of her terrible state of mind' (quoted in Spark 1988: 62). Godwin (who could not even remember his grandson's age) instead wrote to berate Shelley and to ask for more money to help him fight a litigation. A second letter from him directly to Mary Shelley proved equally insensitive; instead of consolation for the loss of her child, Mary Shelley found herself threatened once more by the withdrawal of her father's love. 'Remember too', wrote Godwin, 'though at first your nearest connections may pity you in this state, yet when they see you fixed in selfishness and ill humour the family cease to love you and scarcely learn to endure you' (quoted in Spark 1988: 62) – harsh words and eerily reminiscent of Frankenstein's own harsh words to the creature when he pleads with his creator to be heard by him: 'Be gone! Relieve me of the sight of your detested form' (Shelley 1818: 104).

The characterisation of the creature draws heavily on Mary Shelley's own personal experience of her attempts to win her father's notice and approval and the rejection she endured. Even more striking is the way in which Mary Shelley's early traumatic loss of her mother reverberates throughout the novel (Rubenstein 1976). Dead and absent mothers dominate the narrative. Felix and Agatha's mother is dead, so is Sophie's, and the creature, of course, has no mother, only a so-called father who abandons him to his fate. Frankenstein's own mother was an orphan taken in by his father and his adoptive sister (whom he later marries) was also an orphan. Throughout the novel the absence of the mother as a loving, admiring mirror is thus acutely felt. This absence can also be traced in the stories of the patients who view their body as undesirable. The predicament of Frankenstein's creature draws attention to the potentially destructive consequences of a loss that cannot be mourned.[5] The creature's rejection is painful, but we cannot ignore the way in which his sorrow becomes perverted into a wish to spoil the love that he perceives others to behold. The *self-made phantasy*, which I am suggesting fuels some people's need to remodel the body, results from just this kind of 'perversion of loss' (Levy and Lemma 2004).

Beauty and the beast within

The question of what constitutes beauty is a complex one and I will not be able to do justice to it here – it deserves a book in its own right – but it deserves at least some mention. When it comes to beauty, research studies have repeatedly confirmed that we appear to be drawn to symmetry and baby-like features: the large eyes and mouth set against the small nose.[6] Moreover, we are actively unsettled by asymmetry in others' facial features particularly. This would suggest that beauty denotes a state of harmony and, indeed, the importance of harmony or symmetry can be traced in many definitions of beauty. The implication appears to be that what is perceived as beautiful presents us with an image of completeness and balance rather than of difference. Descartes defined beauty as 'an agreement and equilibrium of all parts so exact that no one part dominates the other' (quoted in Pacteau 1994: 82) – a definition later echoed by Diderot: 'In finding objects beautiful I mean nothing other than that I perceive, between the parts of which they are composed, some order, arrangements, symmetry, relations' (Diderot 1751, quoted in Pacteau 1994: 83).

Leonardo da Vinci's detailed study of the human body, born of his meticulous examination, measurements and then representations of bones, muscles, tendons and veins, led to a description of the beauty of the body that, as Pacteau (1994) draws attention to, underlines the absence of lack:

> Though human ingenuity may make various inventions . . . it will never devise an invention more beautiful, more simple, more direct than does Nature; because in her inventions nothing is lacking, and nothing is superfluous.
>
> (Leonardo, quoted in Pacteau 1994: 82)

In Leonardo's work each limb, each organ was perfectly designed, fit for purpose: the arm described a perfect circle; the body as a whole was contained within a square and a circle. How far removed this perfect body is from the real body we all have to live with. As such it brings into focus the need we have to find reassurance in the external bodily form of some kind of predictability, order and sameness. A disfigured body, or a missing limb, are unsettling reminders of our own physical fragility: this probably accounts for why we find physical disfigurement so disturbing, yet compelling. We may feel the need to both look (to locate the ugliness firmly in the other) and to look away, as if afraid this perceived ugliness might be somehow contagious and what we have projected will force itself back into us.

Asymmetry seems to impose a particularly heavy demand on the mind. Why might this be so? Here Matte Blanco's (1975) description of the bi-logic mind is very helpful. He distinguishes two modes of thinking: the asymmetrical mode (i.e. conscious, logical thinking) and the symmetrical mode (i.e. unconscious thinking which treats asymmetrical relations as if they were symmetrical creating an illusion of timelessness). These represent two modes of knowing the world. We might surmise that symmetry is appealing because it resonates with a timeless universe, where feelings of infinity dominate, where we experience ourselves as 'one' with our object(s) without the disjunctive experience posed by the perception of difference (i.e. of asymmetrical relations). Asymmetry, by contrast, places a much heavier emotional demand because it requires us to tolerate difference and, ulti-mately, our finitude.

In many cultures respect for the body is based on a respect for order, boundaries, purity and wholeness. According to Bakhtin (1984) the bour-geois classical canon that evolved in Europe during the Renaissance emphasised an aesthetic of beauty based on a clean and orderly body. This 'classic' body is separate from other beings, distinguished by its symmetry and its divorce from any connections to birth, death or daily profane functioning. Crucially, the inner processes of absorbing and ejecting are not revealed. In contrast the 'grotesque body' transgresses this classical cannon and is very strongly associated with daily bodily functions, birth and death: 'It is unfinished, it outgrows itself, transgresses its own limits' (Bakhtin 1984: 24–30). In other words, it is the body in the process of becoming – but it is also a body that through its very attempt to transgress its own limits, actually concretises them and reminds us of them.

Whatever 'ugly' represents for us, this always seems to point to something we want to set ourselves apart from. In many films, characters who are visibly different tend to be associated with evil or monstrous behaviour, as in *Frankenstein*, as we have seen. Ugliness is all too often depicted as bad or evil. Perhaps there is something so terrifying about that which we call 'ugly' that it somehow deserves a category apart from 'good' or 'bad' – who is ugly can therefore not also be 'good', and is different from just being plain 'bad'. What is ugly is often someone or something that is felt to pose danger to the self – someone or something we want to distance ourselves from. In other words, I am suggesting that when we perceive something to be ugly, we are really referring to something that we cannot integrate into our perception of ourselves and which we deposit in the perceived-to-be-ugly other.

The etymology of the word monster is relevant here for it derives from the Latin, *monstrare*, meaning to warn or to show. What is monstrous or ugly is then perhaps something we need to externalise (i.e. show), to mark as 'other' so that we are no longer connected with it lest it would threaten to show up something in us that we would rather not see. Paradoxically, we also know, of course, that what we most want to set aside is what we unconsciously often end up drawing close to us so that we can control it. When we perceive someone or something to be ugly, Rickman (1957) thus draws attention to the hold this has over us:

> we cannot treat it with indifference. It rouses our deep-set emotions and its horror lingers in the memory. . . . It is something which stirs fantasies so profoundly that our minds cannot let the object alone.
>
> (Rickman 1957: 86)

We need monsters and beasts – we always seek to mark as other to ourselves the person, for example, who is envious or 'evil' (the latter being the predilection of the tabloid media) so that we can keep an eye on it from afar and not be contaminated by it. We feel compelled, and provoked, by our perception of the ugly, the intensity of the reaction a telling sign of our implication in the ugliness that we are simultaneously distancing ourselves from: 'The ugly object is felt to be both disturbingly familiar and utterly foreign' (Hagman 2003: 983).

Through Frankenstein, for example, we can observe how he becomes inseparable, and at times indistinguishable, from his 'ugly' creation. Indeed, this is because, as Hagman (2002) points out, neither beauty nor ugliness are intrinsic properties of the other, but they denote an internal emotional experience that is projectively identified into the body of the other: 'a sense of beauty is interactive and intersubjective' (Hagman 2002: 668). And we might add the same for the sense of what is ugly.

To feel beautiful is to feel whole and lovable and to relate to one's objects as such too (Lee 1948). By contrast, the perception of ugliness seems to denote a rupturing into consciousness of disturbing, frightening feelings or phantasies typically linked to aggressive or sexual impulses (Hagman 2003) that need to be projected into the object.

I want to suggest that we turn our eyes away from what is perceived as 'ugly' because it stands for that which we can never resolve: it threatens us with the reality that dogs us throughout life, that is, that the experience of wholeness – the experience of beauty – can never be total, permanent or the product of omnipotent creation.[7] An embodied existence forever reminds us that the experience of integration and unity will inevitably give way to experiences of disintegration and differentiation – that is, for each of us, it will expose at various times the core experience of insufficiency that lies at the heart of human subjectivity. The best we can hope for is that we do not lose the capacity to have this perspective on our predicament. When we do, we are more likely to seek quick solutions to these psychic problems.

The tyranny of beauty

I would now like to illustrate the intersubjective nature of 'ugliness' through the experiences of Ms A., whom I met when she was in her early thirties. I saw her over a period of four years in twice weekly therapy.

Ms A. was an attractive, immaculately presented woman, who struck me as very stiff in her bodily movements. She also had the habit of constantly ironing out her clothes with her hands (as if ironing out imaginary creases), and of touching her hair (as if to check that everything was still in place). She had come into therapy following the breakup of a relationship. She had left her partner of three years because she claimed that he was forever subjecting her to the 'humiliation of his flirtatious manner' with other women. I had been very struck by these words, and the pain as well as grievance that under-pinned them, as she conveyed how readily she felt exposed as ugly if he as much as looked at another woman. Ms A. told me that the end of the relationship had nevertheless at least freed her from the 'tyranny of looking good'. When I invited her to expand on this, she described how in three years she had never once let her boyfriend see her without make-up. This meant that she always had to wake up before him, allowing at least one hour to apply fresh make-up, so as to ensure a fresh application before she could let him see her.

As we started to work together, I soon came to know first hand the 'tyranny of looking good' because it proved very hard, for a long time, to engage Ms A. in a more real exchange with me in the room. As well as hiding her face behind layers of make-up, Ms A. manicured our relationship. But the 'pretty' exchanges she so much wanted to ensure between us were very fragile and threatened by the eruption of a more aggrieved part of her. She was extremely sensitive to any misattunement between us as if any rupture in her phantasy of us, as a mutually admiring, always together couple, was felt to herald a catastrophe. At first she was very politely curious about my other patients, but some months into the therapy she was affronted when I was unable to meet a request to change the time of one of her sessions. On this occasion I was able to see how easily paranoid she could become as she imagined that my inability to accommodate her must surely point to a much more desirable patient in my mind.

Ms A.'s mother was described as very loving but also critical. She had experienced her mother as particularly critical of her attempts as a teenager to make herself look attractive. The mother invested a great deal of attention in Ms A.'s appearance, often spontaneously buying her clothes, for example, but she seemingly could not tolerate that her body could be enjoyed or desired by others. Ms A. described her mother as very dismissive of her boyfriends, just as she had been of Ms A.'s father. She felt that her father – a much older man who had died when Ms A. was an adolescent – had never loved her mother or her. She was sure that he must have had numerous affairs. She sensed that her mother had felt humiliated by this state of affairs and had recruited her into a kind of campaign against her father, turning to her daughter not only for comfort, but also as a substitute partner.

There were strong homosexual currents in their relationship. Ms A. recalled that her mother, well into her late teens, would walk into the bathroom when she was having a bath or sitting on the toilet. Ms A. spoke about this almost fondly, but she seemed aware as she disclosed this to me that I might not view this as such a positive state of affairs. In fact, I felt that she both feared that I would point out to her that this was not so loving or normal, and at the same time she desperately needed me to do precisely that, something that her own father had not been able to do.

Ms A. felt that her mother wanted her to look good, but it became clear that there was an embargo on being desirable except *for* her mother. Ms A. had became trapped in the pursuit of her mother's loving and approving gaze at the cost of renouncing being separate from her and becoming a woman in her own right. The pressure to protect this special position in the object's mind was imperative.

While discouraging the assertion of Ms A.'s sexuality, the mother had actively encouraged her to have cosmetic surgery on her nose, aged nineteen, so that she could be 'really pretty'. When I enquired as to whether she had disliked her own nose, Ms A. became strikingly confused. I thought that her confusion revealed the extent to which her body was not in fact her own such that she had never really properly looked at it independently from her mother's eyes.

As the work progressed, and she could reveal to me more of her unmade-up self, we came to understand how her mother's discomfort with her own body and sexuality had been directly projected into Ms A.'s body. Ms A.'s body had become both the site for improvement, aided by the mother's dubious support, and a dangerous place in her own mind.

A year into the therapy Ms A. brought to a session photos of herself before her cosmetic surgery. This proved to be a very painful, if important development in our work. It was plain to see that Ms A.'s nose, by most standards, was absolutely fine, but that her mother had projected the hated aspects of herself into her daughter's nose. One might well construe similar cases where the parent actively supports surgery in a young person as Body Dysmorphic Disorder by proxy.

Whatever the ugly nose represented in the mother's mind, for Ms A., the surgery had held the promise that she could somehow ensure her ongoing desirability in her mother's eyes – a desirability that relied on her not being her true self. Her expectation that the object would not be able to look at anything ugly was strikingly apparent in the transference. If ever she was very distressed, but particularly if she felt angry, this would elicit panic that I thought anticipated my inability to bear such ugly feelings and 'look' at them with her.

The projective identification into Ms A.'s body had been so extensive that Ms A. had never been able to experience her body as separate. However, it also became clear that Ms A. had identified with the more controlling aspects of her mother. Her wish to recreate a fused, idealised relationship with me presented considerable challenges to the therapeutic work, and to any relationship she tried to establish. She was keen to please me, often complimented me on my appearance and taste, and I felt she tried to draw me into more friendly exchanges with her as she arrived and left the consulting room – all of which had the effect of making me feel controlled and, importantly, scrutinised and at the mercy of her gaze.

As Ms A.'s case illustrates, the mother's perception of ugliness was mediated by projective processes. Ugliness may be consciously felt to denote an individual characteristic relative to some familial and/or cultural norm, but it is invariably also an intersubjective experience – a point that is lost on many of the patients I have worked with. It is only through helping them to move away from a focus on the body as an object to be manipulated, towards thinking about a relationship with the object in their mind, that progress can be made.

Chapter 3

Mirrors

'Mum, look at me . . .' 'Mum, watch me . . .' – these commonplace and charming instructions, invitations or appeals (depending on the mood of the day) by the young child direct the mother's admiring gaze onto ME. Not that we ever grow out of such longings, of course, but as we grow older we mostly shy away from this more undisguised demand for the other's admiring gaze. The desire to be looked at, and to be admired, requires the presence of an other willing not only to look, but above all to also take pleasure in the self's desirability. In Chapter 2 I suggested that early on this desirability is typically rooted in the body and mediated interpersonally through the gazing relationship. For example, it may be felt to be on account of a physical achievement: 'LOOK, I can jump down four steps today', or on account of aesthetics: 'LOOK how pretty I am in my princess dress'. In other words, by far the most common reason for our felt desirability in the early years is somehow mediated by the bodily self and requires a witness: someone who looks at us.

The self's earliest experience of itself will therefore be partly dependent on the quality of the libidinal cathexis of the body by those closest to the baby. The quality of the (m)other's desire, and her capacity to enjoy the baby's body, shapes the subjective experience of being-in-a-body, and hence of the self's desirability. Crucially, if all goes relatively well, the early exchanges between (m)other and baby install internally a benign observer – an other who sees us for who we are, 'warts 'n' all', and *still* loves us. The saying 'love is blind' is then perhaps misleading: love is *perception* coupled with acceptance of what is seen.

The body is 'living memory' (Resnik 2005): our history is inscribed in our body. The traces of our infantile modes of relating can be discerned in our idiosyncratic physical and gestural patterns, in how we relate to our body as the site for loving exchanges or for the expression of hatred, in how the body may be experienced as a source of pleasure or of anxiety. All of our attempts at the modification of the body speak to these early experiences.

In this chapter I will focus on the mother's role as mirror to the baby and explore the function of the earliest physical exchanges between mother and baby in establishing a stable representation of the body. To this end I will chart the basic milestones in the development of the body representation. Understanding the role played by vision, touch and mobility allows us to develop a more comprehensive view of how our body bears the imprint of the earliest affective exchanges. Although these are milestones we all traverse, the *meaning* – particularly the unconscious meaning – of biological changes and development will vary for each one of us.

The (m)other-as-mirror

The history of the mirror itself is a telling one and provides a powerful metaphor for the important psychic function of feeling mirrored by the other. The original, proper, mirrors were manufactured in 1460 by the Venetians – the first to create clear glass. These mirrors became prized possessions, and their manufacture a lucrative business. In 1507 two Venetian brothers, Andrea and Domenico del Gallo, improved on the quality of the original mirror by using a flat glass plate backed with tin or silver amalgam. They fiercely guarded their invention, which was widely sought after and remained a secret for 150 years. It proved to be such a commercial success, and evidently spoke to such passionate, human longings to find one's own reflection, that by 1664 spies were sent by other countries, most notably by Louis XIV's ambassador to Venice, to 'steal' the secrets of mirror-making from the Venetians (Bates and Cleese 2001). The appropriation of this 'secret' was bloody: kidnapping and murder punctuate the history of mirrors. Having access to a reflecting surface was seemingly felt to be urgent, necessary, worth killing for, echoing the urgency and violence that some patients express when their search for the loving gaze of the other is thwarted.

The notion of the mother-as-mirror represents one of the most important analytic contributions to understanding the dynamics of the earliest relationship and of the development of the body self. As many authors have noted, the mother's face is the child's first emotional mirror (Searles 1963; Winnicott 1967; Lacan 1977). The dynamic, affectively laden, visual interplay between mother and baby shapes the baby's earliest experiences of object relating, which are then internalised and lay the foundations for the child's inner world (Wright 1991). At this early stage, what the mother mirrors back is 'reality' for the baby (Krueger 1989).

In healthy development the experience of the mother looking at her baby with loving eyes is internalised as a benign experience, not only of being taken in, that is, of being received by the other (we speak, for example, of welcoming eyes), but also of being reflected back. In this process of being seen and of finding in the other's eyes receptiveness and understanding, the self's experience is transformed. Wright (1991) speaks of the good-enough mother who *'looks after'*, underlining looking as an active process whereby the mother not only 'claims' (Alvarez 1999) her baby through her gaze and invites him to engage, but also 'looks after' his needs, which as yet have no words. 'Being seen' by an other, therefore, has a potentially containing function.

Throughout life, mirrors – actual and symbolic ones – remain important. One of the most important theoretical contributions to the developmental function of the mirror is to be found in Lacan's account of the *mirror stage*. Lacan's (1977) understanding of the self's complex relation to its mirror image is noteworthy. His work is especially relevant for understanding the dynamics of body modification and of body image disturbances because, through the register that he calls 'the Imaginary', Lacan prioritises the visual field and the specular relation that underpins the child's (and later the adult's) captivation in the image.

The child's recognition of absence is the pivotal moment around which the mirror stage revolves (six to eighteen months of age).[1] As he is now constituted within 'the Imaginary' (i.e. the order of images, representations), the child identifies with an image outside of himself. Lacan makes two important suggestions with respect to the mirror image. First, he draws attention to how the baby's body is an uncoordinated aggregate, a series of parts, zones, organs, sensations, needs and impulses rather than an integrated totality. He notes how the body matures unevenly, forming the basis for the child's experience of its 'body-in-bits-and-pieces' – a fragmented body. Hence he argues that the child's image in the mirror has a coherence the child's own body actually lacks. Second, Lacan suggests that the child recognises himself at the very moment that he loses himself in the other, that is, the self recognises itself as subject in an exteriority. Lacan's mirror stage thus brings to the fore the tension between the fragmented or 'fragilised' body of experience and the solidity and permanence of the body as seen in the mirror.

Lacan adds a further layer to his understanding of the mirror image. As we have seen, he suggests that the gestalt in the mirror reflects back a unified picture of the body. In identifying with its mirror image, the baby introjects it into the ego; yet Lacan emphasises that the child's relation to the image is also alienated: the image both is, and is not, an image of itself. The image is 'false' in so far as the self and the image are not one and the same. In other words, it is because the child takes as its own an image that is 'other' that this lays the foundations internally of an alienating structure. For Lacan, establishing one's identity is therefore always a process of alienation. To speak of alienation, however, may overlook a more funda-mental issue, that is, that what the mirror stage describes is the way in which the child has to relinquish the unity with the mother that he now replaces with the (inevitably illusory) image of unity in the mirror. In this sense, we might say that the body is forever a reminder of, and potentially a substitute for, the loss of a fused state with the mother.

The notion that the image of the self always comes from outside is especially helpful. For Lacan, the image in the mirror becomes the blueprint for the ego. The self thus internalises otherness – the other's desire – as the condition of his own desirability. This dynamic is very important. For some patients with marked body dysmorphia, the other's desire has typically been felt to be inaccessible and unfulfillable by the self, thereby reinforcing a sense of insufficiency at the core of the self (see Chapter 4). For others, it has been felt to control or usurp the self (see Chapters 5 and 8).

The problem posed by otherness is plain to see when we focus on the specular image because this image is not isomorphic with one's own representation of the body, that is, they are never neatly superimposed. The most concrete example of this is that we can never see the back of our heads, or the end of our spine, even though we do have an inner experience of them. It is actually only the other who can see these parts of ourselves, albeit a perception inevitably filtered through their own unconscious. Perhaps this is why the experience of paranoia is so aptly conjured up by the feeling of someone looking at us 'from behind' – looking at us from a perspective we can never have on ourselves, and hence that we are not able to control.

The way the other looks at us is therefore inscribed on the body and shapes the perception we have of our body. The perception of our body is then inextricably object-related. An important implication of this is that the other's look is a potentially destabilising influence on the evolving body representations; it is indeed this experience that comes to the fore in patients who modify their bodies.

When all is going relatively well in development, the other is felt to be both the foundation and support of our identity as well as what necessarily destabilises us because it needs to present us with the reality of separateness. In these patients, however, the other is *primarily*, or sometimes *only*, experienced as a destabilising internal presence affecting their very experience, and perception of, the body and it undermines a stable, coherent sense of self.

Lacan's mirror stage draws attention to how the mirror image provides a promise or anticipation of the self-mastery and control that the child lacks, and that the mother provisionally covered over in gratifying the child's needs. Libidinal relations thus establish the ego through a fantasised identification with others, particularly the mother (the child strives to be the object of the mother's desire), and an illusory corporeal cohesion founded on a mistaken identification of the child with its visual gestalt in the mirror. The apparent completeness of this image affords a sense of mastery over the body, but Lacan cautions that:

> the functions of mastery, improperly called the ego's synthetic functions, institute on the basis of a libidinal alienation the subsequent development – namely . . . the paranoiac principle of human knowledge.
>
> (Lacan 1953: 351–356)

The ego, for Lacan, remains an inauthentic agency, whose function is to conceal an otherwise unsettling lack of unity.[2] The baby's identification with its specular image represents an attempt to seek an ideal, future identity in the coherence of the totalised specular image. The mirror stage is thus a drama 'whose internal pressure pushes precipitously from insufficiency to anticipation' (Lacan 1977 [1949]: 78).

An important limitation of Lacan's notion of the mirror is that it is not elaborated in the context of the vicissitudes of the early mother–baby relationship. There is an additional problem. Lacan, as we have seen, suggests that the child takes as its own an image that is 'other' and that this then inevitably lays the foundations internally of an alienating structure. This represents, in my view, a very good description of what happens when things go wrong in development, rather than necessarily providing an account of normal development.

Lacan essentially suggests that the mirror propagates a kind of lie (i.e. 'your body is *not* fragmented') in the face of what is otherwise a deeply disturbing reality. Although Lacan is right to stress that the reality of being-in-a-body poses a challenge since the body's integrity is always only ever temporary, and our idealised image of it is just that – an ideal – he dismisses too readily, in my view, the importance of what might be recognised as a necessary defensive narcissism. Here it is timely to turn to the other significant theoretical voice on the question of the mother-as-mirror, namely Winnicott's, where we find a rather different account of the mirror.

Winnicott (1967) sensitively draws out how the baby comes to know himself through what he sees on his mother's face. He emphasises the crucial role of the mother in helping her baby to come to know himself through his relationship with her and what she is able to reflect back to him in digested form. Assuming that what the mother reflects back to her baby is not distorted by her own difficulties, she will provide a reliable, loving mirror that will allow the baby to develop a sense of being at home in his body and in his mind.

Bearing in mind Lacan's notion that the mirror lies, I would now like to take one step further Winnicott's notion of the mother-as-mirror and suggest that when all is going well in development, the good-enough mother's loving gaze needs to hold up a *benignly distorting mirror*, that is, she needs to bear the reality for the baby of the inescapable fragmentation and fragility of the baby's body (a fragility that can never be completely overcome, except in phantasy, as Lacan described) *and* she needs to be adept at promoting a kind of benign 'lie' in order for the baby's bodily self to feel whole, robust and desirable, given that no one can ever be 'ideal'. In other words, for the baby's sake, she 'glosses over' the true state of affairs. In this sense what Lacan refers to as an 'inauthentic ego' may be precisely what is partly protective against the development of body image disturbances. This is borne out by research on body-image disturbances where it has been suggested that the problem is not a distorted body image as such, but rather a lack of a distorted body image, that is, the absence of a self-serving body image bias (Jansen et al. 2006). In this study the control subjects rated their own bodies more positively than others rated them, whereas the eating disordered patients were the harshest of all in their self-ratings.[3] I want to suggest that when the mother cannot help the child to install internally a pair of 'rose tinted glasses' (Lambrou, 2006), a more persecutory gaze may dominate the internal world. The self may become overly reliant on image and mirrors in order to feel whole and may also feel compelled to modify the body in order to achieve an idealised form – this is most readily apparent when working with some patients with marked body dysmorphia, as I will discuss in Chapter 6.

The development of the psychic-libidinal map of the body

Our experience of the world is inevitably mediated from the unique perspective of our body. To understand the relationship between the body and the mind, we have to think on the boundary of the real and of the imagined body, on the boundary of one body and of two or more bodies.

The body's anatomy is an incontrovertible fact: we are organs and bones, but how we put these together in our minds to form a representation of our body only partly depends on actual anatomy. Rather, as I have been suggesting, it also depends on how the body is seen by others, on how it is experienced in relationship with others.

Body imaginings

Aged twenty-eight, Mr S. was involved in an industrial accident. As a result he had lost his left arm. When I first met him, he walked into the room, barely looking at me, and sat on the edge of the chair in a distinctively skewed manner, with his upper body noticeably leaning to the left. He recounted the details of the accident and his ongoing pain in his left arm. He spoke about his left arm as if it were still a part of him, but he made a passing reference to the fact that, of course, he knew that his arm had been amputated. Yet, the pain at times was intense – a kind of burning sensation which distressed him. He had been unable to work since the accident and had withdrawn from those close to him. He said he felt that others either stared at him, and this made him feel uncomfortable, or they pretended nothing was wrong, and yet he refused to wear a prosthesis so it was obvious to all that something *was* wrong, he said. Mr S. poignantly described how every time he experienced pain in what he felt to be his left arm, this distressed him *and* he also experienced a feeling of comfort, which he could not explain to himself.

For Mr S., as for others who suffer phantom limb pain, the pain had become a reassuring signal that he still had his arm. If he were to relinquish the pain he would be confronted with the reality of the loss of one of his limbs.

This book is not about work with people who have lost one of their limbs, but I am choosing this example because the experience of phantom limb sufferers powerfully conveys how we need to develop and protect a coherent representation of our bodies in our minds. We need to do this because it supports our sense of who we are. And we strive to protect this image even in the face of an incontrovertible reality – the arm *is* lost. In our own idiosyncratic ways we all do what Mr S. was having to manage: we all struggle to maintain a coherent image of our own body as it continually changes. Throughout development, particularly at nodal points such as puberty, or as our bodies age, we need to construe a new bodily imaginary to accommodate the changing body.

Schilder (1950) stressed that the body gestalt is structured by psychological, not anatomical requirements. Indeed, the psychic/libidinal map of the body is organised not only by the laws of biology, but also by the meanings and phantasies we associate with the body – our own and other people's. It is in fact more apt to say that we are dealing with an imaginary anatomy. The term *body image* is now widespread in both lay and professional circles. Schilder (1950: 11) defined the body image as 'the picture of our body which we form in our mind, that is to say, the way in which our body appears to us'.

His early, pioneering work in this area emphasised the 'elasticity' of body image, noting how it fluctuates (e.g. in terms of perceived size or feelings of lightness and heaviness) and affects our relationship with others. Moreover, the body inevitably fails us through illness or pain or a feature we dislike. These experiences unsettle the coherent representation of the body and can malignantly distort the perception and experience of the body.

And yet, whilst the felt experience of the body is in flux, it is also the case that out of the early experiences of body states and physical exchanges with others we develop a representation of our body that is more or less enduring, and that contains both perceptual and evaluative components. Damasio (2000) likens the representation of the body-self to a map in the brain that provides continuity across different states. It also provides the essential continuity in the quality and range of the affective core (Bucci 2008).

In order to underline what I consider to be the essential *dynamically unconscious* dimension of the representation we have of our bodies, I prefer

to use the term *body imagining(s)* in the sense that the internal representation we have of our body is always of an *imagined* body.[4] This term thus
more accurately denotes the potential fluidity in our body image and its
relation to our mental states at any point in time. It also underscores that
the representation of the body in the mind is an unconscious psychic
organisation powered by particular phantasies of the self-in-interaction-
with-an-other. Body imaginings grow out of the earliest internal bodily
experiences, for example, of pain and pleasure, in relation to others and so
colour the individual's experience of his *body-self*. The body imagining – as
I am defining it here – is therefore the image we have of our bodies in our
minds at any given point, as Schilder noted, resulting from the idiosyncratic
meanings with which the body has been endowed through these earliest
exchanges. It is built on projective and introjective mechanisms. Importantly, this representation of the body is fundamentally a function of
libidinal cathexes. In other words, the way we represent our body in our
mind is inevitably object-related, and its original source lies in the body's
physicality:

> From that first union between the psychic representative emanating
> from the body and the memory traces of the image of the object, a new
> entity is created: the object representation. In this new mixture, the
> subject has worked out all inherent subjectivity, not only because of the
> projection, but also because of something stemming from the inner
> sense of the subject's body feeling, to which he or she has given a
> conceivable and meaningful form.
>
> (Green 2004: 120)

The extent to which the body may then be felt to be a hospitable or
inhospitable home for the self will therefore reflect the quality of the earliest
identifications. These identifications will bear the imprint of the physical
experiences of being-with-an-other mediated by vision, touch and movement.

Touchstones in the development of the body-self

Sam has just finished feeding. He is resting calmly on his mother's lap as she
gently strokes his bald, large head. His eyes flutter, as if he is on the brink of
falling asleep. He yawns and pulls his right hand close to his face, placing it
then in his mouth to suck on it. Then suddenly he twists his neck backwards,
drawn by the bright light that his little brother has just switched on from
behind the sofa where Sam is positioned with his mother. He scrunches his
eyes shut, as if to keep out this brightness, and then starts to cry, arching
his back, stiffening. Perhaps it was too much: the bright light, the noise of his

mother scolding his brother for putting the light on, his mother's abrupt movement as she turned towards the brother which, in turn, pushed Sam to the side of her hip, out of her view. His mother responds to his distress calmly, but assuredly. Her physical movements are confident and fluid as she holds on to his trunk and draws him back across her lap and looks into his eyes: 'That was not nice was it? Horrible light! You were trying to get off to sleep', and then she resumes the gentle, rhythmic stroking. Within seconds Sam stops crying and looks at her, pushes his head into the generous folds of her stomach, and falls asleep.

Sam was six weeks old at the time of this observation. Within a very short space of time he was transported from tranquillity in his bodily experience – he was satiated and in close, contiguous contact with his mother – to a hyper-alert state, which marks a discontinuity in his experience. This brief excerpt from a year-long baby observation illustrates an ordinary moment of extraordinary importance because it is punctuated by the dynamic, affective interconnectedness of two bodies and minds. In this example, the sensitive mother soothes her baby not just with her understanding and words, but also with her physical movements that are as eloquent and containing as her words.

The baby enters the world as a body and mind waiting to be met by the minds *and* bodies of those who will care for him. His outer surface and inner organ sensations are constantly being received and stored in the mind. These sensations interact from the outset with the environment. Bodily experiences provide the primary vehicle for relationships with others. Nowhere is this more apparent than in the early relationship between mother and baby.

The first exchanges between a mother and her newborn baby are primarily tactile and visual ones: they touch and look at each other. The quality of the mother's looking is reinforced through tactile and vocal exchanges as she relates to the baby's body. The baby's experience, for example, of grasping or sucking, of pain and pleasure, and how this is responded to by the mother through her gaze, touch, interest and understanding, will all contribute to the development of the body-self and of the body image (Glover 1956; Spitz 1965; McDougall 1974; Krueger 1989; Schilder 1950). The earliest sense of self is then embedded;[5] it is mediated through bodily sensations. If all goes well, physical sensations come together to form a more integrated experience of the body-self (Glover 1956; Spitz 1965).

Newborn babies probably have some rudimentary sense of their body. Already in utero, complex patterns of spontaneous sequences of movement are present even though bodily interactions at this stage are limited and largely consist of hitting against the maternal abdominal wall.[6] The earliest representations of the body are probably linked to high-tension physio-logical needs and stress experiences such as hunger or pain (Lichtenberg 1975) which are, however, always experienced in relationship-with-an-other:

> The tactile sensations that a baby has while being nourished at the breast (especially in the oral and perioral zones in the hands, which are ready to grasp the breast and anything within reach of the palms, such as garments near the breast) become in this way some of the first fragmentary (focalized) experiences formed by the primitive mind.
>
> (Gaddini 1987: 321)

At birth, Greenacre (1960) suggested, that the alternating states of tension and relaxation formed a kind of central core of awareness of the body. Neuromatrix theory (Melzack 1990) further proposes that we inherit a 'neuronal signature' of our bodies which produces an implicit sense of the body. This is consistent with the observation that newborns can imitate orofacial and head movements (Meltzoff 1990). The newborn's ability to identify specific bodily movements and to reproduce them with the corresponding part of their own body suggests that they indeed do have some sense of their own body.

A large body of evidence supports what we have long intuitively recog-nised: the importance of touch in early development. Bodily contact has a significant effect upon the development of the central nervous system and of the endocrinum. It has been suggested that the sensory experience of touch aids the process of separating 'me' from 'not-me' and plays a part in the libidinisation of the body by the mother (Hoffer 1949, 1950).

There now exists an extensive literature on the effects of early handling on the subsequent development of various species and on preterm infants (for a review, see Barnard and Brazelton 1990), ranging from effects on resistance to stress and immune function, to the growth of the brain, and on brain chemistry itself. Maternal contact, for example, inhibits the baby's pituitary-adrenal response to stress (Stanton et al. 1987). There is also evidence to suggest that early handling alters the concentration of gluco-corticoid receptors, which are involved in terminating the stress response (Stanton et al. 1987).

Harlow and Zimmerman's (1959) pioneering studies with baby rhesus monkeys imprinted on us the powerful image of the wire mesh 'mother' whose provision of milk did not suffice to entice the baby; rather, the baby monkeys preferred the so-called 'cloth mother' who provided contact comfort only through a terrycloth ventral surface. These studies underscore the widespread view that touch is a fundamental, and most likely necessary, component of the earliest attachment bonds. Anzieu (1989) expands the role played by touch and the skin, suggesting that the ego is primarily structured as a 'skin ego'. He argues that the baby acquires the perception of a bodily surface through the contact with the skin of the mother when he is being cared for by her (e.g. during breastfeeding) (see also Chapter 8).

Not only is touch instrumental in the development and maintenance of attachment, but also the experience of touch appears to play a part in regulating physiological systems in a manner not dissimilar to that afforded by attachment (Reite 1990).[7] There is evidence to suggest that in order to acquire cognitive and affective awareness of the body, a substantial level of tactile arousal may be necessary (Weiss 1990).[8] Physical contact per se is important, but it is the *quality* of the touching, and the meaning it therefore acquires for the baby, that are vital to determining its impact on the body imagining. Indeed, the quality of the touching interaction is a main factor in the later development of attachment relationships. Parents derive their attitude towards touching their children from their own history of body-related relationships (Main 1990).

The combined agency of touch and vision are then central in the baby's development in first year of life. Vocalisations, visual and skin contact are primary mediums through which the mother resonates the baby's affective state. Of course, this works both ways, that is, the baby also affects his mother through his physical responses.

One of the fundamental skills that the mother imparts to the baby through these exchanges is the acquisition of self-regulation. In the first year of life psychic organisation is determined by the so-called 'neonatal behaviour state'. State organisation reflects the interaction of all the baby's sensorimotor and neurological systems. Sander (1988) thus even speaks of a 'state self' as the precursor to the body self.

From the outset the baby's adaptation to the external world is dependent on his interaction with the mother because it is through this relationship that the baby's experience is organised (Stern 1985). At the most basic, physical level the baby gradually has to adjust his regulatory systems (for example, breathing and digestion) to the outside world, and the mother supports him in reaching the physiological equilibrium necessary to survive. In the first month of life the baby's infantile state organisation is thus influenced by the quality of the mother–child interaction. The connection between change of state and the experience of interaction with an actual other is therefore not only a psychic process, but it is also 'characterised by *biological processes of exchange*' (Lemche 1998, my italics).[9]

Because of its role in emotional development, it has been suggested that state development impacts on the development of psychic structures. When the baby can manage basal self-regulation of states, he can change his state to protect himself from over and under stimulation. The capacity for state regulation in newborns has been found to be an important predictor of social emotional and cognitive ability at eighteen months (Lester et al. 1984).

The mother's own experiences of being-in-a-body will also affect the baby. Throughout pregnancy, and following birth, the mother has to adjust to her maternal body, which is likely to carry unconscious meanings for her. Depending on the nature of the mother's phantasies about her body – that is, her own body imagining – it may be more or less available for the baby in terms of the quality of its presence and receptiveness to the baby's own physicality. In turn, the baby will experience the impact of her body tensions, changes in her smell, her breathing, the rhythm of her movements and her speech. Physical exchange with the mother is, crucially, an affectively laden interaction: the way her body moves, the quality of her gaze, the tone of her voice, the softness of her touch, all convey her affective state.

Even in the best possible conditions, however, for example in the feeding situation, it is impossible (and developmentally it would not be desirable, even if possible) to maintain a relation of perfect reciprocal regulation. In the earliest stages of development the baby's body repeatedly comes up against discontinuities in his sensory experience since even the best of mothers will not always be available when the baby needs her to be. The baby will therefore have to endure interruptions and derailments that will, it is hoped, then be followed by the re-establishment by the mother of the baby's bodily regulation – 'it is hoped' since it is through them that he will experience that it is possible to transform inevitable discontinuities into positive feelings about his own bodily regulation in the relationship.

The overall experience of physical reciprocity within which the baby's states are regulated is central to the development of the body imagining. The accurate mirroring by the parent of the sensations and feelings experienced by the baby as coming from inside his body, or on the skin surface, and what is coming from the outside (i.e. establishing body boundaries), will form the core of the body imagining (Krueger 1989, 2004).

While touch and vision are closely connected, it is vision in particular that plays a key role in facilitating separation. Vision delineates the external object and is crucial in the negotiation of distance from the object (Wright 1991). Of all the senses, vision most readily confirms the separation of baby from mother and throughout life performs a potentially distancing and controlling function. Greenacre (1960) considered vision to be 'indispensable' in establishing the boundary between self and non-self:

> touching and taking in of the various body parts with the eyes (vision) helps in drawing the body together, into a central image beyond the level of more immediate sensory awareness.
>
> (Greenacre 1960: 208)

Tactile and visual contact with the (m)other, of course, coexist alongside the baby's own motor actions. In the early months the baby can perform only a limited number of self-initiated motor actions such that his experience of his own bodily movements is inextricably bound to a relationship characterised by close physical contact and dependence. The baby practises his own motor skills within a close, physical relationship, for example, pushing himself away from his mother while all along still being close to her as she holds on to him (Lemche 1998). Greater motor control, and the experience of contingency between inner proprioception (i.e. the perception of the position and movement of the body), and outer movement perception, are central to the development of a cohesive experience of the body in the first few months.

The baby's increasing mastery over his movements gives rise to the important experience of integration in his movements, which expresses itself in the baby's evident and contagious joy when this is achieved successfully. Increasingly, the baby can now initiate physical contact.

Gradually the baby experiences his body as an important vehicle for the satisfaction of his wishes. Successful movement of his body, a more developed capacity to manipulate external objects, and attempts at locomotion all contribute to a more unified body imagining.

At this stage of motor development the intentional nature of grasping movements is in the process of being fully established and the child then takes his first momentous, independent steps. Crawling is a physical and psychical watershed that shapes the experience of the body in a new way. It heralds a new quality in relationships too. The child can now 'play' and experiment with spatial separation.

By this stage the child is actively invested in securing mastery over his body, eventually enjoying running fast, jumping and more generally experimenting with his ever sophisticated motor skills. The experience of exerting increasingly voluntary control over his inner bodily functions and over his motor movements provides a steady source of self-esteem. Even the temporary loss of this feeling can generate shame and embarrassment. Indeed the earliest recalled prototype of the experience of shame for many people tends to be anchored in a physical action – in the body – which exposes the child's relative smallness or loss of continence. This perhaps explains why the content of much humour, and that which elicits the heartiest laughs in young children, are jokes or situations that locate in the other the experience of physical limitations or incompetence – this is the essence of much slapstick comedy (Lemma 2000).

The development of language marks another important milestone and is itself rooted in motor development. There are important links between motor and vocal development (Kelly et al. 2004). For example, rhythmically organised motor and vocal activities such as the onset of first gestures (e.g. pointing) predicts the appearance of words (Lemche 1998). The use of language facilitates the exploration of spatial separation as words make it possible to bridge physical distance. Similarly, the child becomes increasingly able to use language to express and resolve uncomfortable or distressing states that previously could be managed only through physical action.[10]

Once relationships are mediated by language, curiosity about the body and the anxieties it generates can also now be spoken about. At this stage many children display intense curiosity about the body and its functions. From approximately the age of three onwards a representation of the interior of the body, including that of internal organs, such as the heart or lungs, develops gradually (Lemche 1998).[11] In my experience, the more sophisticated the knowledge and understanding of a body with organs that work to keep it alive (such as the heart), the greater the anxiety in the child related to the body's potential vulnerability.

The combination of language and mobility heralds a developmental revolution and affords the child an exciting sense of mastery over his objects and the world more broadly. Now the child can mediate the distance between himself and the (m)other both verbally and physically. His experience of his body as boundaried begins to consolidate and notions of 'private' parts of the body start to make sense and often promote questions about why some parts of the body are more private than others.

During the second and third year particularly, the gradual increase in genital feelings (clitoral and phallic) introduces further complexity to the evolving body imagining. As Greenacre (1958) observed:

> With the gradual intensification of these endogenous phallic sensations this part of the body [genitals] assumes greater importance . . . identity although generally having a stable core both in body and psychic structure and functioning, is nonetheless subject to various changes at nodal points of development, roughly following stages of body and maturational achievement with their accompanying emotional problems. Consequently, no sense of adult functional identity can be completed until after adolescence is well past and assimilated.
>
> (Greenacre 1958: 616–626)

The extent of the visibility and accessibility of the genitals most likely plays a part in the respectively different experiences of the girl and the boy, and the genital anxieties that may then be triggered (Bernstein 1993). These gender differences shape the development of the body imagining because they will also invariably attract particular familial and cultural projections related to the emergent sexual body.

During the early latency years the child develops an increasing sense of control of his body. At puberty the predictability and (illusory) experience of control, changes – overnight, it can feel like to some young people. The advent of puberty, with its dramatic physical changes, necessitates the integration of the sexual and aggressive urges of the post-pubertal body into the body imagining, and so into the representation of the self.

Body imaginings are very reactive to actual changes in our bodies, such as those caused by illness or accidents, as well as the natural and inevitable changes brought about by physical development, such as those of puberty. Whereas at birth the mind may be said to develop from the body, in adolescence the body presents itself forcefully to the attention of the mind (Ferrari 2004). Erections, masturbation and menstruation intrude on an oasis of relative calm in the physical domain of the pre-pubertal stage. For many young people, for example, the experience of an orgasm becomes a focal point around which a sense of the reality of the genital can be further organised, accompanied by a sense of volitional control in the seeking of sexual satisfaction. But the demands made by this inevitable developmental transition can simply be too much to bear for some young people (Laufer and Laufer 1984).

At the best of times this is a complicated and unsettling process. It is all the more so where the quality of the early relationships have contributed to a fragile, undercathected body-self, or to entrenched splitting of the body imagining such that body parts may have become identified with bad, terrifying objects. In these cases an internal or external organ can be experienced as an alien object residing within the body rather than as an integrated part of the body self. Body sensations may then need to be kept separate from the image of oneself as sexually mature. Consequently we are not surprised that the modal age of onset for a range of body image disturbances is in adolescence.

Meltzer (1967) refers to the 'confusional anxiety' that he regards as typical for all adolescents:

> the confusion centres on their bodies and appears with the first pubic hair, the first breast growth, first ejaculation and so forth. Whose body is it? In other words, they cannot distinguish with certainty their adolescent state from infantile delusions-of-adulthood induced by masturbation with attendant projective identification into internal objects. This is what lies behind the adolescent's slavish concern about clothes, make-up and hair styles, hardly less in boys than in girls.
>
> (Meltzer 1967: 98)

Laufer (1968) echoes the question of ownership of the body that is latent in so many clinical presentations during adolescence: is it felt to belong to the young person or to the mother? In order to assimilate the pubertal body into a coherent sense of self, the adolescent frequently has to create an experience of concrete ownership of the body, fashioning it in his way, thereby erasing the imprint of the (m)other. Hence, the modification of the body during adolescence, through tattoos, for example, is not necessarily, per se, an indicator of pathology. Much will depend on the extent to which the modification of the body becomes necessary and compelling.

Particular developmental stages thus re-'present' the body to us in its altered form and require us to integrate the changing body into our existing representation of the body, so that it can be updated. This is not just the case during adolescence, but it applies equally to the psychic impact and meaning of the natural ageing process.

The transgenerational transmission of body imaginings

As we have seen, the body is not just a physical reality: the way we experience it is inevitably defined by our earliest fears and desires because the body also reflects unconscious introjective and projective processes. The way we feel in our body is shaped by the meanings and phantasies of others, hence our body tells the story of several generations.

Our body imaginings result from the internalisation of the (m)other's body imagining through the unconscious transmission of gestures, posture, mannerisms, rhythms – all of which contain affectively laden representations of self-in-interaction-with-the-other:

> A pre-verbal infant absorbs not the words but the implicit intentions of communication. . . . This register is conveyed through physical contacts, facial expressions, gesture, vocal tone.
>
> (Raphael-Leff forthcoming)

In order to understand how the body imagining can be transmitted inter-generationally we need to take a brief detour into the functioning of memory.

The early physical experiences that I have highlighted as core to the establishment of an appropriately libidinally cathected body-self are stored as procedural memories. Memory research has delineated two kinds of memory systems: declarative and implicit (Schacter 1987). Declarative memories can be recalled and verbalised and give us the narrative of our lives. Implicit memories, by contrast, are pre-verbal (typically relating to the first two or three years of life) and therefore cannot be directly accessed and cannot be repressed on account of the slower maturation of the brain structures necessary for explicit memory – in other words, they are descriptively unconscious, not dynamically unconscious (Clyman 1991).

The implicit memory system includes procedural, emotional and affective memories. This is of central importance to how we represent the body because the earliest sensorimotor experiences, which stimulate emotions and carry affects, are most likely encoded as procedural memories of my-body-with-an-other. They are thus most likely stored in the non-repressed unconscious. These memories – also referred to as 'emotion schemas' (Bucci 2008) – incorporate representations of other people validating or repudiating the child's body-self. An emotion schema can be activated directly by sensory features in perception or from memory. This is clinically relevant because it suggests that what we need to be attuned to is 'subsymbolic communication' that is embodied (Bucci 2008), that is, we are talking about somatic and sensory processes that can be neither verbalised nor symbolised and that may operate outside of intentional control or organised thought.

Procedural memories of physical experiences are then rooted in physical experience-with-an-other and will stamp how the baby will experience his body and so views himself. Feeling merged with the mother's welcoming body, or feeling unheld by her, will be accompanied by intense affects that most likely do impact on memory, wish and phantasy (Pine 2000).

Just like her baby, the mother will have internalised (and stored as a procedural memory) an experience of her body-with-an-other. As I mentioned earlier, the mother's experience of her own body will, in turn, influence how she relates to the baby's physicality. Infants who are classified as anxiously attached frequently have mothers who demonstrate an aversion to close body contact (Ainsworth et al. 1978). Main (1990) underlines that the amount of touching has no observable consequences, but the manner in which the baby is held (e.g. affectionately versus awkwardly) does. She found a significant relationship between the parent's own reported experience of rejection by the mother during childhood and subsequent observed aversion to physical contact with the baby. One of the most important communications in terms of the development of the baby's body-self is whether the mother can take pleasure and enjoy her baby's physicality and sensuality.

The immediacy of the physical contact with her baby will most likely activate the mother's own latent, primitive sensations, phantasies, wishes and anxieties that will reflect her own early experience. In other words, what the mother sees as she looks at her baby, how she is able to avail herself to him both physically and mentally, will be shaped by the quality of the relationships felt to reside inside her, not least the quality of the relationship between, and with, her own internal parents. The extent to which she is 'occupied' (Rhode 2005) by her internal objects may lead the baby to experience her as preoccupied and absent or as overflowing with her own projections (Fraiberg et al. 1975; Williams 1997) such that, either way, the baby experiences no room in his mother's mind. Brazelton and Cramer (1989) have correctly pointed out that during pregnancy parental conscious and unconscious expectations, and the past experiences of the parents, exercise significant influence upon the attachment relations that develop once the baby is born. The baby's experience of his own body is thus mediated by what he experiences as the mother's relationship to his body (Laufer 1981). And what she feels about his body will be mediated by what she feels about her own body. As Raphael-Leff (forthcoming) suggests, the body is amenable to external influences 'but is also deeply rooted in parental ascriptions'.

The father's role is also clearly vital:[12] he needs to 'look after' the relationship between mother and baby and the baby's attempts to find himself in her eyes. Father therefore provides another 'pair of eyes' that look both at the self and at the self in relationship with mother. When the paternal eyes are missing or 'blind' in some way to what transpires between mother and baby, this may place the baby at risk. The baby may then be exposed to only one view of himself and may therefore struggle to separate from the early picture of himself that he finds in mother's eyes. This kind of impingement is all too apparent in the experience of patients presenting with body dysmorphia, to which we will turn in Chapter 4. Where this has been the experience early on, the therapeutic relationship can provide a vitally important additional 'pair of eyes' that can allow for a more benign perspective to begin to take root in the self.

Chapter 4

Being seen or being watched[1]

'Devil . . . you dare approach me? . . . be gone, vile insect! or rather stay
that I may trample you to dust'.
'I expected this recognition . . . all men hate the wretched: how then must
I be hated to be a miserable beyond all living things! Yet you, my creator,
detest and spurn me, thy creature to whom thou art bound by ties only
dissolvable by the annihilation of one of us . . . you my creator, abhor
me. What hope can I gather from your fellow creatures who owe me
nothing?'
'Be gone! Relieve me from the sight of your detested form'.

(Shelley 1818: 102–104)

Body dysmorphia

Small said to Large, 'But if I turned into a bug would you still love me
and give me a hug?'
'Of course', said Large, 'bug or not, I'll always love you no matter
what'.
'No matter what?' said Small. 'What if I was a crocodile?'
Large said, 'I'd hug you close and tight, and tuck you up in bed each
night'

(Gliori 2003: 10)

Bugs and crocodiles are not the prettiest of creatures. This evocative story
speaks to every child's anxiety about whether what the mother sees when
she looks at her child is felt to be beautiful and lovable *in spite of* all his bug
and crocodile feelings, which, of course, we all have. We often speak of ugly
feelings as if feelings can be seen and judged to be appealing, pleasing to the
mind's eye, or else repellent. One of the functions of the good-enough
mother is to help the child bear such ugly bug or crocodile feelings in
himself because they can be seen and accepted by her. Beauty, in this sense,
is indeed in the eye of the beholder.

As psychotherapists we are probably all accustomed to working with patients who display a dysmorphic body image and/or for whom their physical appearance is a source of varying degrees of anxiety and distress. Because patients with this kind of preoccupation will have the ring of familiarity for many therapists, it is important to be clear about the specific characteristics of the patients I am concerned with in this chapter. In so doing I hope to delineate a spectrum of difficulty that we will encounter clinically with respect to both the distress about the given body and the measures taken to alter or conceal it in some way.

The patients for whom body dysmorphia and hatred of their body is a core, primary features represent only a minority of patients with body image disturbances. For these patients, however, the hatred of a body part(s) occupies their minds and the therapy sessions, often stripping meaning away from any interaction through the concretisation of both the problem (i.e. a flawed body part) and the solution (i.e. cosmetic surgery). Through this work I became interested in the different qualities of transference and countertransference that I noted and that I will elaborate on later.

These patients display a *heightened* preoccupation with some typically minor or altogether imagined flaw in their appearance. The preoccupation with the ugly body part is prominent, persistent and very distressing and needs to be distinguished from more transient anxieties about physical appearance or discomfort in one's body, if only because of the severity of these patients' symptoms, which can have implications for treatment. These individuals present with a significant impairment in functioning because the preoccupation with the body leads to obsessional, and sometimes very extreme, attempts to conceal and/or change their appearance, either through surgery or so-called 'DIY' (do-it-yourself) surgery, often placing the individual at risk of harm (e.g. using sandpaper to remove scars or bleach to lighten the skin).

Many find it hard to leave the house for fear of being seen or only go out at night when darkness provides much needed cover from the other's gaze. As I reread *Frankenstein* I was reminded of this as Frankenstein's creature also 'travelled only when I was secure by night from the view of man' (Shelley 1818: 142). For patients with body dysmorphia, this enforced seclusion contributes to feeling that they are somehow set apart, another species – not unlike the way Frankenstein's creature felt. Some avoid mirrors altogether convinced that the reflection will only confirm their sense of being ugly and different, while others manage only by checking their appearance obsessionally in mirrors.

Frankenstein's creature discovers himself as different once he catches his reflection in the water:

'I cherished hope, it is true, then it vanished when I beheld my person reflected in water'.

and

> 'At first I was startled back, unable to believe that it were indeed I that
> was reflected in the mirror.'
>
> (Shelley 1818: 133)

As Brooks (1995) suggests:

> in a scenario that mirrors and reverses Lacan's . . . the outer image –
> that in the mirror – presents the body in its lack of wholeness while the
> inner apprehension of the body had up until then held it to be
> hypothetically whole . . . the mirror image becomes the negation of
> hope, severing the monster from desire.
>
> (Brooks 1995: 88–89)

I would argue that the creature never felt whole. The mirror fails to deliver its promise of illusory unity precisely because of the creature's early experience of Frankenstein's disgusted look and subsequent rejection (see Chapter 2). When the earliest physical exchanges between the baby and the object of desire inscribe ugliness into the body, the specular image can only confirm what is already prefigured on the body through projection. This is painfully lived out by patients with marked body dysmorphia where the reliance on the mirror to reassure themselves that they have concealed their ugliness is both anticipated as a source of relief, and invariably experienced as confirmation of their ugliness once they set eyes on their reflection (whether in actual mirrors or through what they imagine the other sees).

Some interesting research suggests that patients with body dysmorphia reveal a bias for misinterpreting other people's emotional expressions as negative (Buhlmann et al. 2004). Pertinent to this discussion is the observation made by the authors that these patients, relative to controls, rated significantly more neutral emotional expressions as contemptuous, suggesting that the gaze of the other is invariably felt to be hostile to the self.

Whilst there will almost certainly be some degree of shared narcissistic pathology underlying these types of presentation, my experience is that there are also qualitative differences amongst these patients that may have clinical implications. In other words, I am suggesting that body dysmorphia needs to be considered along a spectrum of severity, where the more severely disturbed patients may prove to be less accessible in analytic treatment and/or may require other types of help alongside analytic treatment because of the risk of self-harm and/or psychotic breakdown.

The literature that exists on patients with a diagnosis of Body Dysmorphic Disorder (BDD), who share descriptively the features I have just outlined, is of note in so far as it consistently underlines the severity of the functional impairment in patients who present with a primary, all-consuming preoccupation with an ugly body part or parts: some patients, for example, are unable to leave the house because they feel too ugly or may spend several hours putting on make-up and checking themselves obsessionally in mirrors (Phillips et al. 1993; Neziroglu et al. 1996; Phillips and Diaz 1997; Dyl et al. 2006).[2] Importantly, the psychiatric literature alerts us to the potential risk of self-harm in these patients. Suicidal ideation and attempts are common, with lifetime suicide attempt rates of 22–24 per cent (Veale et al. 1996; Dyl et al. 2006). A study looking at the suicide rate among 200 adolescents diagnosed as having BDD found that 44.4 per cent had attempted suicide (Dyl et al. 2006).

Although I am suggesting that the psychiatric literature on BDD is of some relevance to analytic practice, clinical work with these patients soon exposes that the diagnosis obfuscates important qualitative differences between individuals who ostensibly present with similar preoccupations about the body. Importantly, the diagnosis neglects the fundamental feature of these presentations, namely the *hatred* of what the reviled body part unconsciously represents. This takes us to the heart of the matter: to understand and help these patients it is important to understand the prevailing quality of their unconscious identifications.

In my experience with patients whose hatred of a body part or parts is all-encompassing two qualities of the 'mother-as-mirror' have emerged through the transference and my countertransference: she (the internal mother) may be felt to be providing a one-way, blank mirror *or* to be actively distorting and/or rejecting (either looking at the baby with hateful eyes or she is inappropriately narcissistically invested in the appearance of the child's body). These distinctions are, of course, never so clear-cut in practice; rather, they are used here as attempts to conceptualise some of the states of mind – diversely inflected by the relative stronghold of a 'super'-ego, as I shall go on to describe later – that can be observed through the unfolding of the transference with these patients. The distinctions should be read as denoting degrees of difficulty along a spectrum where hatred of the body is a primary feature of the patient's presentation. They may help us in understanding why only some of the patients with a dysmorphic body image are compelled to pursue cosmetic surgery and may prove highly resistant to thinking about their pain.

The one-way-mirror-mother

The first group of patients that I am proposing appear to be preoccupied with an internal object felt to be inaccessible or unavailable: a *one-way-mirror-mother* who is 'opaque' (Sodré 2002) and hard to read. Repeated exchanges with an actual mother felt to be inaccessible, for whatever reason, may contribute to the establishment of an internal tormenting experience of uncertainty about her feelings towards the self.[3] The search for absolute certainty in relation to what the other 'sees' when looking at the self may lead to desperate attempts to create the ideal body that will guarantee the other's loving gaze.

When these individuals seek help they do not present necessarily with an obviously traumatic history, but as the transference develops one is left with the feeling that they failed to make any real impression on the mother as in some way special and attractive. Trauma around the birth, actual physical flaws in the baby or postnatal depression may all complicate who the mother sees when she looks at her baby. Instead of welcoming eyes, I think that these individuals were met by emptiness or absence – a blank mirror – nothing on which to 'impress' and so build an image of themselves as appealing and special.[4] Kilborne (2007), in his discussion about appearance anxiety, notes that those individuals who cannot find themselves in the eyes of another need to compulsively control their appearance so as to 'make themselves intelligible' (Kilborne 2002: 27).

In a number of cases I have been led to formulate the patient's early experience as one of relating to a 'dead' mother (Green 1983). In these cases, as Green (1983) has highlighted, after a certain limit of time, the mother is experienced as being definitely dead, whether absent or present. This means no contact can be re-established when she is back. These patients' presentation also resonates with the description of 'essential depression' characterised not by sadness or pain, but by lack of desire: the patient is 'tired' (Aisenstein 2006).

As I suggested in Chapter 1, at the core of each of us there exists a painful yearning to know the inside of the mother who, by virtue of her separateness, can never be fully apprehended and possessed by the self. From the outset, as Meltzer (1988) suggests, we are all confronted with a painful state of uncertainty. We find more or less adaptive ways of reconciling ourselves to what we cannot see and can never know with any certainty about those we are closest to and hence, too, about what they see in us. If this experience is, however, reinforced in actuality by a mother who holds up an opaque, one-way mirror then the task of bearing what Meltzer (1988) refers to as her unknowable 'enigmatic interior', may expose the baby to tormenting doubt about what it is that the mother sees in him.

For some the uncertainty thus generated may lead to the need to control the object as a means of eliminating any doubt about what the other sees; the more the mother is felt to be withdrawn or inaccessible or ambiguous, the greater this imperative. It is striking to note in some patients how the certainty of the conviction of one's ugliness appears to be preferable to the torment of uncertainty.

Control over the 'other' may be expressed through attempts to remodel the bodily self, thereby creating an illusory certainty that the self 'knows' and so controls what the other sees when looking at the self. In this respect I understand the underlying dynamic in this group of individuals as similar to that found in what I have described elsewhere as 'self-preservative lying' (Lemma 2005). Like those lies used to serve up a fantasised, more attractive version of the self, so as to manage the anxiety generated by the object's inscrutability or unavailability, the pursued 'new' nose is a kind of lie that is felt to guarantee an admiring, loving gaze. In these cases cosmetic surgery is an enactment of the perfect match phantasy. The highly dependent and idealised relationship some people establish with cosmetic surgeons (before disappointment sets in), gives some clue as to what is being enacted: the search for a 'transformational object' (Bollas 1987) who will give birth to a new and improved version of the self.

An inscrutable, blank or absent mother appears to contribute to the failure to establish a securely based internal observing object who looks at the self with benign eyes.[5] Instead, a more critical, scrutinising other may have the upper hand in the patient's mind. Nevertheless, my sense is that this particular group of patients can more readily free themselves from the identificatory grip with this persecutory object. Although they feel very ugly and humiliated, and so hide from others, they are less likely to pursue cosmetic surgery. They report contemplating it, and may even become very preoccupied with it at various points, but overall the patients who are mostly relating to this kind of internal object are more likely to find their way to psychotherapy and probably will be able to make use of it. Although they display a relatively greater capacity for thinking, within the same session, these patients will most likely fluctuate between thinking and a defensive retreat into the concreteness of the bodily preoccupation.

The distorting-mirror-mother

The second group of patients that I am proposing convey through the transference an experience with a more distorting, intrusive, hostile object: a *distorting-mirror-mother*. These individuals typically present with more obviously difficult early histories characterised by the presence of inter-personal hostility. This also contributes to a deficit in the early libidinal cathexis of the body, but with an added noxious twist: the baby's body not only is undesired, but also becomes the receptacle for the mother's pro-jections. The hostility may be quite overt: as she looks at her baby this mother sees something 'ugly' (i.e. unacceptable) in herself, but locates this ugliness in the baby, relating to the baby's body as something 'bad' and 'ugly'. This mother uses her gaze to project 'ugly', unwanted parts of herself into the baby only to then condemn the baby for not matching up to her ideal. Such exchanges then expose the baby to an other who critically scrutinises what is now *his* 'ugliness' and badness. The hostility may, how-ever, be more implicit in the mother's failure to receive the baby's projec-tions of his so-called 'ugly' feelings. This may result in a marked deficit in the development of symbolic thinking making it more likely that undigested projections become concretely located in the body.

In the presence of a distorting-mirror-mother, and in absence of other receptive eyes/minds, the baby may be forced to include the mother's distorted image of him into his own emergent sense of who he is, including both the hated and hating aspects of the object. In these circumstances the mother's image of him acquires a persecutory quality. The source of the paranoid anxiety may then be concretely attributed to an ugly body part. Here, the reshaping or removal of a body part may be best understood as a hostile attack on a bad internal object, now felt to be quite concretely occupying the body. The body is indeed often felt by the patient to be the persecutor exposing the ugliness of the self to the world. The phantasy is that this persecutor is killed-off through the reshaping or removal of the reviled body part – this is the only way of separating from the other felt to now 'reside within the self' (Fonagy and Target 1999). We might say that these patients are in the grip of what Meltzer (1964) described as the somatic delusion, which he defined as:

> the physical and psychic expression of (a) a wide and deep split in the self, whereby (b) an expelled portion becomes represented by, and takes possession of, the function of a particular body part; (c) this part is then felt to take up a life completely of its own, totally ego-alien in orientation and powerfully effective in its interference with all good internal and external relationships.
>
> (Meltzer 1964: 246–247)

In these patients we can readily observe the actualisation of the self-made and reclaiming phantasies. We are effectively talking about a violent state of mind in the patient: violence is being perpetrated against the hated 'other' who is now concretely identified with the hated body part. This is probably why these individuals are more likely to pursue cosmetic surgery, sometimes repeatedly. The patient who wants to be rid of a body part is in identification in his mind with an omnipotent object who, through a process of splitting, incorporation and idealisation, is invested with the power to rescue the self from further rejection by proffering 'surgery' – a literal cutting off – as the alternative to thinking and so integrating painful, 'ugly' feelings towards the self and the object.[6]

A subtype of the distorting mirror mother is what I am calling the *you-are-me-mirror-mother*. In this group the patient's history and the quality of the transference that ensues suggests an experience of relating to a mother who was very narcissistically invested in the patient's body and appearance (sometimes with clear sexual overtones), undermining attempts at separation. This mother overstimulates the baby's body leading to a hypercathexis of the body ego. The surface of the body is over-invested with concern, attention and projection of the mother's need for admiration. It is, to use Joyce McDougall's (1989) term, a case of 'one body for two'.

It is probably appropriate to view this group of patients as relating to a particular version of the 'distorting-mirror-mother' since the object is indeed distorting, but I am highlighting this subgroup since their early histories are somewhat different. Not infrequently, these patients relate stories of experiencing the mother as concretely physically intrusive (e.g. no respect for the need for physical privacy during development), and as exerting pressure to 'look nice', often 'fussing' over their own and the child's appearance. They do not so much project ugliness into the child's body as target the body as a site for intrusive inspection and improvement. As one of my patients put it, her mother would look at her and say: 'If you only had a smaller nose then you would be really very pretty'.

These patients convey a sense that the body never felt like their own, but rather that it felt like the mother's 'commodity'. They often present with eating difficulties alongside a more specific preoccupation with a part of the body they want to change. These patients frequently undergo cosmetic procedures during late adolescence, often at the instigation of the mother, in an attempt to conform to what is expected of them and to appease the object.

Thin and thick skinned body dysmorphia

So far I have been suggesting that some patients relate mostly to an internal object felt to be absent, resulting in an undercathexis of the body, while others relate mostly to an object who projectively identifies 'badness' into the child's body, or an object who is experienced as narcissistically fused with the self, controlling of the body's appearance. Most likely all these three kinds of objects are experienced as persecuting to some degree, but even so, the transference that develops with these patients suggests that there are some different nuances in how they relate to themselves and to the object through their relationship to the body.

Of particular note are the differences between these patients in the extent to which the body (and therefore the object with which it is unconsciously identified) is attacked, in reality, through unnecessary cosmetic procedures. It is therefore probably more appropriate to speak of a spectrum of narcissistic disturbance underlying the symptom of body dysmorphia.

The distinction proposed by Rosenfeld (1987) between thick and thin skinned narcissism offers a helpful way for thinking about this spectrum. I would like to suggest that the patient who is *predominantly* relating to a 'one-way-mirror-mother' presents typically as more 'thin skinned'. He is more immediately vulnerable, fragile, hypervigilant of other people, and easily humiliated. The patient who is *predominantly* relating to a 'distorting-mirror-mother' typically presents as more 'thick skinned' and is harder to engage in treatment. I am emphasising the predominant nature of the quality of these internalised relationships because as several authors have noted, the division between thin and thick skinned is not a fixed one, with most patients moving from one to the other position and back, often within the same session (Bateman 1995; Britton 1998). Indeed, once the patient resolves to pursue cosmetic surgery (even if this is not followed through) this represents an attempt to create a thick skin. At such points the concreteness of this pursuit makes meaningful engagement with such patients very difficult.

In the thick skinned group the preoccupation with, and actual pursuit of, cosmetic surgery can acquire a manic quality. The body has become successfully objectified and is no longer the site of an embodied self. Rather, it is there to be manipulated, triumphed over or attacked. The disregard displayed by some patients for the physical risks associated with a number of cosmetic procedures is suggestive of an identification with an object who was felt to be uninterested or even repelled by the baby's body.

The quality of the identifications underpinning these disturbances lies at the heart of the overlaps and differences between the two positions on the spectrum of body dysmorphia. A particular process of unconscious identification appears to be at work in these patients: through an introjective identification the patient takes into himself a felt to be hateful and hated object that cruelly scrutinises the self. The patient-as-object now vilifies himself as object, that is, he turns against the split off part of his ego identified with the object (Freud 1917). Along with this narcissistic identification there is, in these patients, a further process of splitting and identification whereby what the object is felt to hate (and so, now, the self in identification with the object also hates) becomes projected into, and concretely identified with, the reviled, ugly body part. The body thus becomes an object. A part of the body becomes projectively identified with a confused mixture of parts of the self and parts of the object.

These patients are in the grip of paranoid anxieties. It is the relative pervasiveness of the paranoid-schizoid grip on overall mental functioning that distinguishes the two groups: the thick skinned group of patients are more rigidly identified with a cruel, scrutinising object, a point I will return to later. Additionally, in this group, there appears to be a far more violent attack on the link to the body that is now the container of the spilt-off projections, thereby creating greater obstacles to thinking about what is happening internally.

I would like to suggest that the patients who pose the greatest risk to themselves, who display greater compulsiveness in their attempts to conceal and/or alter the 'given' body and who are hardest to engage (and possibly also to help in analytic treatment), are more likely to display the underlying dynamics just described.[7] In the consulting room, we are often faced with a part of the patient who is malignantly identified with a harsh and ruthless observer, where looking is in the service of destruction, not love. The therapist may be experienced as a harsh, shaming observer who will surely humiliate the self or the therapist may be herself subjected to the patient's cruel scrutiny and denigration. The psychotic part of the personality has a greater stronghold on the patient's overall functioning than in the group of patients I mentioned earlier. The transference can be deadlocked in the oscillations between the patient's experience of being hated by the therapist or of hating the therapist, precluding the possibility for any meaningful contact to be made between the patient and them.

Being seen or being watched?

The primary anxiety voiced by patients who perceive themselves as physically flawed is of being scrutinised by the other and judged to be ugly and unlovable.[8] Humiliation is a painfully common experience as they feel perpetually exposed to the harsh, watchful gaze of the 'other'. This leads us to consider the role of the superego.

The literature on patients diagnosed with BDD describes how they often describe that they are not seeking an ideal body; they just want to be 'normal' and 'fit in'. While this is true in the sense that in most cases the individual feels that all he is trying to do is to change one or more imperfections to make himself 'normal', the unconscious phantasy is that this change will make the self perfect in the object's eyes. The sometimes relentless pursuit of cosmetic surgery highlights the self's identification with an abnormal superego that lures the self into believing that there can exist such as a thing as an 'ideal ego', that is, a perfect, idealised self. This is quite different to an 'ego-ideal', which has a more benignly aspirational quality (Hanly 1984).

In cognitive research studies BDD patients, relative to healthy controls, have been found to view themselves from an observer perspective (Osman et al. 2004). This is not, however, the healthy perspective taking that flows from the resolution of the Oedipus complex, where one can take the third position of observer of the self. On the contrary, some of these patients seem to be in identification with a harsh observing object, an ego-destructive 'super'-ego (Bion 1962). But the temporary relief from anxiety that submission to such a terrifying superego serves up as consolation, in fact, serves only to magnify anxiety, feeding into escalating cycles of cruelty and punishment. This pathological 'super'-ego watches the ego from a 'higher' place and is fundamentally against the pain that comes from thinking and understanding (O'Shaughnessy 1999). It is the rule of the tyrant.

David Veale, who has contributed extensively to our understanding of patients with BDD from a cognitive perspective, argues that they have lost, the 'rose tinted glasses' (Lambrou, 2006) – the self-serving bias that protects many of us from too many narcissistic wounds as we look in the mirror (Veale and Riley 2001; Lambrou 2006). We might say that the rose tinted glasses are imparted by the good-enough mother who 'looks after' her baby with loving eyes. The rose tinted glasses are the benign loving superego (Schafer 1960) that partly develops out of the mother's early care, love and concern with the bodily self.

Clinically, it is the extent and rigidity of the identification with an ego-destructive 'super'-ego that differentiates between the two groups proposed here. In the more 'thin skinned' group, we observe a less absolute identification in this respect. Even though the individual often feels at the mercy of a harsh, scrutinising internal object, these patients convey a greater degree of hopefulness that their pain will be received by the object. Their longing for the object's desire is at times transformed into hatred for the felt to be rejecting object, but it is more possible to engage with their longing and the pain of rejection such that thinking can take place.

In the 'thick skinned' group, it is precisely a more rigid, malignant identification with an ego-destructive 'super'-ego that ensures the thick skin and that presents us, in the room, with the challenge posed by a part of the patient who is against life. I would now like to illustrate this core dynamic first with a brief excerpt from the assessment phase with an adolescent girl, and then with a detailed session from an analysis with an adult patient.

A seventeen-year-old girl, Ms G., was referred because of BDD. She described feeling ugly for as long as she could remember, but this feeling took hold in a particularly vicious manner around the age of thirteen. She felt especially concerned about her skin and the shape of her face. Her skin, she said, was blotchy and uneven. She could not say what was wrong with her face except that it was the 'wrong shape', that somehow it was 'too big'. She was, in fact, an attractive girl with exceptionally smooth skin, as far as I could see. Yet she spent several hours every morning applying make-up and changing in and out of various outfits before she felt able to leave the house. This led her to drop out of college and to disengage from her peer group.

Although the rituals around her appearance were of distress to her, they could also have an enveloping, almost sensual quality, as if in the minutiae of the care taken with dress and make-up, and of obsessionally checking her reflection in the mirror, there was an enactment of a longed for, idealised, primitive interweaving of look and touch between self and object. No matter how much effort she invested in making herself 'acceptable', as she put it, and even if temporarily she felt that she could face the gaze of the other from behind the layers of her disguise, she was all too soon at the mercy of a persecutory gaze and the cycle resumed again.

One of the most striking and disturbing features of Ms G.'s presentation was her obsession with collecting 'living dead' dolls – dolls that are made to look dead, but with open eyes. I am choosing to share an excerpt from the assessment phase because it captures quite vividly some of the themes I have been describing.

Ms G. arrived for the second of four assessment consultations upset and angry. On the way to the session, she had a row with a woman on the bus – it was 'always a woman', she emphasised. This woman had asked her to get off the bus, saying, 'I know what you are up to', and told her she was fat and ugly. My patient shared with me her very violent fantasies about what she would have liked to do to the woman, from which she had refrained only because of the closed circuit television (CCTV) camera on the bus. She said that she had stared back at her and shouted. As it was, she had certainly given her as good as she got, judging from the account she gave me of what she had said to her in reply.

Ms G. went on to tell me that she had felt a bit more positive after our first session, but that now she doubted this was going to help, that what this woman had done had ruined everything. She said that she didn't even know if she would bother coming back the following week for 'another assessment'. She said that the attack had been so unexpected, 'out of the blue'. She emphasised that she had made a real effort to get out of the house to come to see me, but now that she was here, she wondered what the point was. She repeated that the woman had behaved 'unpredictably'.

As she spoke it was clear that she was angry and very defensive. I said that although she had felt better at the end of the session the previous week, now that she was here again, there was a part of her that found the uncertainty about what I really thought about her to be quite cruel. She was now convinced I had seen right through her (like the woman on the bus who says 'I know what you are up to'), and that I had seen something ugly and, as a result, she feared that I was going to tell her at any moment to 'get off', and so humiliate her. She was no longer sitting in the room with someone trying to understand her, but with someone she could not trust, someone unpredictable. She was saying to me she might not come back next week so that now *I* did not know what to expect from her.

Ms G. responded to this intervention by becoming less agitated. She was then able to describe in vivid detail how 'paranoid'[9] she felt in the street, as she was convinced that everyone was staring at her and seeing how ugly she was. She acknowledged that she had felt very anxious about meeting me again because she was not sure what I would make of her.

Ms G's experience of herself was of someone 'living dead' – a powerful and disturbing image encapsulating both her identification with an inaccessible, 'dead', mother, and her hatred of this mother who, I think, she felt looked at her with dead, empty eyes. The use made by Ms G. of her eyes to attack the object was a feature of her exchange with the woman on the bus: she 'stared' her out. This more menacing quality was present, albeit more muted, in our exchange.

In a part of her mind Ms G. experienced the assessment process not as my attempt to understand her and help her, but as me cruelly scrutinising her and withholding my thoughts about her. This made her feel enraged with me and she engaged with me in an angry stand-off where what I had to offer could not be of any help to her and she might not come back. Then there was no space for thinking about what she really felt. In Ms G.'s experience I turned into someone with X-ray vision who would humiliate her – someone I will want to keep outside of my range of 'loving vision'. When my anticipated rejecting response aroused Ms G.'s 'ugly' feelings towards me she felt in the presence of a CCTV-camera-me: I would register what she did and then punish her for it rather than understand the unpredictable part of her that could so ruthlessly and 'out of the blue' attack her and the help she knows she needs.

As with Ms G. the therapeutic challenge with this group of patients lies in titrating interventions that do not feel too exposing and so potentially shaming. This is largely because looking, as in understanding, may be so easily experienced by these patients as being watched from 'on high'. In this work the therapist is frequently projectively identified with a malignant 'omniscience' – an ever-present critical, CCTV-camera-type eye. The self's identification with an ego-destructive 'super'-ego is an attempt to maintain a fragile narcissistic equilibrium in the face of such a harsh, scrutinising object. Submission to this 'super'-ego ensures the needed narcissistic cathexis, but the psychic costs are high since this is an unholy alliance forged with a very destructive part of the self. The 'super'-ego is, at core, a corrupt object: it owns the mind rather than being a part of it. The narcissistic equilibrium thus regained is invariably precarious.

I would now like to illustrate further, and in more detail, this particular dynamic with material from an analysis with an adult male patient, Mr H. He presented with a crippling array of problems of longstanding duration, including marked body dysmorphia, which is the aspect of his difficulties that I will be focusing on here. He had been admitted to psychiatric units from a young age.

For as long as he could remember, Mr H. had hated several aspects of his appearance. As an adolescent he had resorted to 'DIY' surgery in an attempt to alter a particular part of his body. The locus of his body hatred had shifted over the years, mostly affecting his experience of facial features and his skin, but as an adult this concern had spread to the appearance of his foreskin. Although in sessions he would refer in a general way to disliking the appearance of his penis, his distress and anxiety were specifically focused on the absence of a foreskin. The preoccupation with imperfections of his skin extended to the skin on his face and neck. This concern was dominant and associated with ritualistic behaviour that was time consuming (e.g. covering up his neck with scarves even at the height of summer) and led to marked social isolation and obsessional rituals related to his appearance.

This session took place towards the end of the second year of his analysis. The patient had missed the two previous sessions, which had been preceded by a short break in the analysis as I had been away. This had coincided with a stressful family event (his sister's eighteenth birthday party) that he had been dreading.

In this particular session, the third of the week, the patient arrived and asked me how my break had gone. He made no reference to his own cancelled sessions. When I did not reply, he laughed and said he knew I could not answer, but that he wanted me to know that he hoped I had a good time as he was sure that I must be quite tired, that my work was emotionally demanding. He then told me that his sister's birthday party had gone well, but that he had not managed to stay around for long. He had tried to hug her, he said, because that's what he felt he should do, but he really hated physical contact so he had found the whole experience quite stressful. He went on to describe how he found it hard to see his mother pandering to his sister, even though he knew that was the right thing to do because she was younger than him and needed her. He said he felt disgusted by his mother at times, especially when she 'glammed' herself up for these events and paraded his sister as a beauty, 'like it was some fashion show. She says she loves her but this has nothing to do with love'. He paused and then added: 'She is so preoccupied with herself that she has no idea what anybody feels'. He said he hated his mother's emphasis on physical appearance and went on to describe how she was overweight and hated herself.

I said that he had come today feeling pressure to be nice to me, to ask me how my break had gone, but that in fact this 'show' of care and interest masked how he really felt towards this glammed-up me who had left him in order to pander to her own needs.

Mr H. was briefly silent and then said that his sister had a good time at her party. He could remember always hating parties when he was younger because he felt so inept, ugly, 'like a geek'. Instead, he could see that his sister had no self-consciousness; 'She was so relaxed and I have to say that she looked good. She's popular. People want to be with her.' As he described his painfully acute awkwardness when under the glare of others, I detected something more real in our exchange. He spoke about his wish to hide and vividly conveyed how scrutinised he felt. I sensed his pain as he compared himself unfavourably with his sister.

I said that he felt quite hurt at losing my attention over the break and he was still not sure he could count on it now as he was convinced that I had turned my eyes away from him to this much prettier daughter who now occupied my mind.

He replied dismissively that I might have a point. I felt jolted by the sudden severance in the connectedness I had experienced only seconds previously, as if I had been lulled into a false sense of intimacy.

Mr H. added that I knew him well enough by now to realise that he always felt second best. He said that he was full of horrible feelings. He thought his mother wanted 'all the chintz, not the shit'. He then went into one of his obsessional, extremely detailed lists, which at this point in time in the analysis concerned his attempts to alter the appearance of his foreskin.

He went on to say that he had found some very helpful information on the net about foreskins and that if he followed their instructions, this would make a real difference to the look of his penis and so to his mood. He emphasised how good this particular site was at explaining things, unlike other sites he had visited. He had downloaded a brochure from the website and he was very impressed with it. It was especially praiseworthy, he said, because it actually showed you pictures of 'before and after'. He thought it was an advantage that it was written by those who have the problem, 'who know what it really feels like to hate your body, and so it's like a kind of "self-help" group, not those glossy, Harley Street surgeons who are just after your money', he tagged on pointedly. He went into detail, again, about the way the penises looked and he became quite manic. As I listened, I felt the by then all too familiar numbness as he distanced himself from any possibility of a real engagement with me in the room while, as it were, he leafed through the pages of a glossy brochure about penises.

I said that he seemed to find it hard to allow any contact between us today. He believed I was only interested in 'chintz', the gloss, and so that's what he provided me with: a glossy brochure of his experience 'before and after' the break, which protected us both from the rawness of his feelings about it. I said that he had experienced the break as me forcing him to watch the parade of my pretty daughter, whom I chose over him during the break, without any concern for his feelings. And now it was him who was quite excited as he paraded the helpful website: this was my replacement and relegated me to second best.

The patient was silent. When he resumed he said he knew that his wish for a foreskin was not the answer, but that he just couldn't help himself at times: 'It's like a drug. I can't resist it. The image I get in my mind, that I can see when I look down . . . that I will see my penis looking normal . . . it does make me feel better'.

I said that when he felt so full of difficult feelings in his mind it was so much easier if he could comfort himself with the thought that he had this perfect penis. Like a drug, it took the pain away.

He was silent again and then brought the following dream, which he said he had while I had been away:

> A large spider is in a corner of a room. The room is bare, there is nowhere to hide. He looks at the spider and then has to turn away because the spider glares at him. He knows he cannot stamp on it and crush it because it is so big. It has one enormous eye and it feels like it emanates heat that burns his skin, even at a distance. He stands there, frozen on the spot, not sure whether to make a run for it or try to fight the spider.

Mr H. was silent and then said that he had found a spider by his bed the night before. He did not like spiders; the idea of one crawling over his body repelled him; they were 'ugly' creatures. He remembered that as a teenager he used to be afraid of bugs. He said that he was repelled by the idea that they could get right under his skin and eat him from the inside. He laughed and added, 'then they would see what shit was inside me'.

I said that he seemed to feel that I did not want to see what he felt like inside. If he revealed his shitty, 'ugly' feelings about me going away, he feared being exposed to a piercing one-eyed spider-me who would corner him, get right inside his mind and look in disgust at what was inside him.

He was then silent for a long time (quite unusually for him) and then said that some weeks previously he had seen a TV documentary about spiders. The man presenting the documentary had described the spider's web in the most poetic way:

> For a moment it had made me think of spiders as beautiful. I think it's because he got to know them so well . . . years of study . . . I guess that after devoting himself to it he came to love them. . .to see something in them that others can't see.

I found myself very moved by this image. I said that perhaps there was a part of him that could entertain the possibility that I might not look at him with such harsh, piercing eyes – that instead I might see something special in him.

The patient was silent and it took me a few minutes to realise he was actually tearful, which was quite unusual for him:

> I can hear a loud voice telling me that I must go home and get to work on my foreskin . . . that this way it will look just right . . . and then another voice that says it's not the answer. It drives me crazy. Who do I listen to?

I said that this was indeed the dilemma in his dream: when he feels this tension he can either 'make a run for it' back into his fantasies about his improved penis or he can stand up to this powerful voice, but that this was a tough choice. I said that it was so very hard to be inside his mind, having to assuage this demanding voice that promised him this perfect penis. I added that I could see how this voice was really in competition with our work in the room.

The patient agreed and sighed. After a few minutes he said that he knew he would end up going on the website when he got home; it was inevitable, he said, and he retreated into detail, once again, about the stories he had read on the website written by people suffering like him and only wanting to 'look normal'. All this was said with some excitement, as if his brief excursion into reality, and so pain, was now a distant memory and he was, once again, seduced by the promise of concrete solutions.

The crushing rejection my patient felt as a result of my break led to his retreat into his phantasised perfect penis, which would not only be far superior to what I was offered by my 'prettier daughter' during the break, but also ensured that in the session I was left in no doubt about how useless I had become in his experience. I fleetingly felt a more real connection with him as he described his acute self-consciousness during his sister's birthday party. However, by the time Mr H. responds to my intervention, he has retreated into his obsessional lists. I was then left feeling as if I had been drawn into an intimacy, so as to then be made to feel the pain of expulsion. I think that this is how the patient had indeed experienced the break and he is now in identification with such a dismissive, ruthless object. The idealisation of the website, and what it can give him, becomes his way of managing the feelings of hurt that I had tried to think with him about.

By this point in the session Mr H. is in identification with the 'super'-ego that promises him a better penis – offers him the 'drug' that will take away the pain – and relegates me to 'second best': unlike the website, I am no good at explaining things to him and cannot give him a perfect penis. This kind of 'super'-ego breeds only fear and undermines any link to a good object. In turn, I become projectively identified with a 'corrupt' object, here appearing in the guise of an unscrupulous Harley Street surgeon who exploits his pain.

The dream captured a core dilemma in our work: being understood or 'seen' by me to have anything other than 'pretty' feelings (e.g. his so-called concern at the start of the session about my break) did not necessarily bring relief. Rather, it seemed to turn me into a crushing, phallic one-eyed spider that pierced right through him with my burning glare and he simply could find nowhere to hide – the room was bare. I think that in a 'bare', harsh part of Mr H.'s mind, being 'seen' and so understood was experienced as a humiliating exposure of his 'ugly' self. He defended himself against this by himself forging an alliance with a 'super'-ego that crushed me, rendering me useless to him – he only needs self-help.

Towards the end of the session we manage to make some contact again and, quite movingly, he briefly entertains the possibility that like the spider expert, I might see something appealing in him that others cannot see. I thought that at this point he was much more connected with what he felt and was listening to what I was saying. However, as the session ends, I felt him moving away once more, retreating into what he presents as the defeated position: 'I will give in to the lure of a better foreskin'. By this point, probably also because he knew the session was about to end, he had already retreated back into his former, defensively excited state of mind.

Much of the work with the patients across both of the two groups that have been described consists in carefully tracking the patient's identification with a ruthless superego and the projective identification of a scrutinising, harsh and intrusive object into the therapist. This is painstaking work that is repeatedly hijacked by the lure of concrete solutions. These individuals are primed by the very quality of their primary identifications to be especially vulnerable to the media's current preoccupation with physical perfection and the widespread availability of cosmetic procedures to alter one's appearance. To this extent the predicaments of these individuals allow us to appreciate the complex interplay between internal and external forces in shaping individual pathology.

Chapter 5

Occupied territories and foreign parts

Reclaiming the body

> This, at last, is bone of my bones, and flesh of my flesh.
>
> (Genesis, 2:23)

The reclaiming phantasy

The body is the primary seat for the development of the sense of self, as we saw in Chapter 3. It is also the primary site for meeting the other. As such the body imposes itself as both the incarnation of the self's identity and possibilities, and as the ineluctable proof of our interconnectedness with others. The question of the *ownership* of the body emerges in varied guises when working with patients who seek to modify their bodies. But this is not a problem reserved only for the patients we see. It is a problem we are all faced with. All our efforts at body modification, including our daily grooming rituals, are manifestations of this central human dilemma: how to feel at home in one's body. This involves two related psychic processes. First, we need to come to terms with the fact of the shared corporeality of mother and baby – the embodied version of psychic dependency – that ties us to the mother in a most concrete manner. Second, from the moment of birth onwards, healthy development involves the gradual separation of our own body from that of the mother (Laufer 1968). Inevitably, this separation requires relinquishing the mother's libidinal gratification of the body. Being-in-a-body thus both confronts us simultaneously with our dependency on the other *and* with the loss of oneness with the other.

When things are going relatively well, it is hoped that we can develop out of this early dependency to become our own person, with a separate body and mind, but we can never be totally independent of the other. The body is always reminding us that we live in one body, but that this body inevitably bears the trace of the (m)other.[1] The ability to be separate, that is, to enjoy a relatively stable sense of one's own body and mind while also being engaged, and connected, with others is not a once-and-for-all process: at different stages of development this psychic task represents itself and can pose particular challenges. Nowhere is this more so than during adolescence when the tension between the need to separate from parental figures and the regressive pull of childhood longings provides a rocky backdrop for the integration of the changing body in order to consolidate sexual identity (that is, integrating the genitals into the mental representation of the body). Things can go wrong therefore on two fronts: the mother and/or child may experience separation to be profoundly destabilising and may thus seek to remain merged, or separation may only be felt to be possible through very violent means.

Through their careful study of adolescent breakdown, Moses and Egle Laufer (Laufer 1968; Laufer and Laufer 1984) have suggested that if the body cannot be integrated into a coherent image and experience of the self, it may be experienced as 'foreign'. I want to suggest that when the body feels foreign in this way, the modification of the body may represent an attempt to reclaim the body from a perceived invasion by the object. In this chapter I am thus primarily concerned with the problem of the body's *boundaries* and the way in which for some patients the body modification serves the function of rescuing the self from an alien presence felt to now reside within the body, that is, the modification of the body is driven by what I am calling the *reclaiming phantasy*.

This phantasy concerns the *expulsion* from the body of an object felt to be alien or polluting. The subjective experience is of feeling possessed by the object, concretely felt to reside in the body, from which the self must free itself. The aggression that underlines this phantasy is directed at expelling the object, but it is not aimed at triumphing over the object – a quality that is more characteristic of the self-made phantasy (see Chapter 6).

It is through the body that we experience most concretely the tensions that will arise in any kind of intimacy: between the desire to fuse with the other and the fear of being taken over by the other. This may arouse profound claustrophobic anxieties. Rey (1994) has described a primitive universal position of claustrophobia and agoraphobia, which he roots in the body:

> One of the various manifestations of the body self is its relationship with claustrophobia and agoraphobia. Claustrophobic space is the result of projective identification of the body and its inner space into the outside world. . . . It is therefore the child inside the mother's body who becomes claustrophobic inside the inner space of his mother projected into the outside world.
>
> (Rey 1994: 267)

Along similar lines Glasser (1979) identified an internal scenario – the Core Complex – characterised by the wish to fuse with the object, but this fusion is felt to present a danger of total engulfment, and hence has to be violently resisted. This kind of tension is present in some of the patients for whom the modification of the body then provides the means through which they can reassure themselves that they are indeed separate from the other, and it defends against the wish to fuse with the other. An important aspect of the therapeutic work where the reclaiming phantasy drives the pursuit of body modification is to understand the patient's subjective experience of an internal world where there is only a felt-to-be terrifying mother that is defended against through the manipulation of the body's appearance. Here the body modification is often a defence against the terror of undifferentiation.

The body may also be experienced as a container of the other's projections, and it may then feel like an occupied territory. If this is the case it may then have to be denied (as in anorexia), or visibly modified to create an experience of ownership of the body and so reclaim it from the perceived invasion.

The demands of the body can be experienced as invasive, frightening, or even disgusting, at any stage of life. The body is at once captivating and potentially violently repulsive. We can all too readily come to regard it as a monstrous otherness, forever out of our control. Particular developmental transitions may act as catalysts for a more acute resurgence of anxieties anchored in our bodily nature, for example, at puberty or as our bodies age. While the timing of the onset of a preoccupation with the bodily self may therefore be helpfully related to the particular demands of a given developmental stage, work with patients who feel compelled to modify their bodies invariably also involves addressing their relationship with the maternal object and with the meaning for them of the maternal body, which is the focus of this chapter. In approaching this subject I am relying on the important notion of the body both as physical entity and as an 'internal object' (Egle Laufer no date). This internal object is the representation of the affective relationship with the libidinal body that is shaped by the earliest exchanges between the mother and baby.

The maternal landscape

The baby's own body provides the basis for the development of the ego, but it is not only the baby's body that stimulates development. Klein's understanding of the baby's early experience places the maternal body centre stage as the first site of the baby's concentrated psychical activity. Several of her papers underline the baby's primordial relationship to the maternal body. Klein's (1936) descriptions suggest an early awareness of the actual mother's body.[2] The baby appears to structure a world of meaning around the mother's body, especially through experiences of gratification and frustration, not only at the breast as Klein thought, but more generally through the sensory, motoric exchanges that transpire between mother and baby from the start. The baby's earliest exchanges with the mother are sensory in nature and therefore the experience of the mother's body and of the baby's own body are inextricably linked (see Chapter 3).

The experiences of the oral phase provide the first identifications with the mother and the association of her body and functions with the experience of internal fulfilment. Klein (1936) proposed that the mother's body is felt to contain her gratifying possessions signified by the internal contents of faeces, babies and an incorporated penis. Potential rivals therefore also inhabit the rich, creative space of the maternal body. Consequently, the baby is very preoccupied with ownership of the maternal body and seeks to appropriate it for himself. This is intensified by the epistemophilic instinct – the baby's urge to discover and conquer the internal territory of the mother's body. The early Kleinian baby is thus presented as driven by its bodily needs and oral impulses to secure for himself the sustenance and prized goods that the maternal body houses.

Klein set out how complex processes of projection and introjection help the baby to invest the world with symbolic meaning drawn from his immediate bodily and mental states. As Bronstein (2009: 21) points out: 'The content of unconscious phantasies is intimately linked to phantasies of the mother's body and to how the child has worked through this interaction'.

At its best the bountiful and protective maternal body can become a source of inspiration for introjecting helpful figures. But the archaic maternal body can also be a site for horror:

> devotees of the abject, she as well as he, do not cease looking within what flows from the other's innermost being, for the desirable and terrifying, nourishing and murderous, fascinating and abject inside of the mother's body.
>
> (Kristeva 1982: 77)

Julia Kristeva's notion of *abjection* is central to understanding the meaning of the maternal body and adds to Klein's important contribution by specifying why the maternal body can be experienced as 'horrific'. Unlike Klein who stresses the envy provoked by the maternal body and its prized possessions (see Chapter 6), Kristeva evocatively depicts the dread of the maternal body and hence the fear of falling back into the mother's body. Although her views originate from Lacan, she nevertheless parts company with him on a central point. Unlike Lacan who argues that the baby starts to differentiate himself from the mother during the mirror phase, Kristeva suggests that this separation occurs much earlier (though not from the beginning of life as Klein proposes) when the baby begins to expel from himself what he finds unpalatable. This is the process she calls abjection, that is, a rejecting or jettisoning of what is other to oneself so as to create borders of an ultimately always tenuous 'I'. The abject is what we spit out, almost violently, from the self.

Kristeva's ideas resonate in a particularly helpful way with lived experience of being-in-a-body because she highlights how the physical realm of experience – what she refers to as the semiotic (i.e. the study of signs)[3] – is always potentially threatening to disrupt the orderly symbolic realm. Her emphasis on the violent rejection of what is felt to be alien within oneself, and hence on the violence by which one jettisons phenomena that both threaten and create the self's borders, is also very relevant. She argues that what is abjected is radically excluded and yet it can never be banished altogether. Instead, it hovers on the periphery of our existence, constantly challenging our own tenuous borders of selfhood. In other words, what is abjected is not repressed – it remains as both an unconscious and conscious threat to our own 'proper and clean' (Kristeva 1982) self. This is an important feature of the abject: although we need to exclude the abject, the abject must also be tolerated because what threatens life is also that which helps to define it. Kristeva thus emphasises the attraction as well as the horror of the undifferentiated.

The most pointed case of abjection, according to Kristeva, is the abject mother. In her view, woman is specifically related to polluting objects through menstruation and her role in toilet training. Here she argues that our first encounter with authority is with 'maternal authority' when the child learns through interaction with the mother about his body, its shape, and its 'clean and proper' areas. This way the mother is pivotal is establishing a 'primal mapping of the body' (Kristeva 1982).

Kristeva argues that the first 'thing' to be abjected is the mother's body, that is, the baby's own origin. She highlights how the smooth outer body is a space of rational control and unproblematic instrumentality, in other words 'masculine'. By contrast, the inner body – the mother's body – is unfixed, fluid, secret, evading knowledge and control, in other words, feminine. This inner body with its instincts and passions attributed to it is felt to be other. From this perspective, perfectly healthy body parts can be experienced as parasites – a symptom of the body's status as 'other'. David Cronenberg's films – to which we will shortly turn, and others in the horror genre too – draw on this transformation of the normal, visceral inner body into a site of mutation and disease.

Several authors have emphasised that our first experience is of a realm of plenitude, of a oneness with our environment – a view notably endorsed by Winnicott (1945, 1965), whose good-enough mother allows at first for a complete emotional and physical dependence between her and her baby. By contrast, Klein (1957) stressed that from the outset the baby glimpses that he is not completely always 'at one' with the mother, that is, he has an inborn awareness that there exists a separate, bountiful object. The view that has most face validity for me lies somewhere in between these two versions: I tend to think that in the early weeks and months, the baby only momentarily glimpses that there exist some boundaries that separate him from the mother or, as Erlich (2008) helpfully puts it, from the outset, 'psychic events and contents occur within two experiential dimensions: one based on the separateness of subject and object (Doing), the other on the unity of subject and object (Being)' (Erlich 2008: 57). These dimensions run alongside each other and continue throughout life.

The baby's excursions into the harsh reality of separateness are more than compensated for by the good-enough mother who intuitively titrates the baby's exposure to his separateness from her, so that when all is going relatively well, early life is an experience of satisfying oneness with the mother, punctuated by incremental moments of disjunction between need and its satisfaction.

With the gradual loss of immediate gratification that is introduced by the mother, the experience of lack, or the beginning of need, is felt with greater force by the baby. But even when his needs are met, the mother cannot satisfy the baby's primordial desire: to have all needs met *before* they become needs, hence the baby now experiences a painful gap between need and satisfaction. In Lacan's terms, he is in an ongoing state of desire, for desires that can never be met. The problem is that what the baby wants is much more than he actually needs. This is why the baby, just like the adult later, is always the subject of desire.

If the truth be known to ourselves, what we all really want is to be the object of the mother's unwavering love, admiration and desire. Of course, if we had that we would never become civilised, speaking beings – we would never grow beyond the immediacy of the sensory world of our body embraced by the mother's body. This represents a central psychic tension that is especially apparent in those individuals who cannot comfortably inhabit the given body.

The baby is thus confronted with what may feel like an irresolvable double bind: a longing for narcissistic union with his mother and a need to renounce this union in order to become his own person, living in his own body and mind. He must renounce a part of himself in order to become a self. It is precisely in his attempt to break away that, Kristeva argues, the mother becomes abject. Indeed analytic theory has stressed the developmental necessity of the separation between the body of the mother and the body of the child. The father's role is to facilitate this separation and so challenge phantasies of fusion. This is a vital role because it is so difficult to identify the mother's borders:

> the 'subject' discovers itself as the impossible separation/identity of the maternal body. It hates *that body* but only because it can't be free of it.

That body. The body without border, the body out of which this abject subject came, is *impossible.*

(Kristeva 1982: 60, my italics)

Subjectivity is then founded upon separation from the mother and from her body more specifically. For both sexes, *that body*, as Kristeva put it, is always the body of the mother, the primal home that recalls a state of oneness and completion – its seductions and horrors. The maternal body thus reflects the dual aspect of a fear of an engulfing bodily fusion and of a longing for reunification.

The 'impossibility' that Kristeva refers to accurately captures the corresponding urgency that can underpin the drive to modify the given body so as to create a sense of boundary, as I would now like to illustrate with a brief clinical example.

Ms F. was in her late twenties when she was referred by a very thoughtful plastic surgeon after a request for a rhinoplasty. The surgeon said that he thought he could make some very slight improvement, but that essentially the nose was fine and he was concerned that the patient would be inevitably disappointed. He said that he had discerned during his consultation a rather disgruntled tone and that in his experience this did not bode well for cosmetic surgery.

I met with Ms F. several times before she reluctantly agreed to psychotherapy, though after less than one year she dropped out, convinced that what she really needed after all was to change the shape of her nose. This is therefore by no means a therapeutic success story, but my work with her was very helpful to me in understanding better the dynamics at work in some of these cases.

Ms F. had been very ill as a young baby and consequently had spent a lot of time in hospital in the first year of her life. She grew up on a council estate with her single mother, who had not managed to work due to anxiety. As a young child Ms F. had found school difficult; by the age of ten she was stuck in an entrenched pattern of school refusal, which resulted in her mother's decision to educate her at home. She had never known her father and her mother seldom mentioned him.

Ms F. recalled what she described as a happy childhood. She said she had been very close to her mother with whom she spent much of her time. She described her as an anxious woman who was still afraid of the dark. The mother came across as emotionally absent, but somehow as too physically present, requiring Ms F.'s physical presence to assuage her own anxiety. Ms F.

appeared to have never had much opportunity to have her own physical space.

By thirteen she described feeling very conscious of her nose, which she hated. She also disliked her skin, which she said was rough and prone to eczema. She never enjoyed physical activities and generally conveyed a sense that her body had held her back in life.

In her late adolescence Ms F. pierced several parts of her body and had three tattoos done – all rather discrete and hence not visible to others. At secondary school (into which she was only ever partially successfully reintegrated) she shied away from joining in with her peer group. She only developed what appeared to have been an overly dependent and ambivalent relationship with an older girl who was her neighbour and who also sounded quite troubled. At eighteen she went to study make-up and hairdressing at college, which she enjoyed, and she had worked as a part-time beautician ever since. She had not opted for hairdressing, she said, because it would have involved spending too many hours in front of mirrors.

She had one boyfriend aged eighteen – a rather desultory sounding relationship, which ended after only a few months. She continued to live with her mother. Her main source of enjoyment appeared to be her work, in which she clearly took some pride.

By the time I met with Ms F. she had tried numerous cosmetic procedures on herself, chiefly to improve the appearance of her skin. Like the surgeon, I was quickly aware of the latent grievance as she spoke about her disappointment with the various treatments, which of course now included what I was offering her too.

Her relationship with her mother figured a lot in our sessions. Her mother was described as her main confidante, yet the patient also conveyed a sense of not trusting her. She had, for example, not spoken to her mother about her pursuit of cosmetic surgery. It was a peculiar relationship, peculiar in so far as they spent a great deal of time together, seemingly enjoyed some joint interests and they were reportedly physically close. Yet, whenever Ms F. spoke about her mother, her tone was flat, at best irritated, and her descriptions of what they did together were functional or rather vague such that I struggled to form any picture in my mind of the two of them together. Instead I was left with the impression of two people forced to be in the same space together.

Ms F. hated the space we shared too – a space that she undoubtedly experienced as one that she was *forced* to share with me: as far as she was concerned she came to sessions because she needed to convince the surgeon that she could have surgery, not because she felt they helped her. This was, however, not the case in reality, in so far as my work with her was in no way connected to the surgeon's decision, as he had already decided not to operate on her nose. This was a fact she refused to accept.

I came to understand her attendance at sessions as her way of keeping me accused and responsible for her distress. I was the one depriving her of what would make her better. I was the one who, as she once put it, had been given a 'normal nose' and was preventing her from being at peace in her body. At times she assailed me with the urgency of her plight, displaying the many brochures she had gathered of other plastic surgeons who *would* operate on her. She did consult two others, one of whom told her he could not really improve her nose and the other who said he could, but whose fees were far too high. She experienced the first surgeon's refusal, and my assumed complicity in this, as a cruel deprivation. On these occasions her hatred of her mother was palpable and it became clearer that she blamed her mother for the imperfect body she felt she had given her.

Once she told me that her mother had not been careful with her health while pregnant with her and that this was the cause of her skin problems. She hated the notion that 'genes' were inherited and spoke to me at length about this, as if this tied her concretely to her mother's body and left her feeling very claustrophobic. She told me that her mother was overweight. On one occasion she tellingly described her mother's body in a rather vicious manner, as 'sprawling' in the small flat they shared. With no third party available to create a boundary between them, Ms F. felt concretely invaded by her mother's body. Yet, she felt that she could not manage without her, often turning to her for the gratification of basic, physical needs, such as asking her mother to feed her in bed even when she was not ill.

Ms F.'s experience of the suffocating, boundaryless maternal body was most powerfully conveyed in her dreams. Two dreams, which she had relatively early on in the therapy, and which were not untypical in their affective quality and somatic nature, were followed by renewed urgency is seeking cosmetic surgery. In the first dream, Ms F. told me that she was sitting on a park bench, reading a book, when a hand tugged at her from behind with great force. She described feeling a horrible sensation of being 'pulled'. She dropped her book on the ground. This was an important book to her, something to do with her work, and she was worried that it would now be damaged. She said that she could not see who it was behind her, but she felt like she knew the grip of the hand – there was something familiar about the hand. She said she felt terrified. After a few minutes' struggle she managed to get up off the bench and to free herself from the grip. She turned round: there was no one behind her, but she then realised that there was a slimy, shiny white trail on her shoulder – like that of snails, she said – which made her vomit. The vomit covered her book. She was upset about this, but felt better having thrown up.

In the second dream, which she had a week later, Ms F. recalled being asleep and suddenly waking, feeling herself sinking into a soft, damp mattress. She said she was drowning. In the dream she wanted to vomit, but nothing came out. She awoke from the dream in a pool of sweat, itching all over her body, and anxiously told me that her bed was infested with bed bugs. The terror that had been present in the dream infused the room as she recounted it to me and she was evidently still unsettled by it.

Both these dreams are very rich, and early on they led me to feel unrealistically hopeful that Ms F. could engage in thinking with me about the meaning for her of cosmetic surgery. I am only going to concentrate on one particular aspect of the dreams as it relates to what we have been discussing in this chapter. My own understanding is that they expressed Ms F.'s terror of losing herself in the (m)other, of being pulled back into an undifferentiated state with her mother. For Ms F. this was an experience of being suffocated and literally pulled towards, or into, someone else: the hand that grabs her from behind and the soft, damp mattress that she sinks into and cannot get out of. Importantly, in both dreams, something has to be ejected (the mother) through vomit: in the first dream she manages to expel what would otherwise take her over, while in the second dream she cannot even vomit the mother out and hence she wakes, highly anxious and paranoid, feeling her skin itching and convinced her bed is infested with crawling bugs – the mother is felt to get right under her skin. I think this claustrophobic anxiety was linked with her excessive preoccupation with her skin.

It was apparent that Ms F. had been unsettled by both these dreams and the rupture into consciousness of high levels of anxiety. I thought that they were connected with her experience of the therapeutic relationship and the profound anxiety about being intruded upon by me. Tellingly, following these dreams, she engaged with renewed vigour in her search for a cosmetic surgeon. The threat of fusion with the maternal body that the dreams exposed – and that had been revived by the threat posed by an intimacy with me – was managed by retreating into her pursuit of body modification. This was her way of demarcating her body as quite distinct from that of her (m)other.

Even if the baby manages to negotiate the painful separation from the mother, Kristeva (1982) argues that the abject will continue to haunt him throughout life, a looming presence that we can observe in the fear of falling back into the mother's body – as I am suggesting was the case for Ms F. – and in the fear of losing one's identity. Here Kristeva draws on

Freud's (1919) essay on *The Uncanny (Unheimlich)*. In this essay, Freud approaches the question of aesthetics obliquely by exploring the experience of horror and dread. He equates what is felt to be uncanny or unfamiliar with what was, in fact, once familiar, but has now undergone repression, suggesting that the notion common to all aspects of the uncanny is that of 'origins'. The uncanny disturbs the boundary that marks out the known from the unknown.

Although many readings of Freud's paper single out the fear of castration, Freud in fact suggests that the ultimate *unheimlich* place is the mother's genitals or body, particularly the womb: 'This unheimlich place . . . is the entrance to the former Heim [home] of all human beings, to the place where each one of us lived once upon a time and in the beginning' (Freud 1919: 245). The place of the uncanny is where desire is always marked by the shadowy presence of the mother. Both Freud and Kristeva would agree that this state reflects both the longing to fall back into, and be enveloped by, the maternal body, and the terror of losing one's sense of a separate self.

It is important to note that Kristeva's notion of abjection refers to a process, not simply a passing phase. She refers to the rituals that cultures set up to deal with the recurring threat of abjection. For example, she argues that religions have served the function of purifying or cleansing the self. As religions wane, art takes over the function of purification, often by conjuring up the abject things it seeks to dispel. I would like to suggest that for the patients I describe here, cosmetic surgery, tattoos and body piercings represent just such attempts to purify or create a boundary for the self and so cleanse the self from the threat posed by otherness. In this sense, for some individuals, it is like a kind of religion.

Treacherous flesh: the body in David Cronenberg's films

I first became interested in Cronenberg's films through a patient, Mr T., with whom I worked three and then four times weekly, for nine years.

Mr T.'s father had left the family home when he was a young child. His mother, who suffered from a psychotic illness, raised Mr T. with two of his siblings. Consequently, Mr T. had spent some short periods of time in care when his mother had to be hospitalised. It was during one of these periods that he was sexually abused by one of the carers.

When his mother was not in hospital, Mr T. nevertheless experienced her as very erratic. Either she would neglect him (sometimes not buying food or cooking), or she could become quite manic and then intrusive. This intrusion had a sexualised quality. Very often she intruded into his body, such as tickling him against his will, or touching his knee in a way that he hated, or she walked into his bedroom and watched him getting dressed or undressed. As the therapy unfolded, and his psychotic anxieties about me edged forwards in the transference, it became clear that he felt she had taken over his body.

In his late teens Mr T. developed an obsessive preoccupation with his body, which he found ugly. This prevented him from wearing clothes that might expose his body and from undressing in front of others unless the room was dark. He was very preoccupied in his own mind with his appearance and found social situations very difficult.

For the first few years of the therapy, Mr T. discussed his wish to have cosmetic surgery to change the shape of his nose though I could not see anything wrong with his nose. He eventually managed to see a plastic surgeon on the NHS who concluded that surgery could not really help, essentially because there was not a physical problem that required treatment. Although angry with both the surgeon and myself, he was also contained at this point and did not seek further opinions.

Mr T. was a very bright and articulate man who had sought refuge in his intellect as he was growing up. He loved the cinema and was an avid fan of Cronenberg's films. In the first two years of our work he spent a lot of time discussing these films in the sessions. I started to make contact with him, and his anxieties, through these films. I thought he brought the films in lieu of dreams,[4] which he seldom recalled in the first few years of the therapy. The films seemed to allow some space to be created between him and the terrifying rawness of his anxieties as he approached his body in his mind. He felt somehow understood by what he perceived to be Cronenberg's grasp of the treacherous nature of the flesh, and of the terror resulting from the reality of the body, and hence of a self that can never escape its organic origins – origins that for Mr T. were concretely equated with a felt-to-be inhospitable and intrusive maternal body and mind.

Cronenberg's staple preoccupations with bodily disintegration, disease, sexual confusion and bodily transformation resonated deeply with my patient's experience. For Mr T. the body was a prison from which he wanted to escape. His experience of his body brought vividly to mind Meltzer's (1988) description of the 'claustrum' of the mother's body. Over time we came to understand the relief he obtained when he could envisage himself in a different body. This was an image that held him together when in the grip of more psychotic anxieties.

Cronenberg's films are replete with bodily diseases, mutation, disturbing creatures, violent telepathy, video hallucinations, drug addiction and car crash perverse sexuality. Taken together as a body of work, his films stand

out as providing one of the most affecting studies of the psychic meaning
and inner representation of the body. Importantly, his films remind us that
the body is the site for the most disturbing changes and of the most intense
affects. As such many of them examine the descent into bodily chaos and,
effectively, into psychosis.

Like primal phantasies, Cronenberg's 'biological horror' is concerned
with origins: the origins of the subject, of desire, of sexual difference (Creed
1993).[5] This is one reason why his films are so profoundly disturbing. I am
choosing to focus on his work in this chapter not only because it formed an
integral part of my work with Mr T., but also because his films vividly
illustrate the problematic relationship we can all have with the tenuous
borders of the body-self.[6]

In Cronenberg's films, cancerous or parasite transformed body parts are
unsurprisingly troubling. Yet the distinctive contribution of his films is that
they are concerned with the way in which the so-called 'ordinary' body or
body parts can be deeply troubling too – that the very fact of being-in-a-
body is something we all struggle with, and that generates profound
anxieties against which we develop individual and societal defences. His
films portray, in different ways, the compulsion to change reality by modifying the body. And this, of course, is precisely a core unconscious process
that lies at the root of the more extreme and/or compulsive pursuit of body
modification practices.

The sheer visceral repulsiveness of the film *Shivers* (1975), or *Rabid's*
(1976) vision of a disease-driven apocalyptic revolution, turning normal
citizens into ravening maniacs, is horrific. Aware of my own reluctance to
watch these films again, I realised that these films first register *in* the body;
they are truly visceral in their impact. Representation gives way to a
violently affective, immediate and unmentalised contact, foregrounding the
body apart from the comforting representations that we typically use to
keep it at a distance, for example, through our daily grooming rituals. The
films instead propel us into the life of the body, particularly the challenge
posed by the body interior, felt so often to be disgusting and the very
symbol of a persecuting otherness that feels out of control.

By highlighting the monstrosity of the body, Cronenberg steadfastly
avoids the pitfalls of specular idealisation. He locates himself, and plunges
us, the audience, in the anxiety and insecurity implicit in the state of being-
in-a-body. As Shaviro (1993) incisively observes:

> Cronenberg's 'monsters' are forms of alterity that cannot be reduced to
> the economy of the Same, but that also cannot be identified as purely
> and simply Other.
>
> (Shaviro 1993: 145)

The parasite – an image Cronenberg deftly uses in *Shivers* –

is neither part of me nor apart from me; it is something from which I cannot separate myself, but that at the same time I cannot integrate into my personality.

(Shaviro 1993: 145)

In *Shivers* parasite creatures are developed by a researcher, Dr Emil Hobbes, for medical reasons to counteract estrangement from the body. The parasites then proceed to create havoc in a Montreal Island apartment block, Starliner Towers. Through its modernist, urban architecture Starliner Towers conjures up an oasis of control – an illusion that Cronenberg soon shatters. The parasites are graphic representations of the body interior and what comes out of it: faces, sexual fluids, spittle, blood.

Over the course of the first two years of his therapy, Mr T. brought four Cronenberg films to his sessions, which we explored in some detail. I understood them to be communications both about his own internal world, and about his experience of his relationship with me. The films he singled out as especially meaningful to him were *The Brood* (1979), *The Fly* (1986), *Dead Ringers* (1988) and *Crash* (1996). Through a brief exploration of each I hope to illustrate some of the dynamics that Mr T. was grappling with in his own mind.

In *The Brood*, Dr Hal Raglan's system of 'psychoplasmics' underpins his treatment of patients by encouraging them to give bodily expression to their unconscious anger, the results of which include cancerous growths and the main protagonist's – Nola Carveth – so-called 'brood'. Nola was abused as a child. The 'brood' are actual childlike creatures produced by her body – walking incarnations of her inner feelings of anger and of her wish for revenge. As such, by bringing this film, Mr T. vividly communicated his central preoccupation with the therapy and what I would 'do' to him. It brought to the fore the way in which I was experienced by him as a disturbing version of Dr Raglan, encapsulating his tangible fear that our work, instead of helping him, would bring out the cancerous growths of his violent hatred, which he feared would destroy us both.

The 'brood' literally enact Nola's rage, eventually murdering her parents. The 'brood' is inarticulate (they make gurgling sounds reminiscent of a pre-verbal baby and as such capture unmentalised rage), and it is self-consuming (the creatures do not eat but are nourished by an internal food sac and die of starvation once it is depleted).

It was clear enough that Mr T. was very identified with the main protagonist – Nola – as the victim of abuse and who is then filled with murderous rage that she enacts. The creatures Nola gives birth to are the embodiment both of her suffering and of the way she identifies with the aggressor. Here, then, we find a graphic illustration of how a body part can unconsciously represent unmetabolised psychic content with deadly consequences for the self and for the object of hatred. Indeed, this is how we came to understand Mr T.'s preoccupation with changing his nose, and more specifically, how his wish to reduce its size was an attempt to eliminate the presence in his own body of the large psychic protuberance that was his internal mother. If he reshaped his nose, he cut her down to size too and could reclaim his body, but not without inflicting unnecessary violence to his own body.

When my patient consciously fantasised about his new nose, he entered a psychic space where he could wipe out any trace of his mother from his body: the remodelled nose became a psychic imperative that promised him peace of mind. The day after he had seen the surgeon who refused to operate on his nose – an outcome that, in the short term, had seriously unsettled him and provoked a very acute panic attack – he unusually brought a dream:

> My mother is naked and she is walking towards me. There is a putrid smell. I think it's her but then I realise I am oozing this smell and that's all there is: this terrible smell and it's coming from me.

In this dream we can see how Mr T. experiences his relationship with his mother in a very physical way. She appears here as sexualised and intrusive as she approaches him provocatively. As he perceives the putrid smell, the first question he asks himself reveals his central preoccupation with the boundary of the body-self: whose body is emanating this smell. I will not go into all the associative linkages that emerged in the session, but this is the understanding of the dream at which we arrived: at first, Mr T. manages to separate himself from his mother: 'I think it's her'. But the smell that came from her quickly becomes his own putrid smell. This confusion of bodily boundaries encapsulated the felt impossibility of differentiating himself from her, something that therefore required literal surgical intervention.

The timing of this dream, shortly after the surgeon's refusal to operate on his nose, gives some insight into the way that the shattering of the reclaiming phantasy exposed Mr T. to his mother's intrusiveness. He was confused and terrified that he would now be stuck in a body that felt/smelt like his mother's body – a body that disgusted him and, most importantly, which he feared.

For Mr T. the body was horrifying. He mostly shied away from sex and any kind of physical intimacy, only occasionally engaging in one-off sexual encounters. Yet a longing to be in a relationship was also hazily present and made the work between us just about possible, if always very hazardous. Engagement with Mr T. was a most careful balancing act because a central preoccupation as he approached any relationship was the question of how far was invariably too close.

He displayed a heightened sensitivity to his physical surroundings: he experienced any change in the spatial layout of my consulting room as deeply disturbing. If he perceived my chair to be closer to his (the first three years of therapy were face-to-face because of his profound anxiety about the couch), this provoked intense anxiety as my body was felt to inch closer to his. There was both fear of what I might see and do to him if I got closer, but also what he might see and to do me. Both possibilities were equally disturbing.

Mr T. was very aware of my body. On one occasion, startled by some digestive sounds from my stomach, he became visibly anxious and said, 'Is that you or me?' Mr T. appeared to be profoundly confused about his bodily boundaries and lived in terror that he would merge with the other back into an undifferentiated state that was the hallmark of madness. At other times, he feared that if we were too close, *I* would be repelled by his body. As the work progressed it became clear that his primary concern was not with his surface appearance as he presented it and experienced it consciously; rather, he was quite concretely preoccupied with the interior of his body and with its leaky boundaries.

The theme of the body interior as disgusting and horrifying is central to *The Fly*, one of Cronenberg's more mainstream films. Mr T. spoke to me about this film as the primary association to one of the first dreams he brought early on. This was a nightmare in which a swarm of bees were 'drilling' holes into his body.

In *The Fly*, Seth Brundle, a brilliant, somewhat 'nerdy' scientist, invents a spectacular new teleportation device. The device can revolutionise life through the liberation of interior, visceral forces (i.e. the body). In other words, it is a device to transcend the body's frailty, making it possible to transpose oneself instantaneously without having to endure the aggravation of bodily movement or the passage of time. Brundle claims to develop it partly to free humankind from the unpleasant effects of physical motion (in the film the protagonist suffers from motion sickness). But Cronenberg presents the device as a metaphor for the denial of the body's instability, discomfort and movement towards its own dissolution.

In the film the experiment backfires as Brundle overlooks a fly in the teleportation device and is then genetically fused with it.[7] The relevance of this film to my patient lay in how Brundle's 'condition' takes the form of a horrific physical metamorphosis, one that is presented as extreme otherness and loss of identity.

'Brundle-Fly' is a powerful image: it encapsulates both the aggressor that invades the body and takes residence within it, slowly contributing to the self's destruction, and the self's identification with the aggressor. Importantly, it graphically illustrates how this kind of destructive identification can only ultimately rebound back on the self with deadly consequences. The destruction that ensues is the result of a fusion of two bodies and this, of course, resonated with Mr T.'s experience of an engulfing fusion with his mother that could be resolved only through killing off the mother whom he felt resided so concretely in his body.

Although Mr T. was able to function at work, internally he was often on the edge of self-destructive behaviour. He struggled to sustain any intimate relationships. For him *The Fly* charted in the most painstaking manner the destruction he so feared by the forces of an inconceivable otherness as represented, in the film, by the insect. *The Fly* is a particularly important film because it makes it clearer than any of Cronenberg's previous works that the otherness that is so feared actually resides within the self. Brundle's metamorphosis into a fly makes it appear alien and yet it *is* him, thus emphasising that what is truly horrific – what is ugly (see Chapter 2) – is part of the self and cannot be excised without also destroying the self. This is what Mr T. struggled to grasp, as do many patients, understandably preferring to nurse the phantasy that getting rid of, or altering a body part, will preserve or protect the self (Campbell and Hale 1991; Campbell 2008; Hale 2008).

Cronenberg's study of embodiment is most subtly and movingly elaborated in a later film, *Dead Ringers*, which Mr T. referred to as his 'favourite' film. It was of note that this film came up in the sessions only around the time when we started to think about his terror at becoming in any way attached to me. Mr T. watched this film several times as if he was desperately trying to get his mind round the felt-to-be impossibility of separation that his attachment to me threatened him with.

Dead Ringers is the story of identical twin brothers, Beverly and Elliot Mantle, who are both gynaecologists. Their highly symbiotic relationship is disrupted – with tragic consequences – when Beverly falls in love with one of his patients, Claire, and tries to establish himself as independent of his twin. In the therapy with Mr T. I took up this film as a powerful communication to me of his struggle to allow himself to have a relationship with me (i.e. his identification with the twin who wants to separate from his twin and have a relationship), and the violent pull back into a very destructive relationship with an object that allowed him no freedom.

Dead Ringers can be read as a study of the relationship to the maternal body (Humm 1997). The mother (and father too) is conspicuously absent throughout the film, and yet she is intrusively present in the twins' fused relationship to each other, and in their hatred of women.[8] As gynaecologists, the Mantle twins' psychic equilibrium is managed by their obsessive objectification of, and projection into, women's bodies. Women's bodies are both the target of an objectifying, intrusive technology, and the physical support for their efforts to maintain a coherent sense of their own identity. In one scene, Beverly, seized by jealousy towards a phantasised sexual rival, becomes overtly misogynous, devising strange new gynaecological instruments for treating 'mutant' women, complains that his patients do not have the right sort of bodies (presumably the 'right' sort being ones that remain the exclusive possession of the baby), and he finally injures one of his patients on the operating table, actualising the violent phantasies one imagines motivated the gynaecological interest in the first place.

In the end, neither brother can cope with the challenge of separation. The closing scenes of the film provide a chilling portrayal of a melancholic descent into a world of drug addiction, and eventually of joint suicide, in which the gruesome surgical instruments now rebound back on their own bodies as they are used to effect the felt-to-be otherwise impossible separation.

> Mr T. displayed a gruesome fascination with the strange gynaecological instruments that appear in the film and that are used to violently intrude into the female body. I took this up as his way of letting me know that no sooner had he allowed himself to know something about his wish to be close to me that he felt engulfed by a version of me who would surely take him over and 'operate' on him, cutting into his body and mind. This threat, in turn, aroused a violent reaction in him: for Mr T. separation could only be of the most violent kind. It involved 'killing off' a part of himself as well as the object.
>
> As will be clear by now, much of the time, Mr T. lived in, or on the edge of, a psychotic universe where intimacy had been perverted and his body had become the site for intrusion and violence. Given this, Mr T.'s preoccupation with what could perhaps be regarded as Cronenberg's most disturbing film to date, Crash, is unsurprising. This film proved especially important. Because of the film's focus on the perversion of looking, it enabled us to explore Mr T.'s relationship with me through the quality of the gazing relationship between us. It was of note that it was this exploration that finally enabled Mr T. to use the couch, three years after the start of his therapy.

Crash is an adaptation of J.G. Ballard's novel about sex and automobile wrecks. It starkly depicts characters who 'look', but cannot engage, and for whom bodily engagement is perverted as 'car bodies' dominate human ones. Crash's first person narrator – James Ballard – produces commercial films for television. He is involved in a serious car crash as he collides head on with another car. The driver of the other car, Helen, and James are injured, while Helen's husband is killed. During his recovery in hospital, James experiences powerful feelings that disrupt his previously numbed experience of life.

Post-trauma, the prospect of injury and death is violently spliced with new currents of perverse sexual desire and a new fascination with cars, traffic and accidents. James meets up with the scar-covered Vaughan – a crazed 'prophet' and proselytiser of car crashes and sex: he fetishises car crash injuries or photos and films of car crash scenes. Vaughan draws him into his perverse orbit, providing one of the most disturbing cinematic images substituting two bodies coming together in love with the deadening merger of flesh and metal.[9]

Through Vaughn and his initiates, Cronenberg evokes an intensive, obsessively repetitive, one-note insistence, without context or variation, which captures the essence of a perverse state of mind with greater immediacy than any analytic formulation. The longing for contact with the other is perverted and staged in the bleak, passionless world of multi-lane freeways. The disparity between the awfulness of what is depicted in stark physical imagery, and the frozen modernist formalism with which it is beheld, is powerfully staged.

> This captured very well Mr T.'s way of relating to me: no sooner he experienced a wish to be close, or if he felt understood by me, he would retreat into a more obsessional, mechanical way of relating to me during which he bombarded me with information – not least, sometimes, with the detail of the very films I have been describing. When in this mode, Mr T. would present to me some of the horrors of his own childhood dispassion-ately, or he would describe occasional, one-off sexual encounters that bore the hallmark of the distance I had grown to know well in our exchanges.
>
> As he related these desultory, mechanical, sometimes violent, sexual exchanges, I felt as if I had to witness a horrific car/body crash scene while Mr T. 'looked on' and was spared the pain and horror I had to be exposed to and digest for him. It took many years before we were able to get off these kinds of psychic multi-lane freeways that allowed little pause for reflection or contact. Mr T. nevertheless managed to make some progress. When we ended the therapy due to his decision to move abroad, he was far more stable and able to establish some meaningful relationships.

Cronenberg's original fusion of horror, sexuality and diseased, treacherous flesh is responsible for some of the film critics' interpretations of his films as arising fundamentally from sexual disgust and hatred of the body (Creed

1989; Rodley 1997), particularly the female body. Although some of his films lend themselves to such an interpretation, more fundamentally, I think, they speak to the difficulty in reconciling body and mind as an indissoluble unit precisely because the body, as I have been suggesting, invariably bears the trace of the (m)other. In a revealing statement, Cronenberg observes:

> I don't think that the flesh is necessarily treacherous, evil, bad. It is cantankerous and it is independent. The idea of independence is key. It really is like colonialism. The colonies suddenly decide that they can and should detach from *the control of the mother country*. At first the colony is perceived as being treacherous. It is a betrayal. I think that the flesh in my films is like that.
>
> (Cronenberg, quoted in Rodley 1997: 80, my italics)

The 'control of the mother country' was indeed what my patient Mr T. was trying to manage through altering the body: a way of creating the illusion of independence from the imprint of his mother on the body and hence on the self.

Whatever else one might think of his films, Cronenberg has provided us with disturbing pictures of the unconscious at work. In an interview in which he grapples with what is frightening about his films, he draws a distinction between the kind of horror that a film like *Jaws* is predicated on, and the bodily horror of his films, which he links to an implicit notion of an internal world:

> *Jaws* seemed to scare a lot of people. But the idea that you carry the seeds of your own destructiveness around with you, always, and that they can erupt at any time is more scary. Because there is no defence against it. There is no escape from it. You need a certain kind of awareness to appreciate the threat that there is an inner life to a human being that can be as dangerous as any animal in the forest.
>
> (Cronenberg, quoted in Rodley 1997: 60)

For the patients I discuss in this book, the 'danger' Cronenberg alludes to is felt to be located in a body part(s) that have to be modified, and hence reality is modified. When the phantasy is that reality can be altered by modifying the body, the body becomes the site for the enactment of unconscious conflicts.

Chapter 6

Copies without originals
Envy and the maternal body[1]

> I tried to get control over my life by saying 'I'm me and I had this surgery and this is what I had to do.' And, you know, I thought it was wonderful *not to tell* my mother about the operation (laughs). Just like that. It helped to loosen my ties with her, with my past . . . I guess it also played a role in why I got so much pleasure out of it, secretly, that she didn't know about it, that she had to hear about it from someone else. And that I – well, I became *unrecognisable* for her, too.
>
> (Diana, interviewed by Davis 1995: 105, italics in original)

The self-made phantasy

Diana has had quite major facial cosmetic surgery. This affecting account of her experience highlights, in her own words, the unconscious phantasy that fuels the pursuit of body modification in some patients. She underlines, twice, the pleasure she gained from not telling her mother what she was going to do – a strategy that ensures the disturbing triumph over her mother (disturbing because it is underpinned by violence towards the object) when she becomes, as she says, 'unrecognisable' to her. Becoming unrecognisable to one's own mother must surely rank as one of the worst possible experiences – for most people. However, Diana's experience points to the fact that the only way she can cope (what she calls 'taking control over my life') is to look nothing like her mother, or nothing like how her mother made her, and nothing like the person the mother expects to see.

The body's borders may be felt to define us as separate or they may be felt to be too weak, porous and so the person feels all too readily engulfed by the other, as we saw in Chapter 5. The body poses a particular problem precisely because in order to live comfortably in one's body, feeling that it is whole and has a boundary, involves integrating two key 'facts of life' that, paradoxically, profoundly challenge the notion of a boundaried space felt to be one's own. First, as I have already mentioned, the body can never actually be divorced from its more porous origins, that is, from the relationship with the mother and *her* body with which it is indelibly connected.

I would like to propose that this represents an additional 'fact of life' that might be added to Money-Kyrle's (1968) original list and that cannot be subsumed under the related 'fact of life', namely the reality of the parental couple.[2] Second, as Money-Kyrle (1968) noted, it is a painful fact that the body can never alter its final destination, that is, death.

Being-in-a-body thus requires feeling separate while also acknowledging our dependency on others. It also reminds us of our ultimate helplessness in the face of the reality of a changing body. Both these facts re-present themselves to us all, time and again – painful, recurring leitmotifs of our dependency and transience. The organic foundation of life is a reality that we cannot circumvent, try though we do. But in this chapter I want to focus on the way that the body's *origins*, not only its boundaries, present challenges that are managed by some people through attempts to modify the given body.

I will be suggesting that for some individuals the pursuit of body modification attests to the omnipotent phantasy – what I refer to as the *self-made phantasy* – that it is possible to circumvent the (m)other altogether thereby giving birth to the self. The use made of the body by some of these patients bears witness to the need to remould the body according to one's own specifications without interference from the (m)other. Unlike the *reclaiming phantasy* (see Chapter 4), envy is a primary feature of the *self-made phantasy*. The attempts to circumvent the (m)other are often supported by a state of mind in which the body becomes obsolete, the self is omnipotent and the (m)other is triumphed over.

The unconscious aim of the *self-made phantasy* is to erase all trace of a physical resemblance to the (m)other – but the outcome of the modified bodily self makes it unclear 'who' the person looks like. This brings to mind what Jean Baudrillard (1988) has called 'copies without originals': an ideal image of the self that is aspired to, and that cosmetic surgery in particular promises to deliver, but this image itself cannot be referenced back to an 'original', that is, I am suggesting, to the individual's given body by the (m)other.

For these patients the object's independence is felt to be intolerable. A profound grievance fuels envy of the object who is perceived to have good things that it keeps for itself. Defensively, the self retreats into believing that it can create itself by redesigning the body, thereby circumventing the (m)other, and hence any experience of dependency. This has been a striking feature in my work with three women who underwent cosmetic surgery and who enacted, through the surgery, the unconscious phantasy of appropriating something 'better', that did not belong to the self, and that the internal (m)other was felt to possess and to withhold.[3] In other words, the reclaiming and the self-made phantasy are distinguished by the underlying envious attack on the phantasised maternal body/object that is the hallmark of the self-made phantasy.

Of course, circumventing the reality of one's origins inevitably also entails a denial of the reality of the parental couple – not only of the reality of the shared corporeality of mother and baby. The attack on the parental couple is implicit in the self-made phantasy. In many of these cases it is indeed possible to discern the absence of what Birksted-Breen (1996) refers to as the 'penis-as-link', that is, the absence of the linking and structuring role of the knowledge that mother and father are linked and form a creative couple. Acceptance of this reality allows individuals to come to terms with both the fact of difference and of complementarity, and hence to accept their own insufficiency as well as their need for the other. In the majority of the patients I discuss in this book, the father was conspicuously absent either physically or emotionally. Consequently the father was not available to provide the necessary third perspective and so free the child from the symbiotic tie to the mother (Mahler et al. 1975; Stoller 1979; Britton 1993; Fonagy and Target 1999). These patients suffer from an all-too-present mother and an all-too-absent father (see Chapter 1). For both the male and female patients, there appears to be no space between the self and the internalised mother that could allow for the development of an independent relationship with an other. The solution to this psychic dilemma is found in the enactment, through the manipulation of the body, of a phantasy that reassures the self of its omnipotence and self-sufficiency.

This psychic position might well be termed 'phallic' in the sense that being the phallus represents a psychic state of complete self-sufficiency, and hence is an attack on otherness. Indeed, Birksted-Breen (1996) has suggested that it is the failure to internalise the penis-as-link that underpins a number of pathologies, such as anorexia and suicide, where the body is the site for unconscious enactments.

All the three phantasies that I have outlined so far share a common unconscious aim: to obliterate or circumvent the object's independent existence. The reclaiming and self-made phantasies do this quite explicitly by literally trying to erase any trace of the object by altering the body, while in the perfect match phantasy the object is obliterated more indirectly, yet surely, because the aspiration is to be one with the idealised image such that, in effect, there is no object.

In this chapter I want to focus particularly on the ambivalence, envy and grievance that the maternal body can mobilise. I will illustrate these themes through some clinical material, and also through the body art of Orlan and Stelarc.

Envy and the maternal body

Our sense of who we are is built against a backdrop of loss. The first loss we need to bear is that of the mother, which is symbolised in the physical, bodily separation as 'one body for two' becomes two separate bodies at the moment of birth. The fact of separateness, and hence of loss, is an important dimension of subjectivity and is intimately linked to the experience of envy. When loss cannot be borne, envy can dominate the psychic landscape. In some of the individuals who turn to their bodies for solutions, we can discern how the body modification serves the function of bypassing the experience of being given to, of being dependent in any way on the other.

Steiner (2008) helpfully reinterprets Freud's (1937) notion of the 'repudiation of femininity' as an expression

> of an intolerance of a receptive dependence on good objects, which seems to present similar problems for both men and women and is, in fact, the position that infants of both sexes have to adopt in their earliest relationship to the mother and her breast.
>
> (Steiner 2008: 140)

Steiner's reading of Freud is highly relevant to understanding these patients because the earliest experience of receptivity – of being given to – surely unfolds, not just in the feeding relationship, but more broadly in the context of the mother's relationship to the baby's body. The mother's generosity is conveyed, in part, through her capacity to enjoy the baby's body so that he may enjoy it as separate from hers – she has given him life and makes him feel desirable, but not *for* her. For his part the baby has to 'accept' that his mother – the one who originally gave her body over to him and who then nursed him (what Guignard (2008) refers to as the 'maternal mother') – is capable of making him feel loved and admired, but that she cannot *always* make him feel this way. *Her* desire, ultimately, cannot be fulfilled by him. Awareness of the 'sexual mother' (Guignard 2008) imposes painful distance between the self and the maternal object.

Both mother and baby thus have to manage their way through the anxieties generated by dependence on, and separation from, the object. This is difficult enough when all is progressing relatively smoothly in the mother–baby dyad. But when there are complications in this relationship, this particular psychic process may be perverted. Instead of an experience of dependent receptivity to the object, there may be triumph over the object.

The refusal to acknowledge the imprint of the (m)other, of the experience of being given to, appears in its most concrete form in these patients as a refusal to acknowledge the self's bodily origins, and hence the inevitable tie to the maternal body and to the reality of the parental couple. In these cases the individual's relationship to his body recapitulates the experience with the maternal object: the reality of the body has to be bypassed, just as any trace of the dependency on the maternal object, which is profoundly problematic to the self, has to be denied.

Placing envy at the epicentre of our emotional life, Klein helpfully highlighted how it profoundly shapes the earliest relationship to the breast: 'My work has taught me', she wrote, 'that the first object to be envied is the feeding breast' (Klein 1957: 183). She described how the breast can be felt to be greedily withholding its goodness, thereby frustrating the baby. Envy of this selfish breast can then contribute to difficulties in building up a good internal object. Klein movingly conveys the ravages of envy and details how it undermines a sense of hopeful expectation from life and hence thwarts the capacity for love and gratitude. Klein focuses largely on her notion of 'primary envy' defined by the attack being on a 'good' object *because* of its goodness. This is why separateness from this good object is felt to be intolerable and elicits envy. But an actually depriving object may also elicit envy (Lemma 2008).

The most primitive prototype for envy, according to Klein, is essentially envy of the physical possibilities of the body of the other that are felt to be denied to the self. Envy of the breast's ability to nourish is followed by envy of the maternal capacity to derive sexual pleasure from the father's penis and by envy of the ability to procreate. Although both boys and girls envy and covet mother's body and its phantasised possessions, there is a fundamental experiential difference between the sexes: the girl can take comfort in her knowledge that by virtue of her sex she will mature to attain mother's female attributes. The boy, however, when he learns and acknowledges that he is different from mother, has to accept that his wish to procreate like his mother is precluded by his actual body.

Although the girl's narcissistic mortification appears at first glance to be less harsh than the boy's, at that early stage, inevitably, both boys and girls are faced with the physical impossibility there and then of giving life – that is, of being mother. In this sense they both equally have to bear their relative impotence. The woman, unlike the man, is always potentially a mother; she embodies forever the possibility of a shared corporeality. But even though the girl will later be able to bear babies, like the boy, she will never be able to circumvent the fact that she cannot give birth to herself. The body is 'given' to the child. All our attempts to modify the body express the need to customise the body according to our own – not the other's – specifications.[4]

Our preoccupation with origins is apparent in horror films. Creed (2005) has documented cinema's fascination with the 'intrauterine landscape'. She highlights how films such as *Frankenstein* and Cronenberg's *The Fly* concern man's wish to give birth, thereby circumventing the mother, typically with horrific results. *Frankenstein*, Creed (2005) argues, provides a study of male hysteria as a symptom of Frankenstein's inability to create life. In *The Fly* the implicit narrative is about reproduction in which Seth Brundle, as Robbins (1993) has aptly pointed out, appropriates the maternal function.

But the appropriation of the maternal function is not solely an issue for men. Klein (1932, 1935, 1957) has been foremost in foregrounding the importance of infantile sadism, based on envy, directed against the inside of the mother's body by both boys *and* girls. It was indeed Klein who counterbalanced Freud's focus on penis envy and proposed a theory of womb envy (Zeus' parthenogenic delivery of Athena is a good example of this). She argued that boys and girls experience an early femininity phase in which both sexes identify with the mother and take pleasure in the feminine.

This brings us to the important question of identification – a process that has been invariably disturbed in the patients I am describing. The problem is well illustrated in the ever-popular TV makeover shows. Here, we can observe how the shows support the aim *to become the ideal*, and not simply to strive to *be like it*, as we would expect if a more ordinary identificatory process were at work. The unconscious psychological mechanism deployed by this programme format is what Resnik (2001) refers to as 'physical transvestism'. The self, through projective identification, acquires another person's bodily shape and character, dressing in someone else's clothing, imitating their gestures and looks (as in the shows that invite participants to select their surgery according to the look of a particular 'star').

Imitative identifications of this kind may conceal deep feelings of envy because they are an appropriation of the other through imitation. As Gaddini (1969) has observed, imitation precedes identification and takes place primarily through vision. Such imitations are phantasies of being or becoming the object through modification of one's own body. But there is a fundamentally important difference between the object one strives to be like, and the object one would like to have, that is, the aim is to become an exact replica of the other and so appropriate the other. The latter, according to Gaddini (1969), bears the hallmark of envy. A striking and concrete illustration of the kind of theft implicit in the envious appropriation of the (m)other's body appeared in a women's magazine, *In Style*, which regularly published a column aptly titled 'Steal This Look'. To be able to receive the body one is given involves acknowledging our dependency on the giver (we can't give it to ourselves), and finding a way of then making our own what we know we have been given by the object.

Those who yearn to be the ideal search for an experience of wholeness or unity with the other that is called 'beauty' and that they believe can be achieved through altering the body's surface. Yet the image of the fragmented body is often apparent in the narratives and dreams of body dysmorphic patients (see Chapter 4). Not infrequently this image lays bare the envy that is felt towards those whose imagined bodily integrity and beauty is but a sore reminder of their felt insufficiency. The attacks this gives rise to are often unconsciously aimed at a felt-to-be bountiful, but unyielding maternal body.

Where there has been an undercathexis of the bodily self by the mother, envy of the maternal body may be discerned, though its quality will be more or less virulently destructive in any given individual. Whatever the cause of the mother's lack of interest or rejection, the self may experience this as a refusal to give what is needed in order to feel desirable. Instead, the maternal object is felt to indulge in the withheld goods. Deprived of sufficient gratification, the self then feels hard done by and may hold a grudge against the felt-to-be depriving object. This state of deprivation may fuel the omnipotent phantasy of 'becoming mother', such that any dependency is bypassed. I want to stress here that I have in mind an early experience with an actual object who was in some way depriving.

> For one patient, Ms W., her grievance took the very concrete form of trying to acquire for herself the maternal breast through breast augmentation. Her imperative was to modify the bodily *given*. The core problem as far as she was concerned was not so much the particular way her breasts looked (though this was how she presented the problem to herself and to others), but that she could not accept the breast(s) that she had been given as these were always falling short of the large phantasised breasts that she imagined her mother, her friends and me to be enjoying. The given body was a disturbing reminder of her actual dependency on her mother by whom she had not feel desired. There is perhaps nothing harder psychically than feeling dependent on an other whom we feel does not desire us. This was a painful fact of Ms W.'s life that she tried to circumvent in a very concrete way, bypassing the otherwise inevitable experience of loss and of the guilt she felt towards an object she was forever attacking in her mind.
>
> Ms W. had a very traumatic start in life. She was born prematurely and, due to birth complications, her mother was seriously at risk as she gave birth to her. Both Ms W. and her mother had to be in hospital for several weeks. They were eventually discharged physically healthy, but psychically scarred.[5]
>
> Ms W. was an only child. She recalled growing up in the shadow of these early events. She knew from her father that her mother had become very depressed following her birth and she had taken 'time out', as the family referred to it, leaving Ms W. for some months in the care of her father (who was often away on business) and of her elderly paternal grandparents. Ms W. had therefore spent the best part of the first year of her life without a mother able to be responsive and to take pleasure in her. She made a point early on of telling me, reproachfully, that her mother had been unable to breastfeed her. Behind her reproach I sensed her fear that I, too, would be unable to give her what she needed. As it turned out, this fear was linked to a phantasy that I would not 'feed' her because I wanted to keep all good things for myself. As time went on I became aware that I felt peculiarly self-conscious when I saw her – aware of what I was wearing, what I looked like, as if she was closely scrutinising me to see what I had.

Ms W. had very vague memories of her early years, but she was clear that she had never felt close to her mother. She told me that her mother would frequently talk about the fact that she had almost died giving birth to her. She felt that her mother 'used' this fact to extract guilt from her and to make herself feel better. Although her father was described as a more sympathetic figure, he was largely absent, and I gained the impression that he had been chronically depressed too, but managed this by retreating into his work. Her mother also managed herself by developing various interests outside the family and she returned to university as a mature student when Ms W. was still at primary school.

It was clear from her descriptions that Ms W. felt that the mother had been emotionally unavailable to her throughout her childhood. She described her mother as a very attractive woman. She speculated that this was the only reason why her father had stayed in a marriage that she otherwise (defensively, I thought) depicted to herself as a kind of life sentence for him. Our sessions were often punctuated with barbed asides about her mother. I gained the impression that she remained very preoccupied with her mother in her mind even though she had relatively little contact with her besides the 'mandatory' family get-togethers such as Christmas.

As an adolescent Ms W. had become very preoccupied with what she perceived to be her small breasts. She told me that she could barely think about anything else and that she counted the days till she could have surgery to enlarge her breasts. She felt that the size of her breasts accounted for the lack of boys' interest in her. She hated swimming and the summer months because this exposed her 'disadvantage', as she called it. She vividly conveyed the way in which in her mind the world was full of people with large, plentiful breasts who had access to men, and all good things in life, that were instead denied to her. Aged twenty-two, not long after she had left university and secured her first job, she underwent surgery to augment her breasts. She recalled this being the best time in her life: she felt confident, had her first sexual relationship and she appeared to have been less consciously burdened by the ongoing grievance towards her mother.

I met Ms W. when she was in early thirties and she had just become a mother herself. It was this transition to motherhood that provoked a pronounced depressive breakdown. She found it hard to adjust to her baby's dependency on her and she did not breastfeed her daughter. Her husband was described as very similar to her father: a reliable man whom she felt, however, was not very attuned to the difficulties she was experiencing. Nevertheless, he had supported her coming into therapy as he recognised (quite rightly) that she might otherwise be hospitalised. Ms W. was not sure whether his concern was due to practicalities (how could he work if she was not there to look after their daughter), or whether he actually cared for her. I sensed that Ms W. had such difficulty allowing herself to feel any dependency on the object that she was incredulous that anyone might actually be able to relate to her in this way. She seemed to find it very hard to credit her husband – and me in the transference – with any capacity for care and concern as if the other's ability to give was felt to shamefully expose her insufficiency.

Ms W, had come into therapy somewhat reluctantly, but I sensed that she knew somewhere that she was in a lot of trouble. Nevertheless, from the start, even though she attended regularly, and eventually even took up my suggestion to increase her sessions to three times per week, I was confronted by her marked difficulty in receiving any help from me. As the transference deepened, she became explicitly triumphant and managed to create a scenario in her mind where it was her supporting me by paying my fees. In this conscious fantasy, I had been left by my husband, and I needed patients to keep going with my mortgage repayments. In other words, I was the one with the small breasts and I was stuck with them.

Ms W. had felt that her mother had discharged her maternal responsibility towards her by virtue of having given birth to her. She appeared to have internalised an experience of herself as 'taking' something precious from her mother – quite literally almost 'taking' her life. This was a reality that the mother did not appear able to help her to manage; instead, the mother reinforced the 'damage' done to her by her daughter, leaving Ms W. with unprocessed anxieties and guilt about the damage perpetrated against the mother's body. In Ms W.'s case, neither the symbolic nor the feeding breast were felt to have been given freely. Moreover, what was truly desired by the mother was felt to be located elsewhere; it was not experienced by Ms W. as residing within her. As a little girl she had in fact been deeply wounded by her mother's abandonment of her to turn to her studies. One of the times she recalled as most difficult and lonely for her, as she was growing up, was on the occasion of her first menstrual cycle, when she felt unable to tell her mother about her anxieties about her changing body. This recollection triggered another memory, which she dated some years prior to the start of her menstrual cycle. She had been looking through her mother's drawers to find a necklace she wanted to use as part of a dressing-up game. In the process she came across several medicine bottles. She did not know what these were for, but she thought to herself that her mother must be ill. For several days thereafter, she recalled, she had worried that her mother was going to die. This striking memory illustrated vividly her anxiety about the damage done to her mother's body: as she looks through her drawers/body (i.e. gets inside her), she is confronted with the evidence of her damage to her mother's body.

Ms W. was plagued by both loss and guilt. In order to avert an internal catastrophe she turned to manic defences, and restricted her psychic range to the pursuit of repairing her own perceived-to-be-damaged breasts by literally remaking them, thereby denying her dependency on the object. In an identification with her damaged mother she was also, however, trying to manically repair the damage she felt she had done to her mother's capacity to 'give' to her – I will return to this point in more detail in Chapter 7.

The symbolic breast that Ms W. appeared to have internalised was one that was resentfully present and intimated the existence of something better and more exciting than her baby self trying to feed from it. It was a breast that blamed her for needing it and yet, because it was nonetheless given (in a manner of speaking since the mother did return to the family to fulfil functionally her obligations), Ms W. felt both obligated *and* devalued. In turn, obligation replaced gratitude. Gratitude can flourish only in a relationship where what is received has been freely given. In sharp contrast, the object one feels obligated to is experienced as owning the self: the object and self are thus tied together. The breast augmentation helped Ms W., temporarily, to lift the veil of loss, hatred and guilt, allowing her to actualise the phantasy that she owed nothing to her mother. However, her own motherhood powerfully cast her back into the painful old scenario with renewed vengeance. Fortunately, she managed to stay in treatment long enough to make some important changes.

Orlan's carnal art

I would now like to explore the self-made phantasy through the work of the French body artist, Orlan. Her work has promoted a great deal of academic analysis and there are several strands to it that one could focus on. Of necessity, this chapter will restrict itself to the themes most closely connected with the self-made phantasy. I have been drawn to her work, and selected it for inclusion, because it powerfully and provocatively illustrates the way in which the body can become the site for the self's reinvention.

Orlan's various reinventions of herself refuse to take their identity from the given corporeal form; rather, identity is achieved through the process of making or modifying the body according to her will. The characteristically violent reactions that Orlan's work invites can be understood as a defensive reaction to the violence she exposes us to through her images and acts on her body. However, this is probably also on account of the very challenging question her work raises, namely, what is the body's relationship to the self?

Formerly Mireille Porte (before she changed her name), Orlan is a Professor at the Ecole des Beaux-Arts in Dijon. She is a multimedia artist using video, performance, digital images and sculpture. Her art, which is referred to as 'carnal art', can be seen as displaying a limited number of variants that are constantly reworked through new techniques such as performance, photography and surgery, prefiguring the genetic hybrids that Orlan is currently working on.

Orlan experiments on her body and her image: her flesh serves as a canvas for the representational image. She is thus both maker and model. Stretching over forty years, her work charts a very particular kind of journey to explore the very nature of identity through the manipulation of the body. This begins with her experience of giving birth to herself (through plastic surgery and changing her name), to the invention of her own measuring system (using her body length as measure), onto a kind of pseudo-mystical crisis with reincarnations of various forms, then to the controlled manufacture of new faces leading to total dissolution in the limitless euphoria of digital transformation, morphing the image of her face with (to the Western eye) distorted features of pre-Columbian and African sculptures. Her art reveals a preoccupation with the image and representation of the body, that is, what the mirror sees. What she exposes is a kind of dialogue with the mirror thereby presenting herself as 'the twenty-first century's version of Narcissus' (Zugazagoitia 2004).

Carnal art, says Orlan, is an art in which, 'the body becomes modified, ready-made, because it is no longer a perfect ready-made that merely needs to be signed' (quoted in Durand 2004: 209). The question of the body's signatory is of central concern in Orlan's work. As Durand (2004: 207) observes, Orlan tries to 'reinvent and recast everything based on the principle of oneself, oneself alone'. Orlan herself defines the idea of 'self-sculpting' thus:

> a way of refiguring yourself, of vacillating between disfiguring and refiguring, the idea of not accepting what is automatically inherited through genes – what's imposed, inevitable – but of trying to pry open the bars of the cage.
>
> (Orlan quoted in Durand 2004: 199)

The body as a 'cage' implies a jailor – someone who is felt to control the body. Orlan suggests that it is possible to break out of this cage through modification of the body. Her work speaks powerfully to the themes in this book because it creates the illusion that there are no corporeal limits – effectively, that anything is possible. Orlan argues that even pain – an aspect of bodily reality that reminds us that we are in a body – can now be controlled and bypassed (e.g. through anaesthesia) such that there are no longer obstacles to changing the given body. Pain, she thus provocatively asserts, 'is anachronistic' (Orlan quoted in Durand 2004: 199).

Other physical givens and boundaries are similarly challenged by Orlan as when she famously declared 'Je suis *une* Homme et *un* Femme' (I am a man and a woman' would be the literal translation', but Orlan is here introducing additionally a gender confusion by coupling the masculine article with 'Femme' and the feminine article with 'Homme'). Even sexual boundaries collapse as she appropriates both the feminine and the masculine sex. In the *Self-Hybridisations* series, which consists of digital melds of her own face with pre-Columbian and African sculptures, Orlan explores the myriad possibilities inherent in the visual realm, once again indulging, it can feel, in the limitless possibilities for reinvention offered by the virtual realm.[6]

It is Orlan's cosmetic surgery performances, however, that probably represent her best known, and most provocative, work. The operating room in which Orlan's surgery is performed is essentially her artist studio from which originate the works of art: blood-drawings, reliquaries containing Orlan's flesh, shrouds, photos, films. Each surgery has been captured on video and fed to live international audiences via satellite link-ups, and it has been exhibited in a number of galleries in Europe, the United States and Australia.

Her surgery performances are carefully choreographed. Famous fashion designers, such as Paco Rabanne and Issey Miyake, have designed costumes for Orlan to wear during the surgeries. Poetry is read and music is played while she lies on the operating table, fully conscious of the events taking place (only local anaesthetic is used). The use of local anaesthetic triumphantly abolishes any notion of pain, suffering or fear of the body interior or exterior. Instead, it is the audience who is faced with the abject body and has to digest it for her while she 'willingly' engages in what she clearly views as an act of total freedom. Images from the *Omnipresence* series show her laughing on the operating table and smiling in apparent pleasure as the scalpel cuts away at her face, leaving the viewer disturbed and assaulted. As one critic aptly put it: 'We are the ones who suffer for her art. She at least has the benefit of anesthetic' (Jim McClellan 1994, quoted in Ince 2000).

Orlan is the first artist to use cosmetic surgery to divert it from its habits of embellishment and rejuvenating. Carnal art is not against cosmetic surgery as such; rather it is against the stereotypical attributions that are then inscribed on the female flesh in particular, but also male (Ince 2000). Orlan claims that her aims are not mimetic, that is, she does not aspire to resemble another image. Instead, she combines features from a number of Renaissance and post-Renaissance paintings of idealised females, for example, Leonardo's *Mona Lisa* and Botticelli's *Venus* to reinvent her self through surgery.

One important way in which Orlan's work is distinctive is that she is not undergoing surgery to make herself more beautiful according to normative canons of beauty. Indeed, one of her surgeries involves the insertion of two silicone bumps on her forehead, which are evidently grotesque. Her project is indeed quite other: it is the *process of transformation* that compels her. And this is why her work is so relevant to our discussion here: by undergoing cosmetic surgery in order to remodel her body, to pursue what she regards as a radical definition of freedom, her work, as she puts it, testifies to her 'struggle against the innate, the inexorable, the programmed, nature, DNA and God' (Orlan 2004: 200). This has nothing to do with the pursuit of so-called beauty, or of finding a physical form that allows the individual to 'fit in' (i.e. the frequently voiced explanations for seeking cosmetic surgery). Rather, I am suggesting that her work illustrates the struggle against the reality of interdependence, the earliest prototypes of which are the intrauterine state and the early physical dependency of the baby on the mother.

Orlan's work inevitably raises the question of whether, as Ince (2000) put it, she becomes her own mother or whether she is giving birth to a daughter who has no mother. Either way, what is clear is that any dependency on the object is bypassed. Interestingly, given the theme of giving birth to the self, it is of note that Orlan set out to have *nine* operations, suggesting a possible parallel to the nine months of gestation for a pregnancy, though this connection has not been made by her or in other studies of her work. Another important personal detail that Orlan has shared in interviews, which is relevant to understanding her work, is that the idea of turning the surgical interventions into performances grew in her mind during an emergency operation she underwent in 1978 for an ectopic pregnancy, under a local anaesthetic. One can but speculate as to whether this potentially life-threatening experience, and the painful loss of a pregnancy, could not be processed, but instead had to be instantaneously transformed into an exciting performance during which dependency and loss are triumphantly denied.

In interviews Orlan has discussed her difficult relationship with her mother: 'We were always very distant. I had to tell her, "I'm ill" before she'd start to take an interest in me' (Orlan, quoted in Ince 2000: 12). This highly ambivalent relationship runs through her artistic creations like a leitmotif as she resolutely distances herself from the body that gave her life. In *La Reincarnation de Saint Orlan* (The Reincarnation of Saint Orlan) surgery performances and exhibitions between 1990 and 1993, she describes her understanding of what she is trying to do:

> I am shattering the shell, shattering the marble, breaking open the drapes, and really proposing a new image disconnected from the roots *in which I gave birth to myself*.
>
> (Orlan, quoted in Ince 2000: 16, my italics)

One of her first works, *Orlan accouche d'elle m'aime* ('Orlan gives birth to her loved self') speaks for itself: this work was the origin for self-sculpting and prefigures the later surgery performances, *La Reincarnation de Sainte Orlan*, which extend and concretise these ideas in a highly provocative and visceral manner as we, the audience, are exposed to Orlan's body interior 'live' as we watch, for example, the skin of her face being lifted during plastic surgery.

Orlan powerfully and gruesomely exposes the way in which behind the facelift there is always a knife and an excision. Something or someone is cut out, literally, as the self is remade. Her work thus underlines that it is the process of giving birth to a new self, and the state of mind that underpins such a phantasy that is crucial, not the pursuit of beauty per se. Cultural imperatives to look nice and particular aesthetic ideals no doubt play part in the rise of cosmetic surgery. However, the importance of Orlan's work lies in how it graphically exposes the fundamental (unconscious) motivation for some people that the pursuit of so-called beauty conceals, namely to erase the trace of the (m)other that is felt to reside in the body as an alien presence (i.e. the reclaiming phantasy), or to deny dependency on the object and so bypass the experience of envy and to replace this with the creation of a *phantasy* body of one's own (i.e. the self-made phantasy).

The body that is altered through surgery is always both a phantasised body as well as an actual one. Surgeons operate on the flesh, but of course they are fundamentally reshaping phantasies about the self (Gilman 1999). Orlan forces us to consider the idea that if our bodies are an indispensable part of who we are, can sufficiently radical changes to the body turn us into someone 'new'? Her answer seems to be 'yes' and, of course, this is precisely, what many patients who modify their bodies also claim.

The obsolete body: the work of Stelarc

Like Orlan, the Australian artist Stelarc has tellingly declared the body 'obsolete'. When Stelarc speaks of the 'obsolete body', he means that the body must overcome centuries of prejudices so that it can be considered as an extendible evolutionary structure enhanced with the most disparate technologies, which are more precise, accurate and powerful.

Stelarc is referred to as a cyberpunk body artist whose work raises fundamental questions about how technology impacts on embodied relations. His work is closely related to Orlan's, but cannot be equated with it because he has been primarily concerned with exploring the functional possibilities of the human body (Goodall 2000). Stelarc's artistic strategy revolves around the idea of enhancing the body both in a physical and technical manner.

His starting point is that: 'the body is an impersonal, evolutionary, objective structure',[7] and that 'technology is what defines the meaning of being human, it's part of being human.' Especially living in the information age, 'the body is biologically inadequate', he argues, because humans have created technologies and machines that are much more precise and power-ful than the body. Consciously, Stelarc is referring to the fact that the human body can no longer keep pace with machine and computer tech-nology, but I am suggesting here that he depicts (and one could argue that he enacts) through his art, just like Orlan, an omnipotent state of mind that creates the illusion of total control over the design of the body as he effectively becomes his own creator.

One of the more intriguing aspects of Stelarc's work is that he has declared the body as 'empty' or 'hollow' – a body that is not a site for a psyche or self, but one that can house a sculpture, for example:

> I've moved beyond the skin as a barrier. Skin no longer signifies closure. I wanted to rupture the surface of the body, penetrate the skin. With the stomach sculpture, I position an artwork inside the body [in one of his performances he literally ingests a sculpture]. The body becomes hollow with no meaningful distinction between public, private and physiological spaces. The hollow body becomes a host, not for a self or a soul, but simply for a sculpture.

Stelarc penetrates the body, hollows it out, extends it, expands it, hangs it out of a window and maps out several miles of its interior. What is the next step?

> It is time to recolonise the body with microminiaturised robots. . . . We need to build an internal surveillance system for the body. We have to develop microbots whose behavior is not pre-programmed, but acti-vated by temperature, blood chemistry, the softness or hardness of tissue and the presence of obstacles in tracts. These robots can then work autonomously on the body. The biocompatibility of technology is not due to its substance, but to its scale. Speck-sized robots are easily swallowed and may not even be sensed. At a nanotech level, machines will navigate and inhabit cellular spaces and manipulate molecular structures to extend the body from within.

In one sense Stelarc's work could be read as reflecting what many of us seek in more or less compelling ways through the modification of the body: the constant upgrade of a physical machine that resolutely downgrades us all the time. Yet Stelarc seems to be saying that we do not need to accept this reality, declaring the body obsolete instead.

Stelarc has been 'extending' his body since the late 1960s. His idiosyn-cratic performances often involve robotics or other relatively modern technology integrated with his body. Some of his better known perform-ances include attaching a 'Third Hand' to his body (a robotic third arm), and a pneumatic spider-like six-legged walking machine (which sits the user in the centre of the legs and allows them to control the machine through arm gestures), and so-called 'suspension' events during which he hangs his entire body from hooks piercing his skin, often with one of his robotic inventions integrated. In 2007, he implanted a cell-cultivated ear into his left arm.

His works have been heralded for their ability to embrace a wider audience; the best example of this was his allowance for a worldwide audience to log into one of his exhibitions during which he wired his body electrically and joined his neural responses to remote controls over the Internet that could then be manipulated by others. Playing with the themes of remote control by others, Stelarc's work reads like a treatise on the question of the ownership of the body and the distant, functional relation-ship with the other (he is remotely manipulated or touched by others via the Internet) that may belie the need to modify the body. While his critics approach his work as a socio-political commentary on power relations, which is a legitimate reading of his work, I would like to take this one step further and argue that his work, as with Orlan's, also speaks to the psychic challenge posed by our embodied nature.

As I read published interviews with Stelarc, such as the excerpts just quoted, I am aware that although he is so explicitly focused on the body interior, I nevertheless feel distanced, removed from the messy reality of the body. His technical language has an almost hypnotic, mantra-like quality as though he is trying to reassure the listener/reader/himself that the body can be managed, that it can be turned into absolutely anything one wishes it to be, that it can even house a sculpture. His choice of words is evocative and disturbing:

> I've moved beyond the skin as a barrier. . . . Skin no longer signifies closure. . . . The hollow body becomes a host. . . . It is time to recolonise the body. . . . We need to build an internal surveillance system for the body. . . . Speck-sized robots are easily swallowed and may not even be sensed. . . . At a nanotech level, machines will navigate and inhabit cellular spaces and manipulate molecular structures to extend the body from within.

Stelarc conjures up simultaneously a paradoxical image of infinite freedom and self-determination (skin no longer signifies closure) *and* of remote control (an internal surveillance system, robots that will inhabit us and manipulate us without us feeling them).

The contradictions that emerge aptly capture the contradictions we encounter in some patients. Body modification promises absolute freedom

as the body is remade, customised according to the individual's own specifications, bypassing the experience of dependency. Yet, for many of these
patients, one senses that the body feels always under some kind of inner
surveillance – paranoid anxiety is barely beneath the surface. The imperative to modify the body is fuelled by this nagging suspicion, which has to be
silenced by reassuring the self that it is its own maker, that it can reclaim its
external and internal bodily space. The very notion of a body that might
willingly decide to 'host' a highly designed, and hence controllable, version
of an other (literally a 'sculpture' in Stelarc's work), reverses the intrauterine state, in which the baby is hosted by the maternal body, thereby perhaps
allowing the self to become the mother and so bypass an experience of loss.

Chapter 7

The botoxing of experience

> For Beauty's nothing
> But beginning of Terror we're still just able to bear.
> (Rilke 1989)

David Ely's (1964) novel is the inspiration for the film *Seconds*, which charts the story of Arthur Hamilton's reinvention. Arthur Hamilton is a middle-aged man. His life has lost purpose. He feels disengaged at work, and the love between him and his wife has dwindled. One evening Hamilton receives a late night phone call from Charlie Evans, an old friend Hamilton believed had committed suicide a year before. Intrigued, he follows Charlie's directions and is approached by a secret organisation, known simply as the 'Company', which offers wealthy people a second chance at life. The Company, in the person of Mr Ruby, interviews Hamilton, and resorts to blackmail to persuade him to sign on, foreshadowing the unfortunate consequences of accepting the Company's assistance.

The Company fakes Hamilton's death by staging an accident with a corpse disguised as him. His own 'death' is more costly than Charlie's suicide, but easier on survivors, his guides tell him. Through extensive plastic surgery (and a rather dubious form of psychotherapy), Hamilton is then transformed into Tony Wilson. As Wilson, he has a new home, a new identity, new friends and a devoted butler. The details of his new existence suggest that there was once a real Tony Wilson, but what became of him is a mystery.

Relocated to a fancy home in Malibu, Wilson is literally installed in a new, more exciting life, commencing with his transformed look. He starts a relationship with a young woman named Nora Marcus. For a time he is happy, but soon becomes troubled by the emotional confusion of his new identity and its consequences.

After the initial thrill at the 'second life' Wilson soon develops misgivings, which are compounded by the discovery that his new friends are not real but makeovers like himself: the world that has been given to him is entirely false. It turns out that his neighbours have been sent to keep an eye on his adjustment to his new life. Nora is actually an agent of the Company, and her attentions to Wilson are designed merely to ensure his cooperation.

Wilson manages to escape from the colony and heads for his old life but is captured and taken back to headquarters where he learns the truth about the pyramid scheme of which he has become a part: those that cannot make the transition are dealt with severely lest they topple the pyramid.

With its futuristic vision of plastic surgery as literally the creator of life itself, *Seconds*, seen now through the lens of the twenty-first century's obsession with makeover shows, and the staggering rise in the use of cosmetic procedures and surgery, gives pause for thought. The Company – so reminiscent of Rosenfeld's (1971) notion of an internal 'Mafia'[1] – is an apt and chilling corporate personification of the psychotic state of mind that can operate both at a group, societal level, and at an individual intrapsychic level, in relationship to the seductions of cosmetic surgery, and the central phantasy of quite concretely reinventing the self.

The seduction of the path chosen by Wilson is clear enough. As Wilson, Hamilton manages to temporarily escape his own depression and mid-life crisis through a manic flight into a narcissistic, omnipotent state of mind, supported by the literal physical transformations and the new, improved life this seemingly gives him access to. But in exchange for a new customised self he has to kill off, and to keep killing off, the true self, ultimately leaving him feeling confused and alienated, trapped in an enslaved relationship to the *super*-egoish Company who will not set him free. As soon as he questions his new predicament, thereby challenging the propaganda of the narcissistic self he is violently threatened by the Company.

In violation of 'Company' policy, Wilson visits his old wife in his new persona, and learns that his marriage had failed because he was distracted by the pursuit of career and material possessions, the very things in life that others made him believe were important. He returns to the Company and announces a desire to start again with yet another identity. The Company offers to accommodate him, but asks if he would first provide the names of some past acquaintances who might like to be 'reborn'.

While awaiting his reassignment, Wilson encounters Charlie Evans again, the friend who had originally recruited him into the Company. Evans was also 'reborn', and similarly struggled to adapt to his new identity. Together, they speculate on the reason for their failure to adjust, attributing it to the fact that they allowed others, including the Company, to make their life choices for them. This realisation, however, comes too late, as Hamilton learns that failed reborns are not actually provided with new identities, but instead become cadavers used to fake the next client's death. Only by recruiting more men, as Charlie recruited him, can Wilson avoid the fate of becoming the corpse to fake another man's death and reinvention. This twist captures the savagery of the *super*-ego because there is no escape from this kind of psychic organisation: only submission or death. The perverse quality of this particular psychic position is especially pertinent to the self-made phantasy.

Cosmetic surgery is deeply seductive because it speaks so directly to the phantasy of reinventing the self. Of course, cosmetic surgery also provides solutions to the difficulty in coming to terms with ageing and so with death. I will focus less on the latter in this chapter, however. Even so, it is important to underline that the greater ease with which such procedures can now be accessed to stave off the signs of ageing can undermine the capacity to work through the difficulty we all have in accepting our inescapable transience. Instead, we rely on an ever-increasing number of procedures, for more parts of the body, to prolong a youthful appearance. Why then spend years in psychotherapy trying to make sense of one's experience when the surgeon can reconstruct a 'new' self in a matter of hours – and for considerably less money too. But as Ely's novel illustrates, the psychic costs can be high as the more vulnerable part of the self that needs help is recruited by a psychotic part of the mind that triumphs over any dependency on the object and idealises a 'perfect', timeless state. The pursuit of beauty can thus become a psychic retreat from the pain of loss and guilt (Bell 2006).

As I mentioned at the outset, in the Introduction to this book, there is an inevitable tension when discussing all types of body modification, in reconciling individual meanings and the socio-cultural context in which these individual meanings are elaborated. Yet the more I have immersed myself in this subject, the more persuaded I have become that socio-cultural accounts purporting to explain why people seek cosmetic surgery are skimming the surface of what is a complex intrapsychic problem for some individuals.

I am very sympathetic to feminist perspectives because they shed helpful light on the tyranny of beauty for women in particular (Bordo 2003; Orbach 2009). But they do not provide a satisfactory account of why only *some* women are drawn to surgery, and why it becomes an imperative for only a few. Moreover, nowadays the practice of cosmetic surgery is no longer the sole province of women, with increasing numbers of men availing themselves of Botox and other cosmetic procedures.

In this chapter I will be suggesting that although the pursuit of cosmetic surgery and procedures is by no means, in and of itself, an indicator of psychopathology, it is so in some cases, and not just in the case of patients with BDD, as we saw in Chapter 4. After a brief review of the literature on cosmetic surgery, I will focus in more detail on the intrapsychic meaning of surgery itself as seen through the experience of one female patient with whom I worked as she underwent cosmetic surgery.

A brief history of cosmetic surgery

It should be clear by this stage of the book that across all ages and cultures we find examples of body modification. There is nothing new about our contemporary interest in the manipulation of the body self, and we would be justified in surmising that the body has always held communicative and social functions and has been manipulated accordingly – often explicitly so as to beautify the body. Favazza (1996), for example, reports on the practice of head moulding that was popular among Asian groups in the Punjab for purely aesthetic reasons whereby the back of the child's skull was flattened and tied to elongate the face. A similar practice can be traced back to the Chinook Indians in North America.

The first recorded plastic surgery technique was performed as early as 1000 BC in India to reinstate amputated noses as a result of punishment, or where an adulterous Hindu wife's nose had been bitten off by an enraged husband. The Italian surgeon Gaspare Tagliacozzi is often credited as the father of modern plastic surgery. In the sixteenth century, inspired by the need of plastic operations to frequent duels and street brawls, Tagliacozzi pioneered the Italian method of nasal reconstruction in which a flap from the upper arm was transferred to the nose (Gilman 1999). The origins of cosmetic surgery are therefore to be found in the 'covering up', or repair, of violent interactions – an important point I shall return to later.

The renaissance in plastic surgery was due in part to the significant advances in surgical technique made during the First World War, and in part to the involvement of reputable surgeons in the treatment of war casualties (Gilman 1999). The treatment of soldiers who were disfigured by bursting shells on the battlefield awarded a new, respectable legitimacy to plastic surgery. But the transition from the war battlefield to the more mainstream, often unnecessary, use of surgery to alter a perfectly healthy body, was commensurate with the ascendance of a visual culture first and foremost in the United States (Haiken 1997).

Although cosmetic surgery is now a global product, the history of the beginnings of cosmetic surgery, Haiken (1997) has persuasively argued, maps onto the preoccupations that dominated the United States in the 1920s. The Depression impoverished many Americans, but it did not dent the growth of the cosmetic industry. Through the ever-powerful medium of advertising, a visually dominated culture seized the American psyche. It promulgated the myth that personal appearance made you happy and secured employment. Advertisers played on the idea that first impressions could bring immediate success or failure:

> Americans bought this notion along with their toothpaste and deodor-
> ant. From Dr. West's toothbrushes, (which promised 'a magic road to
> popularity that first winning smile'), to Sherwin-Williams paint, (which

warned 'many a man has been rated as lacking in community spirit . . . even as a business failure – merely because of a paint scarred house'), advertisements alternatively promised and warned Americans that others' first impressions – of themselves, their houses, even their bathroom fixtures, could determine the course of their lives.

(Haiken 1997: 101)

In this cultural and political climate a too prominent nose was all too readily constructed as a problem deserving surgical intervention. By 1941 most plastic surgeons had incorporated cosmetic surgery into their practice. Haiken (1997) argues that this transition was secured and enhanced by the popularisation of the notion of the 'inferiority complex' (that is, low self-esteem). In turn, this all too persuasively legitimised cosmetic surgery on the grounds of psychological problems. This psychological interpretation 'enabled surgeons to portray the specialty as a more serious, and even medically necessary, practice than it might otherwise have seemed: No longer was it nearly vanity surgery; instead it was "psychiatry with a scalpel"' (Haiken 1997: 108).

Once physical appearance came to be seen as closely tied with personality, it was difficult to draw the line separating cosmetic surgery from other forms of self-improvement. The facelift got its own 'facelift', as it were: surgery was transformed into a reasonable, if not essential, solution to the psychological and social problems posed by being-in-a-body, not least the problem of ageing and its purportedly associated social and economic costs (e.g. more difficult to get a good job or to meet potential new partners).

Like the Scarecrow who wants brains, the Tin Woodman who wants a heart and the Cowardly Lion who wants courage, we all travel down the Yellow Brick Road in search of a 'transformational object' (Bollas 1987) who will give us a desirable form. As Elliott (2003) rightly points out,

> when Dorothy and her friends finally reach the Emerald City, they learn that they already have the very things they have been looking for. The Scarecrow . . . is already the most intelligent of the lot; the Tin Woodman . . . is the most compassionate; and the Cowardly Lion . . . is the bravest. Their problems lie not in who they are, but in who they think they are.
>
> (Elliott 2003: 14)

Nowadays, wizards have been supplanted by cosmetic surgeons. Like their early forebears in the 1930s, they justify surgery as the treatment for low self-esteem (i.e. who you think you are). The cosmetic surgeon's raison d'être is not to refer on to the psychotherapist, but to sculpt the body and through this change who the patient thinks he is.

All over the world cosmetic surgeons now wield their scalpels to reveal so-called 'new' bodies, and so 'new' selves. The trend to relate to the body as a project has fuelled the global beauty business that is growing at a rate of 7 per cent per year (Kuczynski 2006). Since 1997 there has been a 465 per cent increase in the total number of cosmetic procedures. Of particular concern are the reports indicating the increase in cosmetic surgery on young people aged eighteen and under which has tripled over a ten-year period to 205,119 in 2007 from 59,890 in 1997 (Dermatology Daily, 15 January 2009).[2] These figures suggest that problems of low self-esteem in young people are increasingly treated with the scalpel.

If we fast forward to the current times, the history of cosmetic surgery is simple yet thought provoking: over time we have more surgeons, more patients and more surgeries on more parts of the body. Across the Western and non-Western world we seem to have embraced cosmetic surgery as a fact of life. The body, like a house or a car, has become yet another commodity that we are prepared to exchange or customise, no matter what. 'I like my beauty hardcore', writes Avril Mair, a journalist in the women's magazine *Elle*,

> I know that creams and lotions and the laying on of hands are not enough. I want to see results, not just hope for them. So I have had sharp pinpricks of Botox injected around my eyes and across my forehead. I have had fat syringes of Restylane slowly released into the tender flesh around my mouth. I have had my breasts augmented and my brows transplanted. I have walked out of dermatologists' offices with sunglasses to hide the bruising. I have cried with pain in taxis on the way home from so-called 'lunch hour treatments'. I have spent a weekend in bed, bandaged and barely able to dress myself. I have endured bleeding, black eyes and swelling. There is little that I won't put myself through.
>
> (Mair, *Elle*, March 2009: 309)

She also adds that for her this is 'not an exercise in self-hatred'. Rather, she views it as a manifestation of the fact that she 'loves beauty'. Like Mair, many cosmetic surgery patients would see this as being their justification for altering the given body. But what does 'loving beauty' mean? It is such an interesting statement. Of course, I do not know Avril Mair, and I cannot presume to know what it means for her. All I know is what 'loving beauty' has meant to some of my patients for whom the pursuit of beauty was a psychic retreat. For some, it was a way of bypassing the guilt for damage done to a hated object, which was instead manically repaired through improving the body's appearance. For others, it was a means for averting the pain of the loss of an object who would love and desire the self.

Psychiatry with a scalpel?

Over the years I have had the privilege to listen to a number of stories of patients who have undergone cosmetic surgery or procedures, or who have contemplated it and then shied away from it. These patients displayed no visible physical problems other than the inevitable signs of ageing. On rare occasions I have worked with patients who have undergone cosmetic surgery to reshape, for example, a markedly disproportional nose, or because they have endured a disfigurement following an accident. In these cases I am quite clear that the decision to undertake cosmetic surgery, which is never without meaning or consequence, was nevertheless informed by a realistic self-appraisal and a stable relationship to reality. Consequently their adjustment post-surgery was good;[3] in these cases it made the difference between an uncomfortable self-consciousness that they felt inhibited them and undermined their confidence socially, and being able to engage with life more spontaneously and self-assuredly. After all, we live in a world where appearances do matter. Whether we like it or not, this is a reality. As one patient who had been disfigured through an accident once put it: 'If your face does not fit, life's tough'. Clearly one could take the stance that such a social reality should be challenged, and that supporting the option of cosmetic surgery simply panders to the notion that beauty matters.

My own view is that within the confines of the consulting room, the primary aim is to help the patient to make choices that are meaningful to them and that are rooted in an appraisal of reality, by which I mean that they are not driven primarily by unconscious phantasy. Under these circumstances, if the patient chooses to pursue surgery, I do not see it as my role to prevent them from doing so.

In addressing the problematic of cosmetic surgery, I am therefore not wishing to suggest that the decision to pursue such surgery is always an indicator of a deep-rooted character pathology. Rather, what I hope to convey is that an important component of what requires understanding when such surgery is requested is the state of mind of the patient in relation to the surgery and the unconscious meaning this holds for them. This is easier said than done because the ease with which surgery can be accessed nowadays, and the popularisation of such procedures, have so normalised cosmetic surgery that to even question its unconscious meaning can be felt by the patient to be redundant, if not ridiculous. Indeed cosmetic surgery's critics have themselves been stigmatised as offering only sour grapes. Similarly, the therapist who invites an exploration of these choices can all too readily be experienced as undermining the patient's perceived solution to psychic pain. Nevertheless cosmetic surgeons too recognise that some individuals who seek cosmetic surgery – the so-called 'insatiable' patient (Goldwyn 2006) – will never be satisfied with the outcome because what they need cannot be delivered by the surgeon. The cosmetic surgeon cuts and reshapes a real body but for the patient it is always a phantasised body and self that are under the knife (Gilman 1999). Given how commonplace cosmetic surgery has become, we can also all too readily forget that, in addition to the psychic work that it bypasses, and the consequences of this for psychological adjustment, most surgery has side-effects, some of which are serious and permanent, and occasionally fatal.

The research literature in this area is ambiguous. Most interview-based studies report evidence of psychopathology in patients undergoing cosmetic surgery, though this is not reliably the case when using standardised psychometric measures (Sarwer et al. 1998). Studies looking at the prevalence rate of mental health problems in those requesting surgery suggest a higher percentage (19 per cent) than that found in other surgery patients (4 per cent) (Sarwer et al. 2004). The rate of patients with Body Dysmorphic Disorder (BDD), which one might expect to be high in this population, has been reported as varying between 9 per cent and 53 per cent – this variability most likely resulting from the use of different measures (Ercolani et al. 1999; Phillips et al. 2000; Aouizerate et al. 2003). What is clear, however, is that there is a greater representation of patients with BDD among cosmetic surgery patients than in the general population, where the rate of BDD is 1–2 per cent. Requests for unusual facial cosmetic changes involving bone contouring, bone grafting or cheek and chin implants (when the face is felt to be too wide or too thin), are typically associated with a significant impairment in psychological functioning (Edgerton et al. 1990).

Of concern are the results of four large epidemiological studies carried out in the United States and Europe that have found a relationship between breast implants and suicide. Across these studies the suicide rate was two to three times greater among patients with breast implants compared to patients who underwent other cosmetic procedures (Sarwer et al. 2006). It is unclear as to what accounts for this finding. There has been a suggestion that the post-operative complications, which are not uncommon following breast augmentation, lead to depression and then suicide. It might also be the case that patients who seek breast augmentations have more unrealistic expectations and/or that they have greater pre-existing psychological problems. This view is supported by a study that found an increased prevalence of pre-operative psychiatric hospitalisation in women who had sought breast implants relative to women who had undergone other kinds of cosmetic surgery (Jacobsen et al. 2004). In my experience of working with patients who have undergone breast augmentation (see Chapter 6 and this chapter), the concreteness of the appropriation of the maternal breast fuels more acute paranoid anxieties of vengeance and retaliation, which may provide yet another explanation for the increased risk of suicide in some of these patients.

Consciously, many cosmetic surgery patients claim to want, and believe that what cosmetic surgery will give them, is the 'privilege of anonymity' (Davis 1995) or 'passing' (Gilman 1999) which makes it possible to exist without feeling intruded by the gaze of the other. In other words, they say that they pursue surgery in order to 'fit in'. But as Gilman reminds us, this is not about becoming invisible, but becoming 'differently visible – being seen as a member of a group with which one wants or needs' to identify (Gilman 1999: xxi). These individuals fear being seen for who they feel they really are. They relate to their body – quite accurately, of course, in one sense – as the embodied narrative of their individual developmental history. After all, even birthmarks, blemishes or wrinkles can be seen to physically punctuate our developmental narratives (Resnik 2005), hence procedures such as Botox can be used to erase this history.

Not all patients for whom cosmetic procedures have become psychically necessary suffer from BDD in so far as they are not obsessively preoccupied with a particular body part(s). Rather, they may present with a more diffuse preoccupation with the body's appearance in the context of a more or less thick or thin skinned narcissistic structure. Although ostensibly it is beauty that is pursued, the inner story reveals that the search for 'beauty' variously translates for some into a search for a sense of a desirable self in the coherence of the specular image (which may become compelling); for others, it represents a wish to sever any connection to the object of desire, hence effectively enacting the self-made phantasy in its most complete form by recreating the body anew. For others still it may express difficulty in managing death anxiety – the pain of coming to terms with the reality of loss, and the pain of guilt (Bell 2006).

Cosmetic surgery: the inner story

To put it crudely, cosmetic surgery allows you to get rid of, or to diminish, a body part (e.g. liposuction or rhinoplasty), or to augment it in some way – breast implants being the most common example of the latter. It has never been easier to alter one's appearance and to enact, for those so inclined, the unconscious phantasies I have been highlighting. I will now focus on a more extended clinical illustration of work with a patient, Ms R., who underwent numerous cosmetic procedures. I will also describe briefly another patient, Ms O.

The case of Ms R. highlights how the phantasies I have outlined may in some cases be present in the same individual, at different points, depending on the state of mind in relation to the anticipated and/or actualised body modification. Her predicament illustrates the way in which the surgery was used at different times in her mind to actualise the perfect match phantasy and the self-made phantasy respectively. More specifically, I want to draw attention to the dual function of cosmetic surgery in her case, namely that it provided both a means for attacking the object (through the violence perpetrated on a perfectly healthy body), and a means for manically repairing the damage done to the object through altering and beautifying the surface of the body, and so erasing any signs of damage – effectively 'making over' a more 'ugly' internal reality.

Ms R. was in her late fifties when I met her. The onset of her depression had coincided with her divorce coming through after several years of an acrimonious legal battle. Her husband had left her for a younger woman and Ms R. had been determined to fight him. The hatred she felt for him, and the fight of the divorce, had staved off the latent depression, but once it was all finalised she collapsed. She felt hopeless about the possibility of meeting anyone else given her age and she anticipated a miserable, lonely old age.

Ms R. was difficult to engage. A depressed, aggrieved state enveloped her and she showed little interest at first in my attempts to reach her. She complained about everything: her husband had betrayed her, her daughter had abandoned her to live abroad with her husband, her friends had deserted her and her body was failing her. It was not long before I was also recruited into this list of disappointments. Her narrative was punctuated by recriminations about other people's negligence and selfishness. She was invariably the victim of others' neglect or cruelty. As Feldman (2009) has emphasised, the aggrieved patient feels that it is the object that must change. I sensed her desperation as she spoke; she managed to communicate that she was actually very frightened of what might happen to her. I think that it was her dim awareness of how fragile she was that enabled her to seek help and to stay in treatment, which she was able to do. Over time she managed to increase from once weekly to three times weekly sessions.

Ms R. focused a great deal on her bodily appearance. She was in fact a strikingly attractive woman who looked much younger than her years. I was to learn later that this was partly on account of a facelift she had a few years prior to her husband leaving her.

As I explored her early childhood, she described distant relationships with both her parents. Her mother was felt to have been 'devoted' to the father and a socialite for whom appearances mattered. Ms R. pointedly recalled that her mother always wanted to be at the centre of attention, spending money on 'extravagant' clothes. Her father, she felt, had been 'devoted' to her mother, but Ms R. was convinced that her mother had never loved him as much as he had loved her mother.

Ms R. did not have any siblings – her mother's first born had died at birth. Her relationships generally were impoverished. They had always been so, even at school, where she seemed to have protected herself from contact with others by hiding behind a superior façade that alienated people. She kept everyone at a distance and yet controlled them, especially her only daughter, of whom she was very critical. I quickly felt that Ms R. demanded absolute 'devotion' and that anything short of that left her feeling bitterly disappointed as if she was thrust back into an intolerable Oedipal scenario in her mind in which a devoted, passionate couple shamefully excluded her. This gratifying union, from which she felt so brutally excluded, was where she desired to be and what she felt was owed to her.

Ms R.'s desperate state of mind was palpable, and along with her general practitioner, I shared a concern about the risk of suicide. She was tormented by thoughts of her husband with his new, younger wife. Part of the torment was fuelled by the dominant version in her mind of the couple: for example, she imagined them mocking her as they enjoyed luxurious holidays together. She would go over such fantasies in her mind again and again, and torture both herself and the couple with her hatred in the process. The combined parental couple (Klein 1952) was forever tantalising and cruel. In turn, this incited her own envious attack on it.

After a few months in therapy, she arrived for her session in a very disgruntled state of mind. She pointed to her eyes and said: 'Look, what *she* has done!' (her emphasis). At first, I was confused as I could not really see anything untoward. This irritated her. Indeed, any sign that I did not understand her immediately became proof that I was not devoted to her in her mind. She begrudgingly explained to me that she had been for her Botox injections (she had been having these every four months approximately though I had not known this) and that the female doctor who had administered the injections had done this wrong. Now her eyelids were droopy.

I was struck by the extent of Ms R.'s rage towards the doctor and she very quickly started to talk about suing her. Ms R.'s usual superior, detached demeanour had given way to an overtly rageful tantrum. I thought she felt deeply humiliated by what had happened as if the doctor had exposed her ugliness to the world. My attempt to understand her was rebuffed with greater force than had been usual as she told me that 'Words can never make me feel better'. She said that the only comfort she had ever got was from looking good. It was then that she told me about her facelift and her use of cosmetic procedures and surgery starting in her late thirties. This then exposed her extensive reliance on all manner of cosmetic procedures, virtually on a weekly basis (for example, dermabrasion, Botox, facials, teeth whitening). Ms R. had effectively created her own psychiatric team comprising facialists, dermatologists and cosmetic surgeons.

The following week Ms R. was calmer, yet very detached, and she announced, casually, that she would be missing two or three weeks the following month as she had booked herself in for a blepharoplasty (to rectify drooping eyelids). As she spoke about the surgery, she conveyed the strong impression that she now felt safer and contained. As she conjured up the image of how her eyes would look, she seemed to enter a space in her mind in which an idealised object was looking at an ideal version of her. As I listened, I gained the distinct impression that I was completely redundant in the room. I understood what was happening between us, and in her mind, as the result of her retreat into a perfect match phantasy.

The surgery promised her an all-enveloping, unbroken psychical skin (Anzieu 1989) – the skin that ideally the mother has given up to the child to guarantee its protection and strength. The anticipated surgery functioned for Ms R. as a kind of second skin: she felt less vulnerable, more in control and, crucially, she felt desirable. The idealisation of the psychic system, of which the omnipotent phantasy is a core component, was central to her psychic equilibrium (Steiner 1993). This was apparent in the way she configured the events to come in her mind and presented them to me: she told me that the surgeon was *the best*; his waiting list was closed but he made an exception *for her*; the operation was not dangerous, no different from having some fillings; she had made sure she would get the most senior anaesthetist and so she would feel *no pain*. And so it went on as she convinced herself that what she was about to do was immeasurably special and safe. This phantasy sustained her. It was important not simply in terms of its promised outcome (she would look so much better), but also in terms of the *process of transformation* itself (she was special and she was, in her mind, elevated as the special patient who got in to see the best surgeon and she would be taken care of). For Ms R., in that moment, the surgery was not experienced as an attack on her body. Rather, it provided her with an opportunity to avail herself of the loving gaze and touch of a surgeon/father/mother who would make beautiful her felt-to-be ugly self and so guarantee that she would not be overlooked.

It proved impossible to engage Ms R. in thinking with me about the meaning for her of the proposed surgery. The sessions of that week were suffused with this rather manic state of mind, which had a chilling quality as if she was now so safely tucked inside a narcissistic cocoon that the other person (me) ceased to exist.

The following week Ms R. reported this dream:

> I can see the beach. I am swimming in calm waters. The sea is clear and beautiful. I can see beautiful, colourful fish swimming underneath me. The

sea is warm, like a blanket. And then suddenly I can hear terrible screams and a little girl is drowning.

Ms R. reluctantly responded to my interest in her associations to this dream, by saying that the sea reminded her of a beach her parents loved. They would go there on holiday at least once per year. They were both keen swimmers and would swim far out, leaving her behind on the beach to play on her own. She then added that the best thing about the dream had been the way she felt 'light', and 'at peace in my body'.

I understood this dream as reflecting the way in which the certainty of the upcoming surgery in her mind functioned as a kind of enveloping, warm sea/ blanket. She now felt safe. Significantly, she is in the sea looking at the beach, so she has taken up in her dream the parental position. It is now her, secure as part of a phantasised, beautiful, colourful couple (colourful conjured up for me her description of her mother's 'extravagant' clothes), who looks on at the desperate girl/mother who is drowning. In the transference I felt that she had projected this experience of being left out into me, and I was indeed to be abandoned to my useless words while she had access to a very special one-to-one with the surgeon/father. Ms R. had effectively assumed the mother's identity − her skin − and she was now loved and admired by her devoted father. In this dream we can discern then the activation of the perfect match phantasy (she is now part of an idealised couple with father), and also the self-made phantasy as she enviously 'drowns' the mother and recreates herself.

The problem with this seemingly 'ideal' solution will be apparent in the dream that she reported in the first session of the following week. Prior to telling me this dream she had indicated that the weekend had been stressful because her daughter was being difficult − which I took to also mean that I was 'difficult' because I had not spent the weekend with her. Ms R. felt that her daughter 'owed' her a visit, and she berated her daughter for not suggesting that she would come over to see her. She then told me this dream:

I am shopping in [a country] I think . . . I see this beautiful fur coat. It's on sale . . . half price and I tell my husband that it's a real bargain. My husband says I have one already, why do I need another . . . and then he says, 'it's just another scam to get people to buy things they don't need'. I feel terrible. It's so soft and I feel cold but he simply doesn't understand. He leaves the shop . . . he hates shopping. I stay and the shop assistant is no longer there and I just take the coat and run out with it. The alarm starts ringing and there is so much noise. I start to feel dizzy . . . can't walk . . . I fall over, I think . . . then I wake up in the dream and I am in a

strange place I don't recognise. I feel sweat pouring down my face but I
say to myself – you are not there anymore.

As she recounted this dream Ms R. became very anxious and distressed. It
was as though her impregnable skin was tearing as she now suffered the
consequences of having so triumphantly appropriated, in her mind, the
maternal role and body. I thought that her daughter's rebuff – a slice of
painful reality – had been very hurtful and she had become yet another
person who, like the ex-husband in the dream, and of course me in the
transference, could not understand her inner state of deprivation. This
external rejection punctured the newly acquired skin that only the previous
week had made her feel less raw.

In this dream it is possible to discern how Ms R. desperately needs a soft,
warm skin to hold her together (the fur coat),[4] and she is trying to communicate her impoverished inner state to her husband/me who instead tells
her she has plenty, that she does not need anything else. Desperate, in a very
paranoid-schizoid frame of mind, then she has no option but to steal the
fur coat.

Cosmetic surgery and procedures, at an unconscious level, may provoke
considerable paranoid anxieties. The kind of paranoid anxiety that gripped
Ms R. following her decision to undergo further cosmetic surgery can also
manifest in the experience, post-operatively, of the new body part feeling
like a 'foreign part'.

Another patient I saw, Ms O., a young woman in her late twenties, became
very disturbed following a breast augmentation. Although she had never
previously suffered from claustrophobia, she developed this symptom a few
weeks after her operation. She felt pleased with the breast augmentation, and
yet she also told me that she would sometimes look at her breasts and not
really feel that they belonged to her. She told me this quite consciously, and
with humour, but I felt that this belied considerable anxiety about what she
felt she had fraudulently appropriated for herself – the breasts felt foreign
because they did not, in fact, belong to her.

Ms O. had started to feel unhappy with her breasts in her late teens. Her
sister was described as much better endowed than her. Once she had
managed to put aside enough savings, she decided that she 'owed' this to
herself and she signed up for the procedure without telling anyone about it.
When I asked her why this needed to be a secret, she said she feared that
people would be critical of her. Through her conscious intent to keep her
surgery secret (which is by no means uncommon) I sensed that Ms O. knew

that she was somehow appropriating for herself something that she recognised as not belonging to her, and which might attract criticism.

Her dreams were laden with paranoid anxiety. Two characteristic dreams from the early phase of our work illustrate the persecutory anxiety generated by theft:

> We are in my old school . . . my friends are all there and we are sharing some sweets. I take two pieces . . . I don't think anyone sees me but then the teacher calls me to the front of the class and tells everyone what I did.

In another:

> My house is burgled but the police cannot find the burglars. They tell me it's because they were in disguise.

In the first dream, it appeared that Ms O. was giving expression to having secretly taken two breasts (two sweets) and then she is exposed for what she has done. The second dream clearly illustrates the way that she identified with having stolen something but her so-called 'disguise' (the new breasts) fools the police. In both these dreams the latent anxiety is one of feeling exposed. Another dream develops this theme further, this time explicitly referring to the breast implants and takes the form of a subjective experience of being invaded by something foreign:

> I am lying in bed and my left breast bursts open and all this pus comes out – I look at it and I can't believe this is part of me. It's smelly and disgusting. I just want someone to take the implant out – get this thing out of me. I'm screaming: It's not mine, take it away.

There are several aspects one could take up in this last dream, but the one closest to this discussion is the way that Ms O. vividly conveys how the much sought after breasts are declared to not belong to her ('It's not mine'), they are now attacking her and she urgently wants to get rid of them ('take it away').

Over time Ms O. was able to think with me about the way in which her own breast augmentation represented her attempt to be able to give herself what she needed, whenever she needed it, and so put right what she had experienced as a kind of injustice: early on in her life she had lost her mother's attention when the mother became very ill. It became clearer that the mother had become depressed following her diagnosis, and quite likely, had been less available to Ms O.

The paranoid anxiety that both Ms O. and Ms R. experienced appears to be the result of the way in which they unconsciously recognised that in altering the given body, they had 'cheated' or stolen something that did not belong to them. A core feature of the self-made phantasy is indeed this appropriation of something that belongs to another, or to put it another way, it exposes the inability to receive what the object has given. The given body is felt to not be good enough while the (m)other is felt to possess the goodness, which can now be literally incorporated through surgery. This, in turn, gives rise to a fear of retaliation and hence paranoid anxiety is triggered. The only way to assuage this kind of anxiety is through the surgery, which temporarily at least, covers up the 'ugly' feelings that fuel its pursuit, through the surface beautification of the body – an oasis of calm after the storm. This reassures the self and the object that no real damage has been done.

Let us return to Ms R. again because her predicament illustrates another important facet of the self-made phantasy. I have been suggesting that the unconscious function of the cosmetic surgery for her was to appropriate the maternal body/position in relation to her father. If her eyes are less droopy, if her face is less lined, then surely she will be the one swimming out to sea with father leaving mother to drown instead of her. But at one level Ms R. recognises that this is what she is doing: that she is stealing something that does not belong to her and hence the paranoid anxiety sets in. Alarms go off, she loses her balance and falls unconscious. The maternal skin that does not belong to her is forever out of her reach – she can try to appropriate it for herself but the alarm rings and she will be caught. In this respect the end of her dream is telling: she wakes up, still in touch with the panic (sweat is pouring), and yet she finds herself in an unrecognisable safer place in her mind in which she can gain some comfort through words rather than actions. I understood this as an important sign that reflected the tenuous relationship she was developing with me and that could provide some comfort despite all her protestations to the contrary.

In the session I took up the way in which she was letting me know how urgently she needed to wrap herself up in luxurious state of mind where she would command the devotion she felt no one was prepared to give her. And yet, I added, a part of her mind (projected into her husband/me) recognised that the fur coat/cosmetic surgery was a kind of scam to get her to buy into something that actually is not what she needs. I then linked this to her upcoming blepharoplasty.

Ms R. went on to say that there were times when she looked at photographs of how she used to be when she was younger and all she could see was a very depressed face – nothing beautiful about it. She now had nothing left – her life was over – why not make herself feel better at least in the only way she knew how to? I observed that my thoughts about her dream had left her feeling exposed to this very depressed, damaged part of her and she was now saying to me: How could you do this, can't you see this is all I have?

Ms R. was briefly silent and then said she was glad I had said that because she did not think she could cancel the surgery. She thought that this was what I thought she should do. She told me that she had been invited to spend a long weekend somewhere abroad a few months down the line (which would coincide with one of our breaks). She imagined that all her friends would be curious to see how she had fared post-divorce. They would be looking good. Already she was the 'divorcee', she said, and this made her feel very exposed and lacking in some fundamental way, so she could not face people seeing her face looking 'so old'.

I will not go into this session further. Suffice to say that Ms R. did proceed with her surgery, but significantly, I think, rather than hiding away from me during the weeks' of convalescing post-surgery (which had been her plan), she asked me if she could still attend her sessions. I saw her in fact only days after the operation. She looked terrible, bruised and swollen, as if she had been beaten up. She recounted to me in minute detail the operation and how sick she had felt after the anaesthetic. The net result was that I felt somewhat assaulted by both her bruised face and the detailed description. I was left feeling distinctly nauseous.

This very visceral countertransference gave me pause for thought. I thought that the change of heart in relation to having the sessions in the immediate aftermath of her operation was over-determined. On the one hand, it signalled that she was able to make more use of me and view the sessions as a place she could come to when she felt very exposed – and she was indeed quite literally exposed with her bruised and swollen face. On the other hand, I thought that there was also a need to show me – to confront me in the transference – with the damage that, in her phantasy, she felt her mother had done to her, and that she knew she had perpetrated against her mother. In other words, I felt that there was a wish not only to communicate something about her state of mind through her visibly bruised appearance, but also to visually assault me with this: a theme I will return in more detail in Chapter 8.

Ms R. stayed in three times weekly treatment for just under four years and made reasonably good progress over this time. She did not pursue any further surgery after the eye surgery. For her, transition into older age was especially complicated: not only was she abandoned by her husband at a particularly delicate stage of life when she would have to integrate the fact of ageing, but also Ms R. clearly had been a very unhappy person for much of her life. Her current predicament recapitulated these early painful beginnings with felt-to-be rejecting objects. As Waddell (2007: 188) has so sensitively traced, there is an 'inextricable relationship between beginnings and endings'.

Ms R. harboured a profound grievance towards her mother, which fuelled her very acrimonious divorce. Getting old terrified her: all she saw ahead of her was a desolate, bleak landscape that she tried to embellish through altering her own body and 'making it beautiful'. We can all potentially look at wrinkles as a remnant of an imperfect past, something to be fixed like a broken tooth or bad vision, but I am suggesting here that a more enslaved relationship to the pursuit of body modification is underpinned by a far more complex, violent state of mind.

My work with Ms R. provided me with many opportunities for thinking about the meaning of 'beautiful' and 'ugly' for her. Rickman (1957), in one of only a handful of analytic contributions to the nature of ugliness, suggests that the perception of ugliness confirms the failure of reparation for the destructiveness of one's own aggressive impulses:

> Our need for beauty springs from the gloom and pain which we experience from our destructive impulses towards our good and loved objects . . . we recognise the power of death when we say a thing is ugly.
> (Rickman 1957: 121)

His views are closely connected to Segal's (1952) understanding of the nature of beauty and of the creative urge as denoting the integrative, reparative processes of the depressive position. The appreciation of beauty, or its creation, restores the damaged object (Lee 1948).

We might understand the manic search for beauty, as manifest in those individuals, like Ms R., who become addicted to cosmetic surgery and procedures, as the actualisation of a desperate longing to merge with an idealised, adoring mother manically repaired from the self's attacks on the hated internal mother. It is this implicit attack that is so well disguised by the surgery. Yet, the frantic search for beauty in these cases lays bare the inner experience that the given body (i.e. given by the (m)other) is not felt to be good enough. The repeated surgeries testify to an ongoing sense of grievance that cannot be worked through: 'You have given me something ugly, and now I will give myself something beautiful'. In these individuals the very request for surgery – that is, to alter the given body – represents an enactment of the grievance towards the mother. At the same time, by making oneself beautiful, the phantasy is that the attacked internal object is reassured and restored: 'I have not destroyed you through hatred'.

There is something poignant in the belief that enough trips to the cosmetic surgeon somehow protects us from other other physical and psychic catastrophes. For some, cosmetic surgery is the perceived cure for the 'disease of being finite' (Cronenberg, quoted in Rodley 1997). I hope that it will be clear by now that I mean this in two senses of finite, namely, that we are temporally bounded (that is, we die) and that during life too we are bounded by the limitations of the body that we are given and its origins. Changing the surface of the body cannot change these truths.

Chapter 8

Ink, holes and scars

The present organ-isation of the body is unnecessary. The solution to modifying the body is not to be found in its internal structure, but lies simply on its surface. THE SOLUTION IS NO MORE THAN SKIN DEEP.

(Stelarc 2009)

Written on the skin . . . tattoos are diary entries, protective shields, conversational pieces, countercultural totems, valentines to lovers and memorials to the dead.

(Mifflin 1997: 178)

'I hate my skin', a young female patient told me. All I could see was the smoothness of her skin, the soft contours of a pretty face, hidden behind a veil of hair. But to her eyes it looked uneven, forever erupting in unsightly spots. This imagined skin exposed what she felt inside: hateful and hated.

The skin – the largest organ – is many things. It is the 'scrim' on which we project our phantasies and fears (Mifflin 1997). It is the first point of meeting the other's touch. It is also a container: it keeps the inside intact. Skin thus acts as a boundary, lending a sense of being an interiority in relation to an exteriority. This boundary can be subjectively experienced as a site for meeting the other, or as a shield protecting the self from the other. The skin could be seen as a kind of 'billboard' (Favazza 1996) where permanent messages are recorded, displayed and communicated to others. The messages they convey are multiple when one surveys the functions that body rituals involving markings of the skin have held historically and across cultures, for example, as signs of physical healing, spiritual salvation, inclusion and difference.

In this chapter I want to focus on three types of body modification that have become increasingly widespread in the West as a means of altering the surface of the body, namely the permanent marking of the skin through the use of tattoos, body piercings and scarification, which I will refer to generically as 'skin markings'.

In approaching this subject from a psychological perspective, I want to avoid the pitfalls of merely pathologising these behaviours, which is how they have been characteristically approached in the psychiatric and analytic literature, scarce though this literature is. Rather, I hope to show that such behaviours are best approached developmentally (Rosenblum et al. 1999) and with due awareness of the social functions that they have served across the ages and cultures (Brain 1978). Having said this, I will not be focusing on the more sociological perspectives in any detail since these are thoroughly covered elsewhere.

I will start nevertheless with a brief cross-cultural overview since these practices have long traditions in the non-Western world, but in this chapter I am primarily interested in how these kinds of body modifications have been used by the patients I have worked with, and hence with the internal world of these patients. To this extent the cases I discuss, and the understanding that I have developed of these manipulations of the skin surface, have occurred in the context of working with patients with varying degrees of disturbance.

To add to my own direct clinical practice I will also, however, make reference to published interviews with tattoo artists and those who have been tattooed and/or pierced or branded. In addition, I will refer to my own interviews with five individuals who have chosen to be tattooed and/or pierced, but who have not any contact with mental health services. Clearly, they are a self-selected group of individuals who perceived their decisions to mark the body as meaningful and worthy of discussion. I am therefore not claiming in any way to have found a representative sample. However, I was keen to learn more about the function of these practices beyond the confines of the clinical setting.

Cross-cultural perspectives

The very diversity of body practices across cultures strongly argues against the notion of a 'natural' body since the body has always been manipulated and is always constructed and shaped by personal and cultural meanings. Indeed people have used ink and ash to decorate themselves for more than 5000 years. Tattooing is a universal practice originating in the Pacific Islands.[1] Subsequently worn by sailors, the tattoo remained for some time the province of a largely male, working-class group. During the latter part of the nineteenth century tattooing was popularised through circus acts, most notably the 'freak' show. It remained therefore a feature of working-class entertainment and it is in this context that tattooing took off as a commercial development. At the turn of the twentieth century tattoos continued to show up in so-called titillating and disreputable places. By the

1950s tattoos became more associated with particular subgroups such as bikers, street gangs and offenders. In the late 1970s and early 1980s tattoos became a rebellious fashion statement popularised by punk rock. Nowadays tattoos are a middle-class fashion accessory sported on the international catwalks.

The evolution of the tattoo from its traditional origins to the fashion catwalks is striking. It provides a good example for exploring the extent to which the same behaviour, as it evolves in different cultures and over time, retains its original function. In many primitive societies the body is an important surface on which the marks of social status, family rank and tribal affiliation are inscribed. Indeed, even in contemporary society, we are well aware that the classification of social status depends on the way we present our body in the social world, through the way we dress and style ourselves (Bourdieu 1984; Turner 2000), which nowadays includes skin markings.

Skin markings have traditionally been integral to rites of passage. Even a relatively cursory overview of rites of passage in non-Western cultures highlights that the ritual transformation of the body marks the transition to a new status. In so-called primitive tribal societies piercings, tattoos and scarification have also been used to mark the creation and consolidation of relationships, or as a mark of courage, and especially relevant to the concerns of this book, they have been used to heal the diseased body and the wounded psyche. Favazza (1996), in a very comprehensive study of various forms of body modification, has documented culturally sanctioned rituals that are organised around various kinds of 'self-mutilation', as he refers to it. For example, among some Aboriginal groups the boy's penis is cut during a rite of passage into adulthood. Scarification, involving the process of deliberatively cutting the skin in order to produce scars, is also not uncommon.[2]

Among the Kagora of Papa New Guinea, scarification is an integral part of the rite of passage into adulthood for boys. The boys are reborn as men and strengthened by the bloody ritual. Interestingly, the ritual is also understood to be a way of ridding the self of the 'polluting' female blood that accumulated in their bodies during gestation and the feeding stage. This resonates with my own view that one of the functions of body modification in the West, as I have suggested in earlier chapters, is an attempt to psychically manage the fundamental challenge posed by the shared corporeality of mother and baby. Along very similar lines the Kagora people's ritual, through marking the body, concretely marks out the self as separate from its maternal origins.

The manipulation of the surface of the body to clearly demarcate an 'old' self from a 'new' self thus has a long established tradition in some cultures, and this is especially relevant to the underlying use of body markings in the West. The anthropologist Van Gennep (1960) suggests that every ritual ensures the transition from one mode of being to another. It is a rite of passage with three stages: an act of separation from previous status or identity, a transitional stage that Van Gennep calls the 'liminal', which is the preparation for the resolution that takes place in the final stage. In many tribal or small-scale societies, specific ceremonies exist to accomplish this passage. In the final stage the person typically accepts social and adult identity, often confirmed by indelible scars or tattoos upon the body. In these rituals, marking the body thus signifies the end of the liminal stage. The marks are often on parts of the body that are essential to communication – that is, they are visible. Turner (2000) suggests that in modern society the erosion of the compulsory nature of tattooing as a means of inscribing social meanings and affiliations onto the body, reflects the secularisation of society. However, as we shall see later, some groups in the West are reclaiming body markings as part of their spiritual enlightenment and self-actualisation.

Mary Douglas (1966) has persuasively argued that religious rites 'promise' to make some change in external events, hence their appeal. The same is often true for secular rituals, of course. As I hope to show, drawing blood, tattooing or any other permanent marks upon the body fulfils the sometimes conscious, but mostly unconscious phantasy of an internal and external change: 'Pain lends the process meaning, while the final "altered" body sustains the illusion that the "old self" has been replaced by a new version' (Hewitt 1997: 39). Most likely the sight of blood and the experience of pain are important components because they provoke awareness of body boundaries and of the self (Hewitt 1997), while it is also the case that pain can be used to promote a feeling of transcendence. For others still, pain is an integral part of a masochistic, erotised experience in which intrapsychic pain is converted into physical pain that is then defensively sexualised.

The body modifications we are concerned with in this chapter represent acts of manipulating the body barrier, that is, of exposing what is inside the body, for example blood, often in a rather provocative manner that under- lines their communicative import. The act of shedding blood is perhaps the most universally powerful example of crossing the barrier between the external and internal body. Blood is intimately connected with practices of body modification and in many cultures it is considered a sacred substance that is frequently used for religious purposes (Hewitt 1997; Favazza 1996).[3] Body fluids that cross the body boundary, for example blood and spit, can be experienced as aggressively intrusive to the recipient (as, for example, in fears of contamination), even if the transmission is accidental or invisible (as in viral contamination).

Rebirthing and reclaiming the self

It is estimated that approximately 20 million Americans have tattoos; the number of people with piercings is likely to be even greater (Greif et al.

1999). Given the prevalence of tattoos and of piercings (less so, scarification) in the West, it seems unlikely that all those who have altered their bodies in these ways are psychologically unwell.[4] A discriminating factor appears to be the extent and context of the practice. We might view, for example, one or two tattoos, or a couple of piercings, as 'normal' because they are now fashionable, and can even be regarded as essential requirements in some subcultures. But we might take a rather different view if faced with someone whose body was entirely covered in tattoos. Take the following example:

> Andrew, a young body modifier in his 20s, has undergone hundreds of hours of tattooing, body piercing, scarification, branding and self-surgery. He studies anatomy textbooks and has performed surgery on his body using laser technology, scalpels, sutures and local anaesthetics . . . he has carefully modified his face, arms, torso, earlobes, genitals, wrists, and ankles, and has added over 100 various piercings to his body.
> (Pitts 2003: 1–2)

It is hard not to be both unsettled and concerned by the scale of Andrew's body modification, though it should be noted that Andrew is not a psychiatric patient. Like many body modifiers, Andrew explains what he does in terms of control: 'You can take control of what you otherwise could not' (quoted in Pitts 2003: 2). As he describes cutting his face, the interviewer asks him, 'Why the face?' to which Andrew replies: 'It is a commitment to being true to myself . . . you can't dress like me, you can't be me' (quoted in Pitts 2003: 171).

Andrew appears to emphasise that for him altering his body is his way of defining himself as different, and hence as separate from someone whom he says might 'want to be him'. To put it another way, his actions could be construed as an unconscious attempt to control an object that might otherwise fuse with him and appropriate his body and mind. For him, asserting his separate self requires very concrete measures: his whole body is marked, cut open, stitched back and redefined. For someone like Andrew, body modification appears to have become an imperative, fuelled by the need to feel in complete control. Following his attempt to sub-incise his own penis, which then required numerous corrective operations, Andrew nevertheless insists that 'the body can do anything' (quoted in Pitts 2003: 171).

A proportion of the literature on body markings is heavily politicised and polemicised; it would regard Andrew's body modification as normal, if not admirable. Because such practices in the West have traditionally been linked to particular subgroups, such as those involved in sadomasochistic practices, there has been a tendency to defend, or to over-idealise, the meaning of these practices in the context of freedom of expression, or of the pursuit of spirituality, individuality and sexual excitement.

The tendency to transpose and normalise traditional practices in a modern context, eschewing altogether the question of pathology, is very apparent in the so-called *Modern Primitives* movement – a movement that supports the search for spiritual fulfilment by taming the bonds of the flesh. The term 'Modern Primitives'

> refers to individuals who, in the midst of technological change and the insecurities of modernity . . . challenge western philosophy's notions of faith in scientific, rational, profit driven progress.
>
> (Lentini 1998: 18)

Those affiliated to this group, through adopting traditional body modification practices, use them as marks of opposition to 'civilised' modernity. One of the problems with this is apparent: if Western modernity is taken to be 'bad', then primitivism becomes invested with what is 'good' thereby appropriating and reducing practices to an assumed relationship to the West, imbuing them with culturally idiosyncratic meanings, which as I suggested in the Introduction, are probably quite distinct from their original meaning. The translation and redefinition this implies is one of the reasons why I think that such practices in the West can still be legitimately questioned in terms of their individual psychic function.

A prime spokesperson for the *Modern Primitives* is Fakir Musafar – a highly articulate individual who has written extensively about his own experiences of taking body modification to extremes. He confesses to an 'urge' from a young age to modify his own body, though he does not expand on the reasons for this urge. In what he refers to as a 'body oriented adventure', he asked, for example,

> trusted friends to pierce my chest with two large hooks and suspend me by these two piercings in the style of the Native American Oglelas Sioux Sun Dance and Mandan O-Kee-Pa ceremony.
>
> (Musafar 1996: 328)

By 1991 the *Modern Primitives* movement was receiving widespread public notice, highlighting the 'globalisation' of primitive forms of body modification (Pitts 2003). Some of the practices described under this banner include scarifications, flesh hangings, 'ball dances' with weights pinned to the flesh and nails driven into the skin. Those immersed in these subcultures hail them as 'tribal' rituals, personal and political statements, and sometimes recognise them as erotic performances. In their accounts they underline the transformative qualities of these practices (see, for example, Wojcik 1985), asserting symbolic control over their bodies. This message resonated deeply among women's alternative communities, such as the lesbian community, who found ways of reclaiming their felt-to-be victimised bodies through similar forms of body modification practices (Hewitt 1997; Mifflin 1997; Pitts 2003).

The theme of control has emerged as salient not only in my clinical work, but also, interestingly, in several of the non-clinical interviews I carried out. One of the striking features of the narratives of those who have marked their skin is their emphasis on the importance of 'taking control', which is typically viewed as taking positive action. In the five interviews I undertook 'control' was a dominant theme in the narratives of four out of the five individuals. People spoke about tattoos or piercings as acts of taking control over their body, or more generally over their life. The only interviewee who did not use this language, and did not appear to have used the two piercings he had done in this way, was a twenty-two-year-old man.

> He probably best represents the more transient use of skin marking as a kind of badge of fraternity with his peers who collectively had piercings done while travelling abroad after taking their final school exams. On his return to the UK this young man kept the piercings in for a few months and then took them out when he started to attend job interviews. He told me that he did not miss them in any way and that he looked back on it as part of the 'crazy time I had . . . the kind of thing I will tell my children'. He had enjoyed what he called the 'transgressive aspect of doing something like this' as it was so at odds with his boarding school ethos, which he had just emerged from.

In other words, this man presented his piercings as part of an experimentation phase, supported by a wish to be like his friends, but this clearly did not hold greater emotional salience except in this more circumscribed way.

> By contrast, another interviewee, a man in his mid twenties, had six tattoos done on his torso and back, starting in his adolescence. He told me that he decided on the first tattoo aged sixteen. At the time he was going through a difficult phase with his parents, particularly his mother, whom he felt was very controlling. He recalled that he had 'wanted to break free of her control' and 'prove to myself that I could do what I wanted'. This also involved experimenting with drugs. However, he told me that he was able to let go of drugs, but that he continued having tattoos done. When I asked him why he had continued with tattoos, he explained that there was nothing more 'liberating' than feeling that he could alter his body.

> Another interviewee, a woman in her early twenties, explained to me that she turned to piercing her body during adolescence as a way of 'taking charge of my life' (she had pierced three parts of her body and had two piercings on her

face). When I asked her in what way a piercing helped her to feel she could do that, she told me that her parents had been so overbearing that she had never exercised any control over the course of her life. The piercings represented her attempt to 'take back control'. She vividly described the sense of elation when she had the first piercing done and how she would look at the piercing(s) subsequently and 'feel that anything was possible'. She described feeling as if she had always operated on the edge of groups, including her own family. The piercings had helped her to 'celebrate my difference in a visible way'. She felt 'proud' of what she had done.

The meaning of marking the skin can lie in the very fact of getting a tattoo, for example, as much as in their content. Often it pertains to both. Even among the five interviewees, none of whom had any history of contact with mental health services, it was clear that tattoos and piercings were meaningful choices. They appealed as emblems of empowerment or rebellion and as badges of self-determination. For some, tattoos and piercings were also spoken about as marks of disenfranchisement from the family group, or from the mainstream social group they had grown up in: they were visual signs to the wider group that they felt different.

The change in status conferred by the body marking(s) sometimes signals an attempt to overcome a challenging experience and to alter the experience itself. This is an especially important function of tattoos or piercings during adolescence as the young person tries to establish a separate personal and social identity and autonomy from parents, taking pride in the 'new' signified identity (Armstrong and Murphy 1997; Rosenblum et al. 1999). Recreating the body by marking it in some way is felt to differentiate the adolescent self from the childhood body, and from familial and cultural mores. In this respect skin markings are no different from other fashion statements that create tensions with parents or teachers, but that nevertheless give scope to young people to demarcate their body as their own and to try to define for themselves who they are, separate from parental figures. In these scenarios, even though the tattoo, say, may be felt to be 'essential', and may be fiercely defended by the young person, it does not typically have the compelling quality that is characteristic of some of the patients that I have been discussing.

In the clinical setting control is invariably an issue where body modification is part of the presentation. Many patients, however, seem to confuse choosing and hence controlling their so-called body art for control over the given body (Pitts 2003) and its unconscious identifications. Although people like the 'professional' body modifier, Andrew, appear to inhabit an internal world where the body can do anything, the sense of freedom and autonomy that he revels in, is an illusion: not only does the body have limits, but also the self cannot be rewritten by writing on the body since the body can never be reclaimed in any concrete sense: a body that has been abused, for example, *has* had that experience. No matter how many tattoos that abused individuals inscribe on their body, part of who they are will always be someone who has endured the experience of abuse and who has been affected by it, somehow.

It is important to note that all the practices I have been discussing are not just ways of marking the body: they penetrate the flesh. They cause pain. Piercing is followed by several weeks of tenderness while healing. Tattooing is also a painful process followed by a period of transformation in which the wound heals and the redesigned body emerges. Scarification involves inflicting a wound so as to purposefully create a visible scar. These forms of body modification accrue psychic significance not simply from the final, visible product, but for some people, perhaps even primarily, from the *process* of physical transformation – a process that mirrors that of birth. Like the birth process, which if unaided by anaesthesia is painful, many cultures consider pain to be a crucial element for imparting meaning to the change to the body. Yoruban scarification, for example, not only is considered aesthetically pleasing, but also announces the marked individual's fortitude and ability to endure pain. Scar tissue is a concrete sign that pain has been endured, as well as providing visible evidence of a healing process, and some individuals underline this aspect as significant (Favazza 1996; Sweetman 2000).

> One of the interviewees I quoted earlier, a man who had six tattoos, told me that he was also a keen runner and liked to 'push my body to the limits of endurance'. I explored with him whether the experience of pain, that is also a part of tattooing, was important to him. He replied that he did not like pain, but that pain was an 'inevitable part of having a tattoo'. Interestingly he followed this up, jokingly, by saying, 'Women experience pain during child-birth, but they keep having babies don't they!' I observed that this was an interesting association to which he replied, very thoughtfully, that he absolutely felt that with each tattoo he had 'brought to life' important aspects of his personality, and that 'the pain was worth it'.

> Similarly, another interviewee, a man in his late twenties, with four small tattoos, explained to me that tattooing was for him an expression of his creativity. When I asked him to clarify what he meant by 'creative', he replied,

> > It's like you have this body and you want to customise it so that it reflects who you really are, and who you are changes over time so my tattoos reflect these changes.

He told me that he spent a great deal of time researching his tattoos and that he felt 'committed to having more done in the future'. I asked him about the use of the word 'committed'. He explained that he saw it as something that he 'owed' to himself, a way of 'taking care of my body, of myself'.

This interviewee introduces the notion of tattooing as a creative act that allows the person to customise his body to reflect his 'true' nature ('who you really are'). It is another way of describing giving birth to a felt-to-be 'true' self, or as another interviewee put it, to 'bring to life' important aspects of himself.

Later in his interview he told me that while he did not regard himself as religious, he experienced being tattooed as having a 'spiritual quality'. I was intrigued by this and followed it up with him. He explained that it was hard to put it into words, but that he felt in some way 'united with the tattooist . . . at peace with myself'. I asked him if it mattered who the tattooist was and he replied emphatically that this was crucial for him, that he needed to feel that the tattooist 'cares about what he is doing'.

One tattoo artist concurs with this, taking up the analogy of 'giving birth' and connects the pain of the process of tattooing with the pleasure of creativity: 'and it's like labour too . . . to go through this pain to create a thing, to get it out of you. The design is inside of you, it just wants to get out' (quoted in Seeger 1993: 7). Here, the tattoo is explicitly likened to a baby that has to be born.

Two of the five interviewees used the word 'intimate' to describe the process of being tattooed. One described the 'relationship of trust' that she had with the tattooist, who would be involved with her in choosing the design. When I invited her to expand on what she meant by 'trust', she said that, 'because your body is touched by the tattooist, how could it not be intimate . . . I don't mean sexual . . . but there is care somewhere in there'. Another interviewee described the experience as: 'spiritual . . . you give yourself over to this other person who will transform your body permanently'.

These descriptions are deeply evocative of a close, warm maternal relationship. The 'caring' touch of the tattooist emerges as a salient part of the experience for some, though there is sometimes a fine line between the so-called caring touch and the actual violence that is being perpetrated on the body. Interestingly, tattooists' own accounts of their work highlights that some perceive a maternal function in relation to their clients: 'It's totally intimate', says New York artist Emma Porcupine. 'The bizarre thing is you have a bond with the people you tattoo and then the person goes. It's like having a child that you won't see again' (quoted in Mifflin 1997: 98).

As in the tattooing procedure, pain is sometimes an important element of piercing. Although some people may glean erotic pleasure from the pain of piercing, others are extremely apprehensive, if relieved, that they can withstand the pain and they emerge from the experience with an enhanced sense of their physical strength and integrity (Jacobson and Luzzatto 2004). Indeed the twenty-two-year-old man who had two piercings done while on his gap year told me that he felt 'terrified' at the prospect of having his tongue pierced, but that he was very pleased once he had managed to overcome his fear. In this sense we might understand one of the functions of these experiences, especially during adolescence, as reassuring the young person that his body is a grown-up body that is resilient in the face of pain.

Myers's (1992) research suggests that many piercees are conscious of a need for a rite of passage that is 'painful, bloody, and mark producing' and recognise there are appropriations of ritual elements of other cultures. One tattoo artist tellingly called her body modification a 'mini magical support system' (Seeger 1993). The painful process and the permanence of the product remains an integral part of the significance of body modification (Hewitt 1997: 93):

> The art of being cut and surviving is a very strengthening and powerful experience . . . to ask to be cut and then bleed and then end up with something beautiful . . . and then it heals and you have it, and you're proud of it – that can be very empowering.
>
> (Vale and Juno 1990: 105)

The way in which skin markings facilitate an experience of giving birth to a 'new' self, and hence may, in some cases, reflect an actualisation of the self-made phantasy, is further supported by the reports of the pleasure gained from looking after wounds.

One of my adolescent patients, who had ten tattoos and twenty piercings, described how she 'enjoyed' nursing her wounds after each tattoo or piercing. For her, this was a central component of the process of transforming her body from one she hated to one she felt comfortable in. She described the care and patience with which she attended to the various rituals to keep her skin protected from infection, as if she were talking about nursing a newborn. In this young woman, the descriptions of her devoted self-care were especially striking as in so many other respects she neglected herself. She had experienced a very depressed mother as she was growing up. Through the transference she conveyed her conviction that the object would not respond to her needs. The only way she seemed to manage was by cutting herself off from everyone and creating the illusion of self-sufficiency, which of course also made it incredibly hard to engage her in therapy. As she nursed her wounds she was able to be both loving mother to her wounded baby self who, through the tattooing or piercing process, was now given a new lease of life. By marking her body she assumed total ownership of it and created the illusion of giving birth to a new body whose ties to the original object were severed.

Envelopes of suffering

In the West skin markings have assumed ritual and therapeutic significance, legitimising the actualisation of what I refer to as the self-made and reclaiming phantasies. I want to focus now in particular on the reclaiming phantasy as it may be enacted, in some individuals, through skin markings.

Women's emphasis on the tattoo in particular as an expression of personal growth has made it very popular with self-help and New Age enthusiasts (Mifflin 1997). DeMello (2000) has persuasively documented the origins of tattoos in a working-class subculture, which, she argues, have now been appropriated into the mainstream trend of self-actualisation and non-professional 'healing'.

No matter how popular they have now become, they are not devoid of meaning. Skin markings invariably tell a story.

A very articulate nineteen-year-old woman explained to me that her decision to pierce her navel and tongue had nothing to do with fashion. For her it represented a 'deliberate' decision taken after her boyfriend left her. When I asked her what sense she made of this sequence of events, she told me that she had been very much in love with her boyfriend and had 'given myself to him body and soul'. This had been her first sexual encounter and deeply meaningful to her. When her boyfriend left her for one of her best friends, she felt devastated. She explained to me that she needed to mark her body as 'belonging to me again' – that's when she decided to have the first piercing. She expressed with vivid poignancy the way she wanted to make her body her own again, somehow undoing the pain of loss by altering the surface of her body.

Like many who turn to various forms of skin marking, this young woman's experience highlights how body modification can be used to reclaim the body, and hence the self, from another's perceived claim on it. Tattoos have also been viewed by some women as providing a way of rebuilding their physical and sexual image post-mastectomy, for example (Mifflin 1997). Aptly, the term 'psychic armour' has been used to describe tattoos acquired during such periods of painful change or transition.

The connection between a history of physical and/or sexual violence and body markings is also well documented (Davis 1995; Mifflin 1997; Pitts 2003). The literature on tattoos is replete with examples of narratives that illustrate the use of tattooing to overwrite an experience of violation that is felt to be inscribed on the body – that is, I am suggesting, the skin markings provide the means for actualising the reclaiming phantasy, expelling from the body a felt-to-be alien, intrusive object. Indeed DeMello (2000) – who is herself tattooed – argues that tattoos 'liberate the body'. Julia Moon, a tattoo artist, describes her art as a way of 'healing that wounded child, that hurt place, the pain that is left over from the slings and arrows of out-rageous past lives' (quoted in Mifflin 1997: 109).

It will be clear by now that skin markings cannot be reduced to one single meaning or function, and that they are not intrinsically a symptom of pathology. The cultural context in which they occur is invariably relevant to their interpretation. Having said this, I am also suggesting that marking the surface of the skin is for many people a very meaningful choice, not just another fashion accessory. At this point I want to refocus the discussion on individuals who have clearly taken body modification to extremes, or who use skin markings as their *primary* way of managing internal conflicts.

In my attempts to understand the function of skin markings I have turned to two key sources in psychoanalytic theory: the ideas of Didier Anzieu (1989) and of Esther Bick (1968) about the psychic function of the skin. I have found their work very illuminating as they both capture the vicissitudes of the dual processes of identification and differentiation as they are lived out in the earliest skin-to-skin relationship with the object of desire.

Bick (1968), in a seminal paper, emphasised the developmental import-ance of a containing object in relation to the most primitive binding of parts of the personality not as yet differentiated from parts of the body. She was clear that the mother played a crucial role in helping the baby to install internally this containing function:

> But this internal function of containing parts of the self is dependent initially on the introjection of an external object, experienced as capable of fulfilling this function.
>
> (Bick 1968: 484)

When the mother could not help in this way, Bick suggested that

> the need for a containing object would seem, in infantile unintegrated states, to produce a *frantic search* for a object – a light, a voice, a smell or other sensual object – which can hold the attention and thereby be experienced, momentarily at least, as holding parts of the personality together.
>
> (Bick 1968: 484; my italics)

Thus Bick highlights the central organising function of skin sensations – that is, that the actual sensations act as a primary bodily container. Bick's 'frantic search for the object' resonates with the experiences of a number of patients for whom the tattoo or the piercing felt imperative, often during periods of crisis, as a means of holding themselves together. Ulnik (2007), based on his work with dermatological conditions, argues that the mutilation of the skin may represent an attempt to maintain the boundaries of the body and of the ego, as well as helping the individual to feel intact and coherent. All the forms of body modification discussed in this chapter represent attempts to lend corporeal solidity to expressions of individuality and of separateness. They are ways of anchoring the self by permanently marking the body.

Bick (1968) argued that disturbance of the primal skin function could lead to a development of a 'second skin' formation through which dependence on the object is replaced by a kind of pseudo-independence. This might result in the inappropriate use of certain mental functions, or the creation of a muscular shell in an attempt to create a substitute for the skin container function. The second skin would therefore be based on muscularity rather than on identification with the containing object. In my experience, skin markings may function as potential second skins. Some patients appear to use the ritual of being tattooed, and the after-care tatoos require, for example, as the kind of substitute container Bick was referring to. The case of Mr Z., that I will describe shortly, is an example of this. A young man with fairly extensive skin markings, he turned to tattooing during our breaks in the therapy as a way of holding himself together.

Anzieu (1989) develops Bick's ideas suggesting that the ego is primarily structured as a *skin ego*. The skin ego, according to Anzieu, is

> a mental image of which the ego of the child makes use during the early phases of its development to represent itself as an ego containing psychical contents, on the basis of its experience of the surface of the body.
>
> (Anzieu 1989: 40)

He suggests that the baby acquires a perception of a bodily surface through the contact with the skin of the mother when he is being fed or cared for. He underlines the vital function of the experience of being held in the mother's arms, caressed, dressed or washed by her and he emphasises that this complements the feeding experience.

At this early stage the nascent skin ego is imaginarily represented as an outer shell that envelops the whole of the psychical apparatus in the same way that the skin covers the body. The skin ego originates in the skin imaginatively shared by mother and child – what Anzieu (1989) refers to as a *common skin*. Ideally this ensures an 'adhesive identification' between mother and baby. The successful surrendering of a common skin is, how-ever, painful. But it is its successful surrender that allows for the internal-isation and identification with a part of the mother that supports the baby's physical and psychical development, 'a supporting object which the child hugs and which supports it' (Anzieu 1989: 90).

When the skin ego is operating well, it fulfils an important protective function; it provides a *narcissistic envelope* that supplies the baby with a sense of security. However, the protective function may be undermined or absent in some individuals who then exist in what Anzieu (1989) evocatively refers to as an *envelope of suffering*. This envelope, for example, may be inscribed with shame, or to put it another way, this envelope bears the projections of the object.

Anzieu's notion of a common skin is particularly helpful. In several of the cases that I have seen, I understood the skin markings to be an uncon-scious attempt to reject an imaginary common skin that, rather than lovingly enveloping the self, was felt to imprison the self.

Mr Z., a twenty-year-old man, is a good example of this. When we first met my eyes were immediately drawn to the top of his left eyebrow where he had three letters tattooed and one piercing, and to his heavily tattooed arms. When we got to my office and sat down, I found his posture challenging, as if he was invading my space. He said he was not interested in talking to a psychologist, that *he* did not have a problem. When I asked him *who* had a problem then, he replied that his mother would have a lot to say, and then he laughed dismissively.

Mr Z.'s initial challenging posture became a fixture, but it did not stop him from staying in treatment, once weekly, for several years. Over this time we talked about his tattoos and the piercings he had on various parts of his body. He started 'taking care' of his body, as he tellingly described the practices of tattooing and piercing, in his adolescence. The only son of a single mother, Mr Z. grew up on a rough council estate. He hated school, and wore his numerous exclusions as badges of honour. He never achieved academically, but he was evidently bright. By the time I met him he was unemployed, finding it very hard to sustain any job longer than a few weeks. He was referred for help by his doctor because he suffered from claustrophobia and had experi-enced two very severe panic attacks while travelling on the Underground. Initially he had felt very ashamed of this and it was hard for him to accept that he needed help. Nevertheless, he had a good relationship with his maternal aunt, who seemed to intuitively sense this young man's considerable diffi-culties and encouraged him to stay in treatment.

Over time Mr Z. began to explore his highly ambivalent and aggressively charged relationship with his mother who had conceived him 'by mistake', herself aged only sixteen. Their relationship was very volatile and he told me that when he was younger, she had been violent towards him. His father was a drug dealer with whom he had little contact after the age of ten. Both parents were described as physically abusive and I gained the impression that he felt deeply shamed, having internalised an image of himself as unappealing and with no prospects. In his interactions with peers he was quick to feel 'got at', as he put it. His physical presentation was simultaneously threatening and diffident as if he was always anticipating some rebuke or abuse.

Mr Z. felt readily encroached on by others. He did not want a regular girlfriend because 'she would want too much'. He ensured he kept me at a distance too, reacting to some of my interpretations, however tentative on my part, as if they were nevertheless psychic invasions he had to protect himself from, typically by missing sessions (we met once weekly). His claustrophobia on the Underground was yet another manifestation of a core claustrophobic anxiety that shrouded his life.

Although Mr Z. experienced his mother as neglectful, conveying to me that she had seemingly never taken any interest in him, he also experienced her as controlling of him and interfering in his affairs. He told me that she 'went berserk' when he had his first tattoo done aged sixteen (interestingly the same age when she gave birth to him) – a reaction that seemed to confirm for Mr Z. the importance of his decision to mark his body in direct opposition to his mother's wishes. He felt that she was deeply insecure and that because of her anxiety she would always find ways of making him feel guilty. When he left home aged seventeen, after a row, she called the police, alleging that he had assaulted her, which he assured me he had felt like doing, but had never actually done.

Mr Z. conveyed an experience with an object who owned him and from whom separation was felt to be impossible. Breaks in our work were invariably stormy junctures as he both relished telling me that he would not miss me, that I 'fancied myself as important', while at the same time they triggered intense anxiety, exposing the psychic underbelly of his idealisation of separateness: the fear of being abandoned.

In the first year of treatment our breaks were literally 'marked' on his body as he seemed to feel the urge to do something to his body and he acted on it. I thought that any hint of dependency on me when we were not meeting was so terrifying that he needed the tattoo as proof, in his mind, that he would not be drawn back into a fused state with me. This helped to reassure him that he was quite separate from me. At first he resisted any interpretation of this behaviour, but over time we came to understand the function of the skin markings in holding himself together during our breaks. In his phantasy he retreated to a place where he related only to himself (i.e. into a monadic as opposed to dyadic body) – his marked body the solid proof of his independence, that he did not need me and that I could not intrude into his physical and mental space.

Look at me: body markings as visual violence

Skin markings allow some individuals not only to reclaim the body, but also, by virtue of their visual nature, they function as a signal to the world; they powerfully communicate that all is not well. The tattoo, for example, can be a visible mark of personal distress – made visible presumably because there exists in the mind an object who needs to look and see the damage. Nowhere is this more painfully apparent than in the case of Stephanie Farinelli, now renowned in the tattooing community, for having elected to tattoo a necklace of penises of various sizes – the number of penises inscribed on her body has now increased to over one hundred (Mifflin 1997). As she discusses her reasons for getting the tattoos done, she hints at considerable inner turmoil as she discloses that she has problems with her body, feeling she is not very sexual or feminine. This is a body, she reveals, that she simply 'just wanted to cover up' (quoted in Mifflin 1997). In covering up she nevertheless exposes her pain for the world to see.

In the interviews I carried out, just as in my clinical work, skin markings appear primarily to provide a means for demarcating the boundary of the body as separate and as belonging to the self. In so far as skin markings tend to explicitly give expression to a wish to be 'different' (Sweetman 2000), on the surface at least, they do not share the same conscious goal of cosmetic surgery, which for many people is quite the opposite, namely to homogenise the way they look to fit in with a dominant aesthetic (see Chapters 4 and 7) and be desirable.

In my experience, people who modify the skin surface are less likely to do so with the explicit or implicit aim of becoming more desirable to the other.[5] I have not seen enough cases overall to be able to make a valid comparison, but my hypothesis is that in this group, relative to the cosmetic surgery group, the psychic function of body markings appears to be primarily a defence against fusion with the object, whereas cosmetic surgery more readily lends itself to creating the phantasy of an idealised version of the self fused with an idealised object.

Some individuals who feel compelled to mark their skin appear to need to do so because of the impact this will have on the other. I can think of no better example of this than that of the aggressive use of the body in the punk culture of the 1970s. Some readers will recall, for example, the striking appearance, and the shocking performances, by the Sex Pistols and Iggy Pop, who included self-mutilation as part of their acts. But closer to the memory and/or imagination of most readers is likely to be the punk in the street.

The punk movement was primarily a visual form of grievance. Punks integrated their self-mutilation and social protest into their daily lives and 'declared the streets the stage' (Hewitt 1997) on which their pain was publicised. They manipulated body boundaries to communicate internal chaos and rage. They revelled in the abject, rubbing the observer's face in it – sometimes quite literally (I have in mind here some of the performances by the Sex Pistols). The 'punk aesthetic of displaying body fluids normally kept inside the body (e.g. blood, spit and vomit)' (Hewitt 1997: 110) is an antithesis to the integrity and hygiene of the Western ideal body. Body piercing and self-laceration accomplished the goal to 'look as horrifying and repugnant as possible' (Henry 1989).

With their insistent exposure of bodily fluids, punks sometimes appeared less as rebellious adolescents than as enraged babies who were calling out to society/mother to take heed of their plight – a plight they exposed in the language of the body. Importantly, they were enraged and *aggrieved*. Their physical presentation can be understood to have been as much about a communication regarding their internal state as about the enactment of visual violence perpetrated on the onlooker.

My own reading of the more extreme forms of punk is that the body was used as ineluctable proof of the harm that had been done to the individual. These were individuals who wanted to be seen and who looked at the other with hatred. The punk state, in its more extreme forms, could therefore be understood as a state of profound grievance.[6] Their striking appearance forcefully imposed itself on the observer, eliciting sometimes a feeling of disgust and of threat. The body was the primary language of recrimination towards an object that was felt to have wronged the self.

Deliberate body modification can communicate a similar state of defiance and, like punks, many body modifiers enjoy the 'shock value' of their changes (Pitts 2003). I am suggesting therefore that the visual impact on the observer is an important part of the dynamic that is being unconsciously enacted, as I will illustrate later through my work with Mr J.

Skin markings serve potentially the dual function of revealing and of concealing. In some patients with marked body dysmorphia, tattoos are the equivalent of wearing a hood to conceal the face one feels to be ugly. One patient with BDD used tattoos, as she put it, to 'distract' the other's gaze away from how ugly she believed she was. On the whole, however, I have found skin markings to more consistently serve the function of marking the self as 'different' from a designated internal and/or external 'other' – and this difference is what is on display.[7]

Andrew, the extreme body modifier I quoted at the start of the chapter, is described by the author who interviewed him as 'visually shocking' to many observers. In his study of the grotesque body in medieval carnival, Bakhtin (1984) argued that 'because the body is a site of investment, control and cultural production, anomalous bodies can be understood as threatening to the social order' (Bakhtin 1984: 98).

But 'anomalous bodies' are psychically threatening too as they expose the inside of the body as much as the outside – they expose us to what Kristeva termed the abject (see Chapter 5), and this has a powerful impact on the one who looks. It is not unreasonable therefore to ask 'who' needs to be shocked, 'who' in the internal world incites the violence that is a part of these practices.

The kiss of fire

For a minority of people, as I would like to now illustrate through my work with Mr J., the extensive modification of the body through tattoos, piercings and scarification aims to shock and triumph over the object.

Mr J., who had been very committed to the punk movement in his youth, helped me to understand that an important function of his body modification went beyond his need to feel in control; rather, his altered appearance had been his main weapon with which to attack the object.

I met Mr J. when he was in his early forties. He was a very bright man, but his life had taken a very bleak turn. His body, ravaged by years of drug addiction, tattoos, piercings and scars, imposed itself as testament of what he later told me was the 'injustice' of his life. He had been off drugs for some years by the time I met him. When he came into treatment he worked part time in a shop and lived in a hostel. He came from a relatively well-to-do family from which he was almost completely estranged. He only had very intermittent contact with his sister, whom he occasionally called. She was a mental health professional and it had been she who suggested he sought help from his general practitioner.

Mr J. had descended into drugs as a late adolescent, at which point he also dropped out of education and left the family home to live in a squat with friends who felt similarly disaffected with life around them. He never went back and seemingly was never asked back. He felt that his parents could never forgive him for 'shaming the family'. Aged seven, he recalled his mother once telling him he was 'repugnant' when he accidentally spilt his dinner all over himself. This memory was one of several shaming experiences that conveyed the strong impression that for Mr J. his skin was indeed an envelope of suffering.

Mr J. was a twin, but his sister was 'the first to be born', he had told me the first time we met. He said that his mother had never coped with the fact of twins and that she managed this by effectively acknowledging only the existence of his sister. He was not sure, but he thought that his mother had been very depressed after his birth. His father was seemingly always working and a very withdrawn man, whom Mr J. recalled would shut himself away in his study and read. His sister was described as a paragon of virtue: she was pretty, bright, 'always doing the right thing'. Although his contempt for her masked considerable envy of her privileged position in the parental affections, Mr J. nevertheless seemed to feel that she never meant him any harm. Over time he was able to see that his rejection of the family had probably caused her a great deal of pain. One of the positive outcomes of his therapy was his ability to re-establish a closer relationship with her.

If I looked carefully at Mr J. I could see that he could have been an attractive man. But Mr J.'s actual physical presentation was striking: he looked much older than his years, his hair was falling out and his face was covered in piercings and a small tattoo. He also had a long scar running down his left cheek, which I later learnt had been self-inflicted.

The impact of his physical presentation was powerful, such that I found that I struggled to keep up eye contact with him (I was seeing him once weekly face-to-face). I wanted to avoid looking, not because I feared being intrusive, but rather because I had the peculiar sensation that *I* would be intruded upon. I also frequently found myself musing about what he must have looked like before he had altered his face. All this preoccupation in my mind was striking, given that Mr J.'s reason for seeking help had nothing to do with how he felt about his appearance. I began to think, however, that the way he looked was important to him because of how it made the other person feel. Related to this was the fact of his poor hygiene, which meant that he filled my room with a terrible smell that lingered for some time after he had left.

To begin with Mr J. spoke about his internal state indirectly through his political convictions. He was critical of the Conservative government (which was then in power); he 'hated' them and he felt profoundly pessimistic about the possibility of a nuclear war. There was no doubt that Mr J. felt very passionate about these issues and was knowledgeable about both history and politics, but it was also clear to me that these passions reflected on his troubled relationship with his family with whom he was at war – he had not spoken to his parents for over ten years. His altered body was his nuclear bomb, which he had exploded in their face, especially when he had his facial tattoo done in his late adolescence.

It was not long after this tattoo that Mr J. branded himself on his back – a practice that he chillingly referred to, and is indeed described in the body modification literature too, as the 'kiss of fire'. This involved using metal strips that are heated up until they are red hot. The hot metal is then applied to the skin. The aim, he told me, was to create a visible scar. As he explained this to me, dispassionately, I could not help but wonder who was being sadistically punished, who was being triumphed over as his body survived this painful procedure.

Mr J.'s father had died two years prior to the start of the therapy and he had not attended the funeral. His mother was now in a home as she had dementia and he had never visited her. He made it clear that he had no intention of 'setting eyes on her again' – a meaningful and charged choice of words given the way the gazing relationship had developed between them.

Mr J. attended his sessions reasonably regularly, he filled the hour with lots of angry words, he filled my room with the smell of his unwashed body, and then he left. He came to see me to talk and not to listen to me. Mr J. made no concessions to the other. There was no alternative point of view to his own, hence my interpretations were at best redundant, and at worst a source of deep irritation that provoked on occasions a contemptuous assault on me. My experience was one of feeling used by him as a kind of 'dump'. Yet, I was also moved by his predicament and the anguish of his life.

For many months I struggled with both the visual impact he made on me and with the smell. Yet, although I was clear that I needed to take this up, it proved very hard to do so because I was anxious not to shame him. It was probably difficult too because I knew that it would have taken us straight to the heart of his hatred.

Over time I came to understand more clearly that through his visual presentation and his smell, Mr J. had effectively repeatedly shown me his offensive: this was how he assaulted the other and punished them for their perceived crime. A key nodal point in our work coincided with my ability eventually to talk with him directly about the use he made of his body. On this occasion Mr J. had arrived to the session smelling worse than usual and I soon realised that he must have trodden in dog dirt. The smell was overpowering and within minutes of sitting down Mr J. remarked on it, looked at the sole of his shoe and said: 'It's shit . . . those bloody dogs'. I had expected/ wanted him to get up and go to the loo to clean it up, but instead Mr J. stayed put, as if he expected *me* to do something about it, as if in his mind I was one of the 'bloody dogs' that had soiled his shoe and I should clean up the mess. I observed that he seemed to feel as if I had brought this awful smell into the room and that I needed to do something about it. Mr J. laughed and said that therapy was about 'dealing with people's shit whoever it belonged to.' This throwaway comment struck at the core of his grievance: he felt soiled by someone else's 'shit'.

I said that from the beginning of our work he had wanted me not only to look at, and actually smell, how shitty he felt inside, but also to know that this was not his 'shit'. I had never spoken with Mr J. in quite this way before but it appeared, for once, to create some space for reflection as he did not reply with his more characteristically contemptuous tone.

He said that he knew he was full of shit. He added that he could see that he had attacked his body 'beyond repair', he feared, but that when he was younger he had felt a powerful urge to transform his body. I observed that he had transformed it in the most offensive way possible – that each time his parents or anyone else looked at it they could only be shocked. Mr J. agreed and said that his body had been his 'weapon', but that now the gun was turning on him. More in touch with the pain of the damage he had inflicted on himself as well as on others, Mr J. said that he could not imagine anyone ever wanting to get close to him, that he was doomed to eternal loneliness.

I said he was letting me know something about how dangerous closeness to another person felt. After a silence Mr J. said that he did not know what it meant to be close. He thought that he had been close to the people he had shared a squat with after he left home, but he had stayed in contact with only one of then. He then spontaneously told me that when he first became a punk, he had been walking down the street and an older woman had shouted some obscenity at him. He had replied in kind. He recalled enjoying this exchange. I asked him why he thought this incident had come back into his mind now. Mr J. at first said he had no idea, but he was then able to tell me that he recalled how pleased he had been that he had made an impact on this total stranger, that this is what he had wanted: to be noticed. He recalled enjoying his days as a punk because people would always stare at him and that made him feel powerful, in control of his life. I put to him that he wanted me not just to notice him, but also to really know first hand about his hatred and how hatred actually held him together. Coming to the sessions unwashed, leaving his smell behind in my room, ensured that I bore the full brunt of it.

I will not go into this session further, but suffice to say that once we were able to develop a dialogue about how he used his body in his relationships with others, including me, this opened up a vitally important area of explora- tion which took us to the heart of the matter: his profound grievance towards his parents, and his mother more specifically, whom he could not forgive for not loving him. An early memory that he reported involved being at the seaside, aged seven, he thought. His mother called his sister over to her. She wanted to take a picture of her because she looked lovely. He was standing nearby but she did not call him. Mr J. returned several times to this memory as if it was emblematic of her neglect of him, which he evidently experienced concretely at the level of his body-self.

More than any other patient Mr J. helped me to understand the other side of his wish to look as offensive as possible: his longing to be looked at with loving eyes. It took me some time to understand this because the destructiveness towards the object was so pronounced that it blinded me to the way in which by attracting the other's gaze through being offensive there was also a hidden longing to be seen to be lovable. This helped me to also make sense of my preoccupation in my mind with how he looked as if I was searching beneath the layers of this assaulted body for the man he *could* have been – the kind of man who could have been more immediately lovable.

As I write this now, it seems, of course, obvious in one sense. But at the time the violent impact of his physicality made it hard for me to see through this visual barrier. Once I was able to do so, this proved to be a very moving aspect of our work as I could then speak with him about his longing for some identification with a positive image I might have of him.

I also came to understand that in some cases, as with Mr J., when the loving gaze and touch of the other cannot be found, the longing for them can become perverted and the body is subjected to painful procedures. In his case, as in others, the function of the body modification was to create a fusion in hatred with the object, bound and burnt forever into the skin. The 'kiss of fire', a body modification practice that is horrifying in its brutality, illustrates the transformation of a thwarted longing for a loving kiss into a kiss that literally burns the skin.

The penetration and marking of the skin may thus be seen to perform a number of unconscious functions. By way of concluding this chapter here is a summary that reflects my own understanding of what may drive the pursuit of the various types of skin markings that have been discussed so far:

- A denial of separation or loss – the unconscious phantasy is of being fused with the object. This concerns the refusal to mourn the body of the lost object – the body itself becomes a kind of haunting – a perpetual return to that which cannot be mourned.
- An attempt at separation – the unconscious phantasy is that the alien other felt to reside inside the body can be overwritten and, in some cases, that it can be ripped out violently or torn off (that is, the self-made or reclaiming phantasies may be operative).
- An attempt at covering up a felt-to-be shameful body – the unconscious phantasy is of distracting, and so controlling, the gaze of the other.

- An attempt to restore an inner sense of fragmentation – the unconscious phantasy is that by attracting the other's gaze some identification with the image the other sees will be possible and will re-establish a sense of inner cohesion.
- An expression of grievance against the object – the unconscious phantasy is of inflicting pain, and hence of punishing the object, by exposing them to the ravaged site of their crime (e.g. the disfigured body, as in Mr J.'s case).

This list should not be treated as comprehensive. It merely speaks to the diverse, unconscious psychic functions of what may ostensibly appear as homogeneous and culturally sanctioned ways of modifying the surface of the body.

Conclusion
An order of pure decision

I began this book with Danny's story and it seems apposite to conclude with a few words about his development. Danny's early life was punctuated by violence and loss and his physical appearance testified to this. Like all the patients I have discussed, Danny's initial difficulty in reflecting on his experience transformed his body into a haunting ground for the pain, loss, terror and hatred that could not be mentalised.

As the work progressed and he allowed me, slowly, to get to know him, the damage he had inflicted on himself, and on his objects, through his attack on the body, became more real for him. It was painful to observe the dawning of an awareness that no matter how much he might now better understand past events (and regret them), his body nevertheless bore their trace – the literal scars of his history. There is a marked contrast between the omnipotent phantasies I outlined in preceding chapters, which sustain the belief that reality can be changed through changing the body, and the reality of a body that visibly exposes inner turmoil through its altered form and/or surface – changes that often cannot be reversed.

Danny did surprisingly well given his inauspicious early experiences. He was aided by his sharp intellect and his likeableness. When he was eventually released from custody, he went to college and pursued a meaningful vocation that allowed him to make some reparation. He kept in touch with me, in writing, for many years. He managed to sustain in his mind a helpful connection not only with me but also with a probation officer he had grown very attached to.

One of the things that Danny wrote to me about was his experience of other people's negative reactions on account of his extensive tattoos. While in custody, a setting in which so many of his peers were similarly tattooed and/or pierced, he was protected from the judgements he had to contend with once he was living in the community again. In one of his letters,[1] Danny referred to feeling 'imprisoned' by his extensive tattoos, as if he felt that no matter how much he tried to move on with his life, what people saw when they looked at him was this traumatic past and, most disturbingly for him, his hatred.

Danny tried to have his facial tattoo removed, but it left visible scarring in its place.[2] For many people who modify their body, the modifications are not reversible; the ease with which nowadays a range of body modifications can be accessed bypasses this important fact. Even modern laser techniques for removing tattoos cause variable degrees of scarring – a concrete reminder that we can never entirely successfully cover up or rewrite the history inscribed on the body.

Danny had to find his own way of integrating this fact into his sense of who he felt he was, and who he aspired to become, and so find a way of living in this scarred body. His experience is sobering, but the painful reality he had to face up to is one that is currently dangerously sidestepped in the rhetoric that supports the cult of self-improvement and self-cure through modifying the body – a trend that we are now witnessing on a broad social scale.[3]

Feeling at home in our body and mind is challenging: it always requires psychic work no matter how good our early experiences have been, though the experience of feeling loved and desired in early life is a noteworthy asset in this respect. When we are not buffered by early loving experiences, this can feel like an impossible task.

Additionally, at a societal level, other forces are operating and impacting on these internal processes. The delicate and intricate processes that support the establishment of a secure sense of self confidently rooted in the body, and the capacity to reflect on experience rather than enacting it on, and through, the body, are undermined by the relentless emphasis on transformation and change made possible by a staggering range of new technologies. These external trends impinge on how we negotiate the task of integrating body and mind into a coherent image and experience of ourselves.

Faced with the external complexity of the demands of the modern world (especially for young people), and the internal complexity and pain inherent in what is psychically required to develop a body and mind that feel one's own, it is tempting to retreat into more manageable self-improvement projects: the body lends itself to becoming just such a 'project' (Giddens 1991). It can become solely an instrument for personal gratification, reassurance and comfort (a monadic body) rather than relating sensuality to communication with others – in other words, a dyadic body (Frank 1991).

The rate of technological and medical advances that allow for sometimes dramatic alterations to the body's surface far outstrips the mind's capacity to reconcile the triumph of progress with the pain of the inevitable limitations of reality – and especially of our embodied nature. As Nature is 'transformed into a field of human action' (Giddens 1991), we have seemingly been freed from the idea that birth is destiny and believe that we can redesign ourselves at will.

Nowadays the body's vulnerability is overshadowed by a host of medical and technological advances that invite us to see our bodies as negotiable works-in-progress.[4] I am not suggesting that science and technology are a 'bad' thing, but like all good things they can be put to 'bad' use. Technology de-abjectifies the human body, banishing the messy, internal body and its expelled or leaked fluids. It creates distance from our organic nature and limitations, protecting us from the crude reality, as Becker (1973) provocatively put it, that we are 'Gods with anuses'.

An important question is the fate of the body in the mind as the very experience of intimacy is being shaped and transformed by medical and technological advances, not least the impact of virtual reality – a form of communication that is predicated on distance. Anzieu (1990) has compellingly argued that nowadays it is no longer sexuality that is repressed; rather, it is the sensual body, the body that comes into being through the other, the body that is denied by technology. The Internet – a wondrous medium for communication – nevertheless has some potentially undesirable psychic implications, because it

> modifies in an entirely new way the feeling of isolation characteristic of each member of the human species; as a result, one's relationship with oneself and the way in which one's internal mental life is cathected are also modified. The Internet facilitates immediate virtual communication in which the difference between the sexes and between generations no longer plays its traditional role. . . . Virtual reality has a completely different relationship to the pleasure/unpleasure principle and to the reality principle from that of fantasy, because it offers an illusion of what is real, thus circumventing the need to process mentally the links and transformations on which is based a positive relationship between the internal mental world and external reality.
>
> (Guignard 2008: 121)

Virtual reality can fuel omnipotent phantasies. In the cosmetic field, cosmetic surgeons can show their prospective patients just how much they could achieve through computerised 'before and after' simulations. From the point of view of the internal world, these virtual images of the transformed self are pseudo-representations of a pseudo-self. They provide compelling visions of a more desirable self and conveniently bypass what would be a far less certain, messy and painful psychic journey.

Just as technological advances promote the *necessity* of digital networks, and 'the circulatory systems of flesh and blood are now relegated as merely accessories of bygone times' (Heartney 2004: 240), so a real relationship to the body, the self and with others can be opted in and out of with ever greater ease. Technology expands the boundaries of our bodies and in so doing changes the very way we relate (Raphael-Leff forthcoming). Indeed, while communication between adolescents through texts and emails superficially may give the impression of close and intimate exchanges, in those young people for whom the body is felt to be terrifying, this virtual intimacy may paradoxically alienate them further from the reality of being-in-a-body.[5] This may create greater difficulties in integrating the sensual and sexual body into a stable self-representation and into meaningful relationships with others.

We start life in our body and it is our first point of contact with the world of other people. Throughout life we have to accommodate the reality of the body – a reality that is infinitively varied since being-in-a-body, as we have seen, acquires idiosyncratic meanings for each of us depending on the complex interaction between our given body and the body imaginings that become associated with it through processes of projection and introjection.

The body is an arena of a potentially terrifying lack of control. Clothing, hairstyles, make-up are established, acceptable ways through which we all negotiate separation and difference, and hence the development of the self. We need only reflect on our own adolescence to see how profoundly fears of intrusion or castration can be expressed, and somehow managed, through the negotiation of dress and hairstyle. These more everyday ways of customising the body are an inevitable aspect of what it means to be human. I hope that it will be clear by now that I regard body modification practices that are felt to be psychically *necessary* as attempts to control an otherwise disturbing otherness in oneself.

As I have been emphasising throughout, the body always bears the trace of the other. This fundamental psychic truth has to be somehow integrated into our image of ourselves. Facing the reality of the body thus involves a paradox: it means simultaneously taking ownership of the body, its desires and limitations, *and* integrating the fact that the body is the site where we meet the other, where we negotiate the meaning of sameness and difference, of dependency and separation.

Of course, death is the ultimate 'otherness' – an otherness in the sense that it reveals to us in the starkest manner that the body we have is effectively only on loan. It can never be said to belong to us in any absolute sense – we have to hand it back, as it were, accepting its indefatigable journey towards death. Much as we try to control our bodies through various kinds of bodily modification, the body has the last laugh: it modifies itself, gradually and inexorably throughout the life cycle. The uniquely human knowledge of the body's limitations – of death – is hard to bear and we institute defences against this knowledge at both an individual and collective level as a society. Elevating our bodies from their flesh and bones reality to a higher plane as objects of beauty is one way in which we try to separate ourselves from the reality of death (Goldenberg et al. 2000).

Like it or not we are all 'terminal cases' (Cronenberg quoted in Rodley 1997). As Freud (1916) grasped in his paper *On Transience*, gratitude for something ephemeral is hard won and requires the work of mourning. Freud (1916) brings home to us the pain and gains to be had from the capacity to mourn. The challenge of acknowledging our transient nature lies in bearing the guilt and loss that 'are essential to the ability to fully apprehend oneself as *existing in time* . . . the pain inherent in the recognition of the transience of all things' (Bell 2006: 803, my italics). Indeed the capacity to face the reality of the body, and the inevitable changes it will undergo through puberty and the process of ageing, facilitates healthy psychic development across the lifespan. When this integration is not possible, the individual's relationship to reality is profoundly affected and psychotic solutions are instituted, and are often expressed through the body.

One way in which we can bypass the psychic work necessary to 'exist in time' (Bell 2006) is to maintain a mind/body split: body modification panders to this. Ostensibly attending to the body through its embellishment, this is a body without a mind. Where body modification is used defensively body and mind are kept apart precluding symbolisation of the psychic pain that drives these pursuits. Those who become very focused on the body's appearance speak about 'taking care of the body', and may genuinely feel that this is what they are doing. But in truth they are sometimes dangerously divorced from the reality of the body, from its porous origins, from its inevitable ties to the (m)other, from its transient nature.

At its best, however, the body is the site for the most loving exchanges and sense of community (Silverman 1996). If we are to experience it thus, mind and body need to be managed as inseparable. We need to reclaim the body from its relative neglect in our subjective experience, in our social life, in our analytic thinking and practice, otherwise thinking itself is not possible.

With this in mind I want to end with the words of the French philosopher, Gilles Deleuze. Influenced by Spinoza and Nietzsche, he posits a parallelism between body and thought, emphasising how the very opacity and insubordination of the flesh is a stimulus to thought. Rather than being an obstacle to be overcome so as to reach thinking, Deleuze (1989) argued, that the body is what

> plunges us into, or must plunge into, in order to reach the unthought, that is, life. Not that the body thinks, but obstinate and stubborn, it forces us to think and it forces us to think what is concealed from thought: life.
>
> (Deleuze 1989: 189)

For Deleuze the body was the most direct reminder that we are only ever one step *behind* ourselves, always in the process of catching up with what we do not yet know, with what we have not yet thought. The body, like the unconscious, surpasses the knowledge we have of it. To highlight the body is not to devalue thought, but rather it cuts down to size the importance we would rather accord to consciousness in relation to our mind. It is the acknowledgement of the reality of the unconscious: '[it is] a discovery of the unconscious, an unconscious of thought just as profound as the unknown of the body' (Deleuze 1988: 18–19).

Notes

Introduction: body as canvas

1 Bronstein (2009) has helpfully distinguished the way in which we can think of the body as being the source and content of unconscious phantasy, and the arena on which unconscious phantasy is enacted.

2 Like many aspects of the frame, the use of the couch is most probably as much for the benefit of the therapist as it is for the patients. Indeed, Freud was quite explicit about this: he is reputed to have remarked that sitting behind the patient, out of sight, was a safe haven which freed him from the burden of being stared at all day (Ross 1999).

3 Perhaps this explains why we appear to have somehow retreated from sexuality and desire too, even though our clinical work attests to the fundamental influence of sexuality, in spite of the obscurity of its manifestations. This has indeed led some authors to suggest that we have 'desexualised' psychoanalysis (Fonagy and Target 2007).

4 Pitts-Taylor (2007: 21) makes the important additional point that 'the sentiment against elective beautification surgery as self-harming, unnatural, or inauthentic [is] an idea based on assumptions about the natural, proper, healthy body as pristine and unmodified . . . and that the self appears more or less fixed'.

5 The impact of socio-cultural and political forces on the individual's experience of the body have been well documented elsewhere, and I will not be concentrating on this in any depth in this book since my aim is primarily to focus on the unconscious function of body modification.

6 Most of our judgements of other people's character are mediated by our perception and evaluation of their body. This process of stereotypical inferencing is evidenced as early as six years of age (Rumsey et al. 1986). Moreover, we use stereotypes freely and unthinkingly, and frequently make inaccurate judgements (Rumsey and Harcourt 2005). Even so, we make them and they can have powerful consequences. It has been repeatedly shown, for example, that attractive children are judged to have more social appeal as well as greater interpersonal competence (Langlois et al. 2000). One of the most common experiences cited by children who are bullied is that this was on account of their appearance, and we know that appearance-related teasing can have enduring negative effects (Tantleff-Dunn and Gokee 2002; Buhlmann et al. 2007).

7 Cross-cultural studies have highlighted the different body ideals that dominate particular cultures. For example, African American men and women have been shown to be more positive about 'overweight' in women relative to white American counterparts (Harris et al. 1991). In a British study that controlled for

the effect of body size, less dissatisfaction with body size was reported among Asian British women relative to the white women (Wardle et al. 1993). However, there is some suggestion that as a result of the widespread influence of white cultural ideals of beauty that Hispanic and Asian women are experiencing greater levels of dissatisfaction with their bodies (Grogan 2008). Other studies (e.g. Lee and Lee 1999) suggest that in China, for example, the more developed the economy in certain provinces, the greater the likelihood of a preoccupation with weight.

Although many cross-cultural studies suggest that different body ideals dominate in different cultures, some studies suggest that there tends to be broad agreement across cultures on which *faces* are considered beautiful (e.g. Jones and Hill 1993). Such studies, however, ignore the fact that what we find attractive fluctuates within an individual, and historically over time. The perception of beauty or ugliness is closely connected with our internal states of mind (see Chapter 2) – the research simply does not do justice to the dynamic interplay between the internal and the external in determining what we consider to be beautiful.

8 A related challenge in writing on this subject is the potential for sensationalising extreme forms of body modification, which invariably arouse curiosity and voyeuristic impulses, probably in all of us.

1 As you desire me

1 Indeed, Lacan's notion of lack is a recent example of the metaphysical tradition that set up a dualism of body/mind and of nature/culture.

2 Kristeva (1995) describes this as the 'semiotic chora'.

3 Kristeva therefore distinguishes between 'the semiotic, which consists of drive-related and affective meanings organised according to primary processes whose sensory aspects are often non-verbal . . . and linguistic signification that is manifested in linguistic signs' (Kristeva 1995: 104). We will return to Kristeva's ideas in more detail in Chapter 5.

4 See Lacan's (1977) very helpful notion of lack (*manque-a-être*).

5 As I mentioned in the Introduction, the content of these projections will reflect cultural processes too.

6 Although it is by no means always exclusively the mother who is the primary caregiver, this is by far the most common scenario for the newborn baby.

7 Olivier (1989) has discussed the deleterious impact on children of both sexes of the all-too-present mother of early childhood and the not-present-enough father. My own views have been very much informed by her compelling argument in this respect and I am very indebted to her for this.

8 I will not discuss all the assessments due to constraints of space, but instead will draw on two in particular.

9 My task was to determine whether these girls were psychologically 'fit' to take part.

10 Some years ago I was asked to advise on, with a view to then screening participants, another show that would involve a complete, invasive 'overhaul' of the participants' appearance through cosmetic surgery. In the event I did not undertake the screenings because I felt uncomfortable with the ethics of this particular programme, but I was very struck to note that a significant proportion of the women who had put themselves forward had been adopted. One can only speculate about the possible unconscious motivations for extensively modifying the body given a history of early abandonment by the birth parents. But this

interesting finding is noteworthy, possibly lending support to the observations I made through assessing the young women. For some of these women, the modification of the body may unconsciously represent an attempt at finding a desirable form – an opportunity to remodel the body to achieve a perfect form – that would protect against the threat, or the actual reality, of being abandoned.

11 Laplanche (1989) refers to 'enigmatic signifiers' to denote an experience that we know is meant to signify something to us, but we do not yet have a 'signified' which we can ascribe to it. He also terms 'seduction' those infantile encounters with the adult unconscious that are inevitably intrusive because the adult does not master them, hence they can be 'traumatic'.

2 The symptom of ugliness

1 The male birth myth is central to *Frankenstein*'s narrative, but it features a great deal in horror films:

> In his attempt to create new life, the male womb monster of the horror film re-creates an intra-uterine mise en scène, a maternal landscape, which is symbolically his womb, his birth-giving place. He gives physical form to an unconscious memory of his first home.
>
> (Creed 2005: 43)

2 The biographical information was collated from the following sources: Bennett (1988), Spark (1988), St Clair (1989) and Hindle (1994).

3 Of course, the 'filthy creation' might also refer to Mary Shelley's view of the Little William who supplants her in her father's affections.

4 Although infant deaths were not infrequent in those times, this is unlikely to have eased the pain of the loss.

5 When I had almost finished writing this book, my attention was drawn to a most interesting, insightful and non-clinical book by Blum (2003) on cosmetic surgery, in which she also refers to Frankenstein's narrative and draws conclusions very similar to my own.

6 Evolutionary theorists suggest that this is probably because symmetry is an indication of genetic fitness.

7 In a related vein, Bell (2006: 804) has suggested that 'aging objects (a fact of life) are thought of as damaged objects (that is, as having been damaged), and so perception of them stirs guilt.' Nowadays looking old is all too readily equated with something ugly, set apart, something that needs to be covered up so that we can bypass knowledge of our own potential, and sometimes actual, destructiveness and the ensuing guilt.

3 Mirrors

1 According to Lacan (1977), the child is born into the order of the Real – an anatomical, natural order. The mirror stage heralds the end of the Real. This gap propels the baby into seeking an identificatory image of its own stability and permanence (the Imaginary) and eventually language (the symbolic) by which it hopes to fill the lack.

2 Lacan describes two poles around which the ego is oriented, *affairmement jubilatoire* and *connaissance paranoiaque*: joyful, affirmative self-recognition (in which the ego anticipates the unity of its image) and a paranoid knowledge produced by a split, miscognising subject.

3 Self-serving biases are prototypical for healthy people and there is evidence to suggest that they maintain mental health and protect against depression (Brewin 1993; Taylor and Brown 1994).

4 For the reasons I outline I am using the term 'body imagining(s)' in preference to 'body image' or 'body representation', but not as distinct from these terms. The body imagining is, however, *not* to be equated with the body of Lacan's Imaginary.

5 Spitz (1961) even suggested physiological 'prototypes' for psychic mechanisms of defence in early development.

6 It has been persuasively suggested that there exists continuity from pre-natal development onward (Piontelli 1992). An interesting question is the extent to which intrauterine touch contributes to the eventual body imagining.

7 Some studies suggest that it is not just touch that is the critical variable. Korner (1990), for example, in a study with human infants, demonstrated that it was the combined effect of touch and vestibular-proprioceptive stimulation that had an impact on infant soothing.

8 An intriguing study investigating the differential impact of maternal versus paternal touch on children's perception of their bodies, indicated that for both genders the tactile qualities later associated with a sophisticated body concept and positive feelings about their bodies were of a 'somewhat vehement, instrumental or dynamic nature' (Weiss 1990: 450).

9 I am indebted to Lemche's (1998) comprehensive and detailed review of this literature, which provides an invaluable guide to what is a vast body of work.

10 Schilder (1950) observed that the voice and language itself are also an important part of the body imagining; for example, they may have the unconscious meaning of bodily excretions or they may be subjectively experienced as 'weak'.

11 Some individuals find the notion of an inner bodily region very threatening and it may therefore be denied, thereby distorting the body imagining.

12 Although I am referring here to an actual father, it goes without saying that if the father is absent, what is important developmentally is the acknowledgement of the reality of the father in the mother's mind.

4 Being seen or being watched

1 A version of this chapter appeared in Lemma, A. (2009) Being seen or being watched? A psychoanalytic perspective on body dysmorphia. *International Journal of Psychoanalysis*, 4: 753–771.

2 The Wolf Man is a good example of this with his imagined defects on his nose and his obsessive mirror checking (see Brunswick 1971).

3 I am suggesting it is a *contributing* factor because I consider that the baby's innate dispositions also invariably interact with the mother's responses.

4 It is of note that in BDD the bodily preoccupation is commonly located above the neck, very frequently the skin surface (75 per cent), but also the shape of the head, hair, facial features (Phillips 2005) – significantly the first physical sites of meeting between mother and baby. I understand this as suggestive of a deficit in the libidinal investment in the body by the 'object of desire' at the level of early skin-to-skin, face-to-face contact. Although concern with genitals is also encountered, this is far less common (approximately 7 per cent of BDD patients). By contrast, in anorexia, the body dissatisfaction is typically located below the neck, in the lower body areas: the more sexual areas such as breasts, stomach and thighs (Cororve and Gleaves 2001). In anorexia the anxiety thus

appears to be linked more specifically to the sexual – as opposed to the sensual – body and its unconscious meaning.

5 This 'observing' other, as Steiner (2006: 942) suggests, is frequently represented by 'an observing part of the primary object, often the mother's eyes'.

6 Unsurprisingly, actual attempts to alter the reviled body part have been shown not to lead to an improvement in how the patient feels: one study found that following cosmetic procedures 50 per cent of patients diagnosed with BDD transferred their preoccupation to another body area (Veale 2000). Mean satisfaction ratings with the outcome of cosmetic surgery also tend to drop after each procedure suggesting that, at some level, in his disgruntled relationship with the cosmetic surgeon, the patient enacts something of the experience with an internal object that can never be satisfied enough and with whom he is now identified. The surgeon now becomes the one who cannot produce the perfect body that will guarantee the patient's approving look. This may account for the reportedly frequent threats of violence towards cosmetic surgeons and litigation by disgruntled patients.

7 This is, of course, only a hypothesis which requires testing.

8 Perhaps unsurprisingly, such patients are typically found to also have a co-morbid avoidant personality disorder (Neziroglu et al. 1996).

9 Although she was clearly in the grip of a psychotic state of mind, she was not psychotic in the psychiatric sense.

5 Occupied territories and foreign parts: reclaiming the body

1 I am emphasising here the imprint of the mother as in many cases she is the first object desire, but clearly there will be individuals for whom the body is felt to be problematic because of the relationship with the father or because of the particular quality of the phantasy of the parental couple – a point I will return to in Chapter 6.

2 Such an assumption is not inconsistent with the developmental studies that reveal how the baby unconsciously processes the facial expressions and bodily postures of the person he is interacting with and is able to match them (Beebe et al. 2003).

3 Kristeva (1995) outlines an important difference between what she calls the *semiotic* and Lacan's *symbolic*:

> the semiotic [which] consists of drive-related and affective meaning organised according to primary processes whose sensory aspects are often non-verbal (sound and melody, rhythm, colour, odours and so forth), on the one hand, and linguistic signification that is manifested in linguistic signs and their logico-syntactic organisation, on the other.
>
> (Kristeva 1995: 104)

The semiotic (i.e. the study of signs) is thus the pre-verbal way in which bodily energy and affects make their way into language. In other words she suggests that Lacan's imaginary realm, rather than being transcended and hence beyond the ken of analysis, is instead discernible (and needs attending to) thanks to its traces in the semiotic. The semiotic could thus be seen as the modes of expression that originate in the unconscious whereas the symbolic could be seen as the conscious way people try to express themselves using a stable sign system (e.g. written or spoken). In this way Kristeva's framework sidesteps unhelpful dichotomies, arguing instead that the semiotic pole (nature/body/unconscious) always makes itself felt, that is, it is discharged into the symbolic realm (culture/mind/consciousness). The pre-symbolic dimension, with its affect-driven modes of signification, is therefore never out of range and remains a companion in the process of signification.

4 I understood this as defensive in nature in so far as the films allowed for a greater distance to be maintained from his own unconscious. The perverse sexuality and violence that he was so preoccupied with could not have been as readily kept at bay if these themes arose from the more incontrovertible, personal productions of his own unconscious through dreams.

5 Our culture's profound ambivalence towards all forms of embodiment and birthing is the source of much horror (Creed 1993; Shaviro 1993) – a point we will return to in Chapter 6.

6 Cronenberg's fascination with the body may well be related to the loss of both his parents, especially his father whom he witnessed deteriorating through a degenerative disease, though Cronenberg himself has always been keen to distinguish between the impact this had on him personally (which he readily acknowledges) and the relationship between these personal events and the content of his films (which he denies).

7 Brundle's genetic fusion with a fly provides a highly original and disturbing twist on our resistance to the reality of the changing body. Seth Brundle's inexorable bodily transformation uncannily parallels the transformations of puberty, vividly illustrating the agonising time of sexual maturation combined with the crisis of identity that accompanies it.

8 In the closing scenes one of the twins brings her to mind as he recalls that 'Mum forgot to buy the ice cream' for one of their parties. In other words, she comes to mind in her forgetfulness, underlining the pain of absence and loss of the mother – a loss that was never mourned.

9 This is a powerful metaphor for the way we increasingly seek to realign our minds, bodies and sexuality to dominant technologies.

6 Copies without originals: envy and the maternal body

1 First published in a slightly altered version in © *The psychoanalytic Quarterly*, 2010, 79(1).

2 Money-Kyrle (1968) identified three 'facts of life', namely the difference between the generations, the parental relationship, and the reality of time and death.

3 I will discuss one case here and the other two in Chapter 7.

4 Of course, paradoxically, fashion represents a customisation of the body's surface that bears a collective rather than an individual stamp.

5 Both Ms F. (see Chapter 5) and Ms W. had both been exposed to early illness and hospitalisation, and hence their earliest experience of the body was its fragility and utter dependency. It would be interesting to investigate, across a larger sample, how frequent such experiences are in these patients.

6 These photos are often unappealing to the Western eye: Orlan's eyes peer through faces characterised by elongated necks and noses or strange protruberances.

7 All these quotes are taken from published interviews with Stelarc, accessible from his authorised website: www.stelarc.va.com.au/arcx.html.

7 The Botoxing of experience

1 This notion is central to Rosenfeld's (1971) view on destructive narcissism which emphasises a gang-like structure in the mind (a destructive component of the personality) whose raison d'être is to sustain the self in the thrall of the superiority and power of destructive narcissism.

2 I am very grateful to Professor Nick Lowe for drawing my attention to these figures.
3 There is evidence to suggest that patients who request breast reductions in particular, for example, display good post-operative adjustment (Sarwer et al. 2006).
4 See Lemoine-Luccioni (1983) and Silverman (1986) for very interesting discussions of clothing as a kind of skin.

8 Ink, holes and scars

1 The first ever tattoo was reported by Captain Cook.
2 In certain African groups, such as the Baugwe of Cameroon, scarifications are performed to enhance beauty and signal social status. In other groups, such as among the Tiv, they also determine territorial rights, suitability as a potential marriage partner, land usage, and hence are central to social organisation.
3 For example, blood is important in Yoruban ritual ceremonies because it contains ashe, the potential to bring things into existence.
4 For a long time tattoos were associated with deviant practice. The psychoanalyst Albert Parry wrote about the significance of tattoos and embedded stereotypes of deviants in the public discourse. He called tattooing a 'tragic miscarriage of narcissism' (Parry 1933). He claimed that tattooing was a substitute for sexual pleasure, evidence of homosexuality and a source of masochistic pleasure. His work had quite an impact and shaped the subsequent interpretation of tattoos by psychologists who tended to view tattooed men and women as evidencing psychopathology. Many of these studies concentrated on people in the military and in the navy and concluded that the tattooed individuals displayed social and emotional maladjustment greater than that found in those who were not tattooed. (Lander and Kohn 1943; Post 1968). Many studies linked multiple tattoos with antisocial personality disorder and increased aggressive behaviour towards others and impulsivity. Methodologically speaking, however, these are not very good studies and, notably, they ignore the effects of the institutional milieu on the decision to be tattooed.
5 However, for some it marks acceptance into a particular subgroup within which skin markings are an important social currency, and therefore could be construed as making the person more attractive in that particular group.
6 By focusing on the individual level of analysis I am not wishing to deny the equally important social meaning of the punk movement – it is simply not the level of analysis that I am concerned with here.
7 Sometimes, as we have seen, this 'other' is society or the mainstream and consequently skin markings have always held appeal for particular subgroups. This is a recurring theme in the published narratives of those who have been tattooed and is consistent with the greater prevalence of tattoos and other forms of skin markings in particular subcultures.

Conclusion: an order of pure decision

1 Danny – not his real name – gave me permission at the time to make use of the work we had done together for teaching purposes. I think it was his way of expressing gratitude for the help he felt he had received.
2 At the time laser treatments for the removal of tattoos were not as advanced as they are nowadays and the results were often very poor.

3 The various interpretations historians have offered of the changing meaning of the body in the twenty-first century in the West suggest that as public life recedes in significance, the idea of control can illuminate our attitudes towards body modification and the commercial growth in this domain (Sennett 1977; Giddens 1991). As the postmodern world steeps itself in greater impermanence, fragmentation and constant flux, Giddens and others argue that we defensively retreat into personal, local preoccupations through the cultivation of the body, thereby removing it from its likeness to other animals, which otherwise roots us in our finite nature (Goldenberg et al. 2000). This more domestic preoccupation with our own body diverts us from the global questions we would otherwise need to face and that would steep us in preoccupations that bring us closer in touch with basic needs and ontological anxieties. Fearful and out of control, we seek to beautify what we think we can control.

4 This point has also been persuasively made by Susie Orbach (2009).

5 Sigman (2009) has drawn attention to the potentially deleterious impact of social networking sites on both relationships and possibly even on biology.

References

Abraham, K. (1924) A Short Study of the Development of the Libido Viewed in Light of Mental Disorders. In K. Abraham (1979) *Selective Papers on Psychoanalysis*. London: Maresfield.

Ainsworth, M., Blehar, M., Walters, E. and Rohl, S. (1978) *Patterns of Attachment*. Hillsdale, NJ: Lawrence Erlbaum.

Aisenstein, M. (2006) The Indissociable Unity of Psyche and Soma. *International Journal of Psychoanalysis* 87: 667–680.

Alvarez, A. (1999) *Live Company*. London: Routledge.

Anderson, F. (ed.) (2008) *Bodies in Treatment*. New York: Analytic Press.

Anzieu, D. (1989) *The Skin Ego*. New Haven, CT: Yale University Press.

Anzieu, D. (1990) *A Skin for Thought: Interviews with Gilbert Tarrab on Psychology and Psychoanalysis*. London: Karnac.

Aouizerate, B., Pujol, H., Grabot, D., Faytout, M., et al. (2003) Body Dysmorphic Disorder in a Sample of Cosmetic Surgery Applicants. *European Psychiatry* 18(7): 365–368.

Armstrong, M. and Pace-Murphy, K. (1997) Tattooing: Another Adolescent Risk Behavior Warranting Health Education. *Applied Nursing Research* 10(4): 181–189.

Armstrong, M., Stuppy, D. and Gabriel, D. (1996) Motivation for Tattoo Removal. *Archives of Dermatology* 132(4): 412–416.

Bakhtin, M. (1984) *Rabelais and his World*. Bloomington, IN: Indiana University Press.

Barnard, J. and Brazelton, T. (eds) (1990) *Touch: The Foundation of Experience*. Madison, CT: International Universities Press.

Bateman, A. (1995) Thick and Thin Skinned Organizations and Enactment in Borderline and Narcissistic Disorders. *International Journal of Psychoanalysis* 79: 13–25.

Bates, B. and Cleese, J. (2001) *The Human Face*. London: BBC Publications.

Baudrillard, J. (1988) *The Ecstasy of Communication*, trans. B. Schutze and C. Schutze. Paris: Galilee.

Becker, E. (1973) *The Denial of Death*. New York: Free Press.

Beebe, B., Knoblauch, S., Rustin, J. and Sorter, D. (2003) Introduction: A Systems View. *Psychoanalytic Dialogues* 13: 743–775.

Bell, D. (2006) Existence in Time: Development or Catastrophe. *Psychoanalytic Quarterly* 75: 783–805.

Bennett, B. (ed.) (1988) *The Letters of Mary Wollstonecraft and Shelley*. Baltimore, MD: Johns Hopkins University Press.

Bernstein, D. (1993) Female Genital Anxieties, Conflict and Typical Mastery Modes. In D. Breen (ed.) *The Gender Conundrum*. London: Routledge.

Bick, E. (1968) The Experience of the Skin in Early Object Relations. *International Journal of Psychoanalysis* 49: 558–566.

Bion, W. (1962) *Learning from Experience*. London: Karnac.

Birksted-Breen, D. (1996) Phallus, Penis and Mental Space. *International Journal of Psychoanalysis* 77: 649–657.

Bloom, K. (2006) *The Embodied Self: Movement and Psychoanalysis*. London: Karnac.

Blum, V. (2003) *Flesh Wounds: The Culture of Cosmetic Surgery*. Los Angeles, CA: University of California Press.

Bollas, C. (1987) *The Unthought Known*. London: Free Association Books.

Bolognini, S. (2008) *Passaggi Segreti: Teoria e tecnica della relazione interpsichica*. Torino: Bollati Boringhieri.

Bordo, S. (2003) *Unbearable Weight: Feminism, Western Culture, and the Body*. Los Angeles, CA: University of California Press.

Botting, F. (ed.) (1995) *Frankenstein*. Basingstoke: Palgrave Macmillan.

Bourdieu, T. (1984) *A Social Critique of the Judgment of Taste*. London: Routledge & Kegan Paul.

Brain, R. (1978) *The Decorated Body*. London: Harper Row.

Brazelton, T. and Cramer, B. (1989) *The Earliest Relationship*. London: Karnac.

Brewin, C. (1993) *Cognitive Foundations of Clinical Psychology*. Hove: Lawrence Erlbaum.

Britton, R. (1993) The Missing Link: Parental Sexuality in Oedipus Complex. In D. Breen (ed.) *The Gender Conundrum*. London: Routledge.

Britton, R. (1998) *Belief and Imagination*. London: Routledge.

Bronstein, C. (2009) Negotiating Development: Corporeal Reality and Unconscious Phantasy in Adolescence. *Bulletin of the British Psychoanalytical Society* 45(1): 17–26.

Brooks, P. (1995) What is a Monster? In S. Botting (ed.) *Frankenstein*. Basingstoke: Palgrave Macmillan.

Brooks, T., Waltz, E., Knight, J. and Shrier, L. (2003) Body Modification and Substance Use in Adolescents: Is There a Link? *Journal of Adolescent Health* 32: 44–49.

Brunswick, R. (1971) Pertaining to the Wolf Man: A Supplement to Freud's 'The History of an Infantile Neurosis'. *Revista de psicoanálisis* 35: 5–46.

Bucci, W. (2008) The Role of Bodily Experience in Emotional Organisation: New Perspectives on the Multiple Code Theory. In S. Anderson (ed.) *Bodies in Treatment*. Hove: Analytic Press.

Buhlmann, U., Etcoss, N. and Wilhelm, F. (2004) Emotion Recognition Bias for Contempt and Anger in Body Dysmorphic Disorder. *Journal of Psychiatric Research* 40: 105–111.

Buhlmann, U., Cook, L., Farmer, J. and Wilhelm, F. (2007) Perceived Teasing Experiences in Body Dysmorphic Disorder. *Body Image* 4: 381–385.

Campbell, B. (2008) The Father Transference during a Pre-Suicide State. In S. Briggs, A. Lemma and W. Crouch (eds) *Relating to Self Harm and Suicide: Psychoanalytic Perspectives on Practice, Theory and Prevention*. London: Routledge.

Campbell, D. and Hale, R. (1991) Suicidal Acts. In J. Holmes (ed.) *Textbooks of Psychotherapy in Psychiatric Practice*. London: Churchill Livingstone.

Carroll, S., Riffenburgh, R., Roberts, T. and Myhre, E. (2002) Tattoos and Body Piercing as Indicators of Adolescent Risk Taking Behaviour. *Paediatrics* 109: 1021–1027.

Cixous, F. (1976) The Laugh of Medusa. In E. Marks and I. de Courtivon (eds) *New French Feminisms*. Brighton: Harvester.

Clyman, R.B. (1991) The Procedural Organization of Emotions: A Contribution from Cognitive Science to the Psychoanalytic Theory of Therapeutic Action. *Journal of the American Psychoanalytic Association* 39S: 349–382.

Cororve, M. and Gleaves, D. (2001) Body Dysmorphic Disorder: A Review of Conceptualizations, Assessments and Treatment Strategies. *Clinical Psychology Review* 21(6): 949–970.

Cowie, E. (1984) Fantasia. *m/f* 9: 71–105.

Creed, B. (1989) Horror and the Monstrous-Feminine. In J. Donald (ed.) *An Imaginary Abjection*. London: British Film Institute.

Creed, B. (1993) *The Monstrous Feminine: Film, Feminism, Psychoanalysis*. London: Routledge.

Creed, B. (2005) *Phallic Panic: Film, Horror and the Primal Uncanny*. Melbourne: Melbourne University Press.

Damasio, A. (2000) *The Feeling of What Happens: Body, Emotion and the Making of Consciousness*. London: Vintage.

Davis, K. (1995) *Re-shaping the Female Body: The Dilemma of Cosmetic Surgery*. New York: Routledge.

Deleuze, G. (1988) *Spinoza: Practical Philosophy*, trans. R. Hurley. San Francisco, CA: City Lights.

Deleuze, G. (1989) *Cinema 2: The Time Image*, trans. H. Tomlinson and R. Galata. Minneapolis, MN: University of Minnesota Press.

DeMello, M. (2000) *Bodies of Inscription: A Cultural History of the Modern Tattoo Community*. Durham, NC: Duke University Press.

Douglas, M. (1966) *Purity and Danger: An Analysis of Concepts of Pollution and Taboo*. London: Routledge & Kegan Paul.

Durand, R. (2004) Texts for Orlan. In R. Durand and E. Heartney (eds) *Orlan: Carnal Art*. Paris: Flammarion.

Dyl, J., Kittler, J., Phillips, K. and Hunt, J. (2006) Body Dysmorphic Disorder and Other Clinically Significant Body Image Concerns in Adolescent Psychiatric Inpatients. *Child Psychiatry and Human Development* 36(4): 369–382.

Edgerton, M., Langmann, M. and Pruzinsky, T. (1990) Patients Seeking Symmetrical Re-contouring for Perceived Deformities in the Width of the Face and Skull. *Aesthetic Plastic Surgery* 14: 59–73.

Elliott, C. (2003) Magic Way to True Self. *The Times Higher Educational Supplement* 30 May: 14.

Ely, B. (1964) *Seconds: A Novel*. London: André Deutsch.

Ercolani, M., Baldaro, B., Rossi, N., Trombini, E. and Trombini, G. (1999) Short

Term Outcome of Rhinoplasty for Medical or Cosmetic Indication. *Journal of Psychosomatic Research* 47: 277–281.

Erlich, S. (2008) Envy and Gratitude: Some Current Reflections. In P. Roth and A. Lemma (eds) *Envy and Gratitude Revisited.* London: Karnac.

Ewald, F. (1993) Two Infinities of Risk. In B. Massumi (ed.) *The Politics of Everyday Fear.* Minneapolis, MN: University of Minnesota Press.

Farrow, J., Schwartz, R. and Vanderleeuw, J. (1991) Tattooing Behaviour in Adolescence. *American Journal of Diseases of Children* 145: 184–187.

Favazza, A. (1996) *Bodies under Siege: Self Mutilation and Body Modification in Culture and Psychiatry.* Baltimore, MD: Johns Hopkins University Press.

Featherstone, M. (ed.) (2000) *Body Modification.* London: Sage.

Feingold, A. and Mazzella, R. (1998) Gender Differences in Body Image are Increasing. *Psychological Science* 9: 190–195.

Feldman, M. (2009) *Doubt, Conviction and the Analytic Process.* London: Routledge.

Fenichel, O. (1945) *The Psychoanalytic Theory of Neurosis.* New York: Norton.

Ferenczi, S. (1938) *Thalassa: A Theory of Genitality.* New York: Psychoanalytic Quarterly.

Ferrari, B. (2004) *From the Eclipse of the Body to the Dawn of Thought.* London: Free Association Books.

Flanders, S. (2009) On the Concept of Adolescent Breakdown. *Bulletin of the British Psychoanalytical Society* 45(1): 27–34.

Fonagy, P. (2006) Psychosexuality and Psychoanalysis. In P. Fonagy, R. Krause and M. Leuzinger-Bohleber (eds) *Identity, Gender and Sexuality.* London: IPA Publications.

Fonagy, P. and Target, M. (1999) Towards Understanding Violence: The Use of the Body and the Role of the Father. In R. Perelberg (ed.) *Psychoanalytic Understanding of Violence and Suicide.* London: Routledge.

Fonagy, P. and Target, M. (2007) The Rooting of the Mind in the Body: New Links between Attachment Theory and Psychoanalytic Thought. *Journal of American Psychoanalytic Association* 55(2): 411–456.

Fraiberg, S., Adelson, E. and Shapiro, V. (1975) Ghosts in the Nursery. *Journal of the American Academy of Child Psychiatry* 14: 387–422.

Frank, A. (1991) For a Sociology of the Body: An Analytical Review. In N. Featherstone, M. Hepworth and B. Turner (eds) *The Body: Social Process and Cultural Theory.* London: Sage.

Fraser, K. (2007) 'Now I am ready to tell how bodies are changed into different bodies. . .': Ovid, The Metamorphoses. In D. Heller (ed.) *Makeover Television: Realities Remodelled.* London: I.B. Tauris.

Freud, S. (1914) On Narcissism. In *The Standard Edition of the Complete Psychological Works of Sigmund Freud.* London: Hogarth (S.E.) 14.

Freud, S. (1915) *Instincts and their Vicissitudes.* S.E. 14.

Freud, S. (1916) *On Transience.* S.E. 14.

Freud, S. (1917) *Mourning and Melancholia.* S.E. 14.

Freud, S. (1919) *The Uncanny.* S.E. 17.

Freud, S. (1923) *The Ego and the Id.* S.E. 19.

Freud, S. (1924) *The Dissolution of the Oedipus Complex.* S.E. 19.

Freud, S. (1937) *Analysis Terminable and Interminable.* S.E. 23.

Freud, S. (1940) *An Outline of Psychoanalysis*. S.E. 23.

Frosh, S. (1994) *Sexual Difference: Masculinity and Femininity in Psychoanalysis*. London: Routledge.

Gaddini, E. (1969) On Imitation. *International Journal of Psychoanalysis* 50: 475–484.

Gaddini, E. (1987) Notes on the Mind–Body Question. *International Journal of Psychoanalysis* 68: 315–329. Reprinted in E. Gaddini (1992) *A Psychoanalytic Theory of Infantile Experience*. London: Routledge.

Gailey, E. (2007) Self Made Women: Cosmetic Surgery Shows and the Construction of Female Psychopathology. In D. Heller (ed.) *Makeover Television: Realities Remodelled*. London: I.B. Tauris.

Giddens, A. (1991) *Modernity and Self Identity*. Cambridge: Polity.

Gilman, S. (1999) *Making the Body Beautiful: A Cultural History of Aesthetic Surgery*. Princeton, NJ: Princeton University Press.

Glasser, M. (1979) Some Aspects of the Role of Aggression in the Perversions. In I. Rosen (ed.) *The Pathology and Treatment of Sexual Deviations*. Oxford: Oxford University Press.

Gliori, D. (2003) *No Matter What!* London: Bloomsbury.

Glover, E. (1956) *On the Early Development of the Mind*. New York: International Universities Press.

Gold, S. (1985) Frankenstein and Other Monsters: An Examination of the Concepts of Destructive Narcissism, and Perverse Relationships between Parts of the Self as Seen in the Gothic Novel. *International Review of Psychoanalysis* 12: 101–108.

Goldenberg, J., Pyszczynski, P., Greenberg, J. and Solomon, S. (2000) Fleeing the Body: A Terror Management Perspective on the Problem of Human Corporality. *Personality and Social Psychology Review* 4: 200–218.

Goldwyn, R. (2006) Psychological Aspects of Plastic Surgery: A Surgeon's Observations and Reflections. In D. Sarwer, T. Pruzinsky, T. Cash, R. Goldwyn, et al. (eds) *Psychological Aspects of Reconstructive and Cosmetic Plastic Surgery*. Philadelphia, PA: Lippincott, Williams & Wilkins.

Goodall, J. (2000) An Order of Pure Decision: Un-natural Selection in the Work of Stelarc and Orlan. In M. Featherstone (ed.) *Body Modification*. London: Sage.

Green, A. (1983) The Dead Mother. In A. Green (1986) *On Private Madness*. London: Hogarth.

Green, A. (1998) The Primordial Mind and the Work of the Negative. *International Journal of Psychoanalysis* 79: 649–665.

Green, A. (2004) Thirdness and Psychoanalytic Concepts. *Psychoanalytic Quarterly* 73: 99–135.

Greenacre, P. (1958) Early Physical Determinants in the Development of the Sense of Identity. *Journal of the American Psychoanalytic Association* 6(4): 612–627.

Greenacre, P. (1960) Considerations Regarding the Parent–Infant Relationship. *International Journal of Psychoanalysis* 41: 571–584.

Greif, J., Hewitt, W. and Armstrong, M. (1999) Tattooing and Body Piercing: Body Art Practices among College Students. *Clinical Nursing Research* 8(4): 368–385.

Grogan, S. (2008) *Body Image: Understanding Body Dissatisfaction in Men, Women and Children*. London: Routledge.

Grosz, E. (1990) *Jacques Lacan: A Feminist Introduction*. London: Routledge.

Grumet, G. (1983) Psychodynamic Implications of Tattoos. *American Journal of Orthopsychiatry* 53(3): 482–492.

Guignard, S. (2008) Envy in Western Society: Today and Tomorrow. In P. Roth and A. Lemma (eds) *Envy and Gratitude Revisited*. London Karnac.

Haag, G. (1985) La Mère et le bébé dans les deux moites du corps. *Neuropsychiatrie de l'enfance* 33: 107–114.

Hagglund, T. and Piha, H. (1980) The Inner Space of the Body Image. *Psychoanalytic Quarterly* 49: 256–283.

Hagman, G. (2002) The Sense of Beauty. *International Journal of Psychoanalysis* 83: 661–674.

Hagman, G. (2003) On Ugliness. *Psychoanalytic Quarterly* 72: 959–985.

Haiken, E. (1997) *Venus Envy: A History of Cosmetic Surgery*. Baltimore, MD: Johns Hopkins University Press.

Hale, R. (2008) Psychoanalysis and Suicide: Process and Topology. In S. Briggs, A. Lemma and W. Crouch (eds) *Relating to Self Harm and Suicide: Psychoanalytic Perspectives on Practice, Theory and Prevention*. London: Routledge.

Hambly, W. (1925) *The History of Tattooing and its Significance*. London: Witherby.

Hanly, C. (1984) Ego Ideal and Ideal Ego. *International Journal of Psychoanalysis* 65: 253–258.

Harlow, H. and Zimmerman, R. (1959) Affective Responses in the Infant Monkey. *Science* 130: 421–432.

Harris, M., Walters, L. and Waschull, S. (1991) Gender and Ethnic Differences in Obesity Related Behaviours and Attitudes in College Sample. *Journal of Applied Social Psychology* 21: 1545–1566.

Heartney, E. (2004) Orlan: Magnificent 'and' Best. In R. Durand and E. Heartney (eds) *Orlan: Carnal Art*. Paris: Flammarion.

Henry, T. (1989) *Break All Rules? Punk Rock and the Making of a Style*. Ann Arbor, MI: UMI Research Press.

Hewitt, K. (1997) *Mutilating the Body: Identity in Blood and Ink*. Bowling Green, OH: Bowling Green State University Popular Press.

Hindle, M. (1994) *Mary Shelley's Frankenstein*. London: Penguin.

Hoffer, W. (1949) Mouth, Hand and Ego Integration. *Psychoanalytic Study of the Child* 3: 49–56.

Hoffer, W. (1950) Development of the Body Ego. *Psychoanalytic Study of the Child* 5: 18–24.

Houghton, S., Durkin, K., Parry, E., Turbet, Y., et al. (1996) Amateur Tattooing Practices and Beliefs among High-school Adolescents. *Journal of Adolescent Health* 19(6): 420–425.

Humm, M. (1997) *Feminism and Film*. Bloomington, IN: Indiana University Press.

Ince, K. (2000) *Orlan: Millennial Female*. Oxford: Berg.

Jackson, L. (2002) Physical Attractiveness: A Socio-cultural Perspective. In T. Cash and T. Pruzinsky (eds) *Body Image: A Handbook of Theory, Research and Clinical Practice*. New York: Guilford.

Jacobsen, P., Hölmich, L., McLaughlin, J., Johansen, C., et al. (2004) Mortality and Suicide among Danish Women with Cosmetic Breast Implants. *Archives of Internal Medicine* 164: 2450–2455.

Jacobson, Y. and Luzzatto, D. (2004) Israeli Youth Body Adornments: Between Protest and Conformity. *Young* 12(2): 155–174.

Jansen, A., Smeets, T., Martijn, C. and Nederkoorn, C. (2006) 'I see what you see': The Lack of a Self-Serving Body Image Bias in Eating Disorders. *British Journal of Clinical Psychology* 45: 123–135.

Jones, D. and Hill, K. (1993) Criteria of Physical Attractiveness in Five Populations. *Human Nature* 4: 271–296.

Kelly, S., Iverson, J., Terranova, J., Niego, J., et al. (2004) Putting Language Back in the Body: Speech and Gesture in Three Time Frames. *Developmental Neuropsychology* 22: 323–349.

Kestenberg, J.S., Marcus, H., Robbins, E., Berlowe, J. and Buelte, A. (1971) Development of the Young Child as Expressed through Bodily Movement. *Journal of the American Psychoanalytic Association* 19: 746–764.

Kestner, J. (1995) Narcissism as Symptom and Structure: The Case of Mary Shelley's Frankenstein. In S. Botting (ed.): *Frankenstein*. Basingstoke: Palgrave Macmillan.

Kilborne, B. (2002) *Disappearing Persons: Shame and Appearance*. New York: State University of New York Press.

Klein, M. (1932) *The Psychoanalysis of Children*. London: Hogarth.

Klein, M. (1935) Contributions to the Psycho-Genesis of Manic Depressive States. In M. Klein, *Love, Guilt and Reparation and Other Works, 1921–1945*. London: Hogarth.

Klein, M. (1936) On Weaning. In M. Klein, *Love, Guilt and Reparation and Other Works, 1921–1945*. London: Hogarth.

Klein, M. (1946) Notes on Some Schizoid Mechanisms. In M. Klein, *Envy and Gratitude and Other Works, 1946–1963*. London: Hogarth.

Klein, M. (1952) Some Theoretical Conclusions Regarding the Emotional Life of the Infant. In M. Klein, *Envy and Gratitude and Other Works, 1946–1963*. London: Hogarth.

Klein, M. (1957) *Envy and Gratitude and Other Works*. London: Virago.

Korner, A. (1990) The Many Faces of Touch. In K. Barnard and T. Brazelton (eds) *Touch: The Foundation of Experience*. Madison, CT: International Universities Press.

Kristeva, J. (1982) *Powers of Horror: An Essay on Abjection*, trans. L.S. Roudiez. New York: Columbia University Press.

Kristeva, J. (1995) *New Maladies of the Soul*. New York: Columbia University Press.

Krueger, D. (1989) *Body Self and Psychological Self*. New York: Brunner/Mazel.

Krueger, D. (2004) Psychodynamic Perspectives on Body Image. In T. Cash and T. Pruzinsky (eds) *Body Image: A Handbook of Theory, Research and Clinical Practice*. New York: Guilford.

Kuczynski, A. (2006) *Beauty Junkies: Under the Skin of the Cosmetic Surgery Industry*. New York: Doubleday.

Lacan, J. (1953) Some Reflections on the Ego. *International Journal of Psychoanalysis* 34: 351–356.

Lacan, J. (1977) *Ecrits*. London: Tavistock.

Lacan, J. (1982) *Female Sexuality*, edited by J. Mitchell and J. Rose. New York: Norton.

Lambrou, C. (2006) Aesthetic Sensitivity in Body Dysmorphic Disorder, PhD thesis, University of London.

Lander, J. and Kohn, H. (1943) A Note on Tattooing among Selectees. *American Journal of Psychiatry* 100: 326–327.

Langlois, J., Kalakanis, L., Rubinstein, A., Larson, A., et al. (2000) Maxims or Myths of Beauty? A Meta-analytic and Theoretical Review. *Psychological Bulletin* 1(6): 390–423.

Laplanche, J. (1989) *New Foundations for Psychoanalysis*. Oxford: Oxford University Press.

Laufer, E. (1981) The Adolescent's Use of the Body in Object Relationships and in the Transference. *Psychoanalytic Study of the Child* 36: 163–180.

Laufer, E. (no date) The Body as Internal Object. Unpublished conference paper.

Laufer, M. (1968) The Body Image, the Function of Masturbation and Adolescence: Problems of the Ownership of the Body. *Psychoanalytic Study of the Child* 23: 114–137.

Laufer, M. and Laufer, E. (1984) *Adolescence and Developmental Breakdown*. New Haven, CT: Yale University Press.

Lee, A. and Lee, S. (1999) Disordered Eating in Three Communities in China: A Comparative Study of High School Students in Hong Kong, Shenzhen and Rural Hunan. *International Journal of Eating Disorders* 27: 312–316.

Lee, H.B. (1948) Spirituality and Beauty in Artistic Experience. *Psychoanalytic Quarterly* 17: 507–523.

Lemche, E. (1998) Development of the Body Image in the First Three Years of Life. *Psychoanalysis and Contemporary Thought* 21: 155–275.

Lemma, A. (2000) *Humour on the Couch*. London: Whurr.

Lemma, A. (2005) The Many Faces of Lying. *International Journal of Psycho-analysis* 86: 737–753.

Lemma, A. (2008) Keeping Envy in Mind: The Vicissitudes of Envy in Adolescent Motherhood. In P. Roth and A. Lemma (eds) *Envy and Gratitude Revisited*. London: Karnac.

Lemma, A. (2009) Being Seen or Being Watched? A Psychoanalytic Perspective on Body Dysmorphia. *International Journal of Psychoanalysis* 4: 753–771.

Lemoine-Luccioni, E. (1983) *La Robe: Essai psychoanalytique sur le vêtement*. Paris: Seuil.

Lentini, P. (1998) The Cultural Politics of Tattooing. *Arena* 13: 31–50.

Lester, B., Hoffman, J. and Brazelton, T. (1984) The Rhythmic Structure of Mother Infant Interaction in Term and Pre-Term Infants. *Child Development* 56: 15–27.

Levy, S. and Lemma, A. (2004) *The Perversion of Loss: Psychoanalytic Perspectives on Trauma*. London: Whurr.

Lichtenberg, J. (1975) The Development of the Sense of Self. *Journal of the American Psychoanalytic Association* 23: 357–385.

Lichtenberg, J. (1978) The Testing of Reality from the Standpoint of the Body Self. *Journal of the American Psychoanalytic Association* 26: 453–484.

Lombardi, R. (2002) Primitive Mental States and the Body: A Personal View of Armando B. Ferrari's Concrete Original Object. *International Journal of Psychoanalysis* 83: 363–381.

Lombardi, R. (2009) Through the Eye of the Needle: The Unfolding of the

Unconscious Body. *Journal of the American Psychoanalytic Association* 57(1): 61–94.

McDougall, J. (1974) The Psychosoma and the Psychoanalytic Process. *International Review of Psychoanalysis* 1: 437–459.

McDougall, J. (1989) *Theatres of the Body*. London: Free Association Books.

McDougall, J. (1995) *The Many Faces of Eros*. London: Free Association Books.

Mahler, M. and Furer, M. (1968) *On Human Symbiosis and the Vicissitudes of Individuation*. New York: International Universities Press.

Mahler, M., Pine, F. and Bergman, A. (1975) *The Psychological Birth of the Human Infant*. New York: Basic Books.

Main, M. (1990) Parental Aversion to Infant Contact. In K. Barnard and T. Brazelton (eds) *Touch: The Foundation of Experience*. Madison, CT: International Universities Press.

Mancia, M. (1994) *L'Eclissi del corpo: una ipotesi psicoanalitica* (Eclipse of the Body: A Psychoanalytical Hypothesis) By Armando B. Ferrari. Roma: Borla. 1993. Pp. 212. *International Journal of Psychoanalysis* 75: 1283–1286.

Marty, P. (1980) *L'Ordre psychosomatique*. Paris: Payot.

Matte-Blanco, I. (1975) *The Unconscious as Infinite Sets*. London: Duckworth.

Meltzer, D. (1964) The Differentiation of Somatic Delusions from Hypochondria. *International Journal of Psychoanalysis* 45: 246–250.

Meltzer, D. (1967) Identification and Socialization in Adolescents. *Contemporary Psychoanalysis* 3: 96–103.

Meltzer, D. (1988) *The Apprehension of Beauty*. Strath Tay, Scotland: Clunie Press.

Meltzoff, A. (1990) Towards a Developmental Cognitive Science: The Implications of Cross Model Matching and Imitation for the Development of Representation and Memory in Infancy. *Annals of the New York Academy of Science* 608: 1–37.

Melzack, R. (1990) Phantom Limbs and the Concept of the Neuromatrix. *Trends in Neuroscience* 13: 88–92.

Mifflin, M. (1997) *Bodies of Subversion*. New York: Juno.

Milner, M. (1985) The Role of Illusion in Symbol Formation. In M. Klein, P. Heimann and R. Money-Kyrle (eds) *New Directions in Psychoanalysis*. London: Maresfield.

Money-Kyrle, R. (1968) On Cognitive Development. *International Journal of Psychoanalysis* 49: 691–698.

Musafar, F. (1996) Body Play: State of Grace or Sickness? In A. Favazza, *Bodies under Siege*. Baltimore, MD: Johns Hopkins University Press.

Myers, J. (1992) Nonmainstream Body Modification: Genital Piercing, Branding, Burning, and Cutting. *Journal of Contemporary Ethnography* 21(3): 290–292.

Neziroglu, F., McKay, D., Todaro, J. and Yaryura-Tobias, J. (1996) Effect of Cognitive-Behaviour Therapy on Persons with Body Dysmorphic Disorder and Co-morbid Axis II Diagnoses. *Behaviour Therapy* 27: 67–77.

Ogden, T. (1989) On the Concept of an Autistic-Contiguous Provision. *International Journal of Psychoanalysis* 70: 127–140.

Oliver, K. (1993) *Reading Kristeva: Unraveling the Double-Bind*. Bloomington, IN: Indiana University Press.

Olivier, C. (1989) *Jocasta's Children: The Imprint of the Mother*. London: Routledge.

Orbach, S. (1978) *Fat is a Feminist Issue*. London: Arrow.

Orbach, S. (2009) *Bodies*. London: Profile.

Orlan (2004) Orlan Interviewed by Hans Ulrich Obrist. In R. Durand and E. Heartney (eds) *Orlan: Carnal Art*. Paris: Flammarion.

O'Shaughnessy, E. (1999) Relating to the Superego. *International Journal of Psychoanalysis* 80: 861–870.

Osman, S., Cooper, M., Hackmann, A. and Veale, D. (2004) Spontaneously Occurring Images and Early Memories in People with Body Dysmorphic Disorder. *Memory* 12: 428–436.

Pacteau, F. (1994) *The Symptom of Beauty*. London: Reaktion.

Parry, A. (1933) *Tattoo: Secrets of a Strange Art*. New York: Dover.

Peringer, J. (2006) The Wish to Look and the Hatred of Seeing. *Bulletin of the British Psychoanalytical Society* 42(1): 18–27.

Phillips, K. (2005) *The Broken Mirror*. Oxford: Oxford University Press.

Phillips, K. and Diaz, S. (1997) Gender Differences in Body Dysmorphic Disorder. *Journal of Nervous and Mental Disease* 185: 570–577.

Phillips, K., McElroy, S., Keck, P., Pope, H. and Hudson, J. (1993) Body Dysmorphic Disorder: Thirty Cases of Imagined Ugliness. *American Journal of Psychiatry* 150: 302–308.

Phillips, K., Dufresne, R., Wilkel, C. and Vittorio, C. (2000) Rate of Body Dysmorphic Disorder in Dermatology Patients. *Journal of the American Academy of Dermatology* 42(3): 436–441.

Phillips, K., Didie, E., Menard, W., Pagano, M., et al. (2006) Clinical Features of Body Dysmorphic Disorder in Adolescents and Adults. *Psychiatry Research* 141(3): 305–314.

Pine, F. (2000) Preface. In M. Mahler, F. Pine and A. Bergman, *The Psychological Birth of the Human Infant*. New York: Basic Books.

Piontelli, A. (1992) *From Fetus to Child*. London: Routledge.

Pirandello, L. (2005) *If You Desire Me*. London: Oberon.

Pitts, V. (2003) *The Cultural Politics of Body Modification*. New York: Palgrave Macmillan.

Pitts-Taylor, V. (2007) *Surgery Junkies: Wellness and Pathology in Cosmetic Culture*. New Brunswick, NJ: Rutgers University Press.

Pope, H., Phillips, K. and Olivardia, R. (2000) *The Adonis Complex: The Secret Crisis of Male Body Obsession*. New York: Free Press.

Post, R. (1968) The Relationship of the Tattoo in Personality Disorder. *Journal of Criminal Law, Criminology and Police Science* 59: 516–524.

Pritchard, S. (2000) Essence, Identity, Signature: Tattoos and Cultural Property. *Social Semiotics* 10(3): 331–346.

Proust, M. (1972) *Remembrance of Things Past*. London: Wordsworth.

Raphaell-Leff, J. (forthcoming) Aliens and Alienation: Mind Invaders and Body Snatchers (under review).

Reite, M. (1990) Attach, Attachment, and Health: Is There a Relationship? In K. Barnard and T. Brazelton (eds) *Touch: The Foundation of Experience*. Madison, CT: International Universities Press.

Resnik, S. (2001) *The Delusional Person: Body Feelings and Psychosis*. London: Karnac.

Resnik, S. (2005) *Glacial Times: A Journey through the World of Madness*. London: Routledge.

Rey, H. (1994) *Universals of Psychoanalysis and the Treatment of Psychotic and Borderline States*. London: Free Association Books.

Rhode, M. (2005) Mirroring, Imitation, Identification: The Sense of Self in Relation to the Mother's Internal World. *Journal of Child Psychotherapy* 31(1): 52–71.

Rickman, J. (1951) Reflections on the Function and Organization of a Psycho-Analytical Society. *International Journal of Psychoanalysis* 32: 218–237.

Rickman, J. (1957) On the Nature of Ugliness and the Creative Impulse. *International Psychoanalytical Library* 52: 68–89.

Rilke, R.M. (1989) *Duino Elegies*, trans. S. Cohn. London: Carcanet.

Robbins, H. (1993) More Human than I am Alone: Womb Envy in *The Fly* and *Dead Ringers*. In S. Cohan and I.R. Hark (eds) *Screening the Male: Exploring Masculinities in Hollywood Cinema*. London: Routledge.

Rodin, J., Silberstein, L. and Streigel-Moore, R. (1985) Women and Weight: A Normative Discontent. In T. Souderegger (ed.) *Nebraska Symposium on Motivation, 32*. Lincoln, NE: University of Nebraska Press.

Rodley, C. (ed.) (1997) *Cronenberg on Cronenberg*. London: Faber & Faber.

Rosenblum, D., Daniolos, P., Kass, N. and Martin, A. (1999) Adolescents and Popular Culture: A Psychodynamic Overview. *Psychoanalytic Study of the Child* 54: 319–338.

Rosenfeld, H. (1971) A Clinical Approach to the Psychoanalytic Therapy of the Life and Death Instincts: An Investigation into the Aggressive Aspects of Narcissism. *International Journal of Psychoanalysis* 52: 169–178.

Rosenfeld, H. (1987) *Impasse and Interpretation*. London: Routledge.

Ross, J. (1999) Once More onto the Couch. *Journal of the American Psychoanalytic Association* 47(1): 91–111.

Rubenstein, A.J., Kalakanis, L. and Langlois, J.H. (1999) Infant Preferences for Attractive Faces: A Cognitive Explanation. *Developmental Psychology* 35: 848–855.

Rubenstein, M. (1976) My Accursed Origin: The Search for the Mother in Frankenstein. *Studies in Romanticism* 15: 165–194.

Rumsey, N. and Harcourt, D. (2005) *The Psychology of Appearance*. Maidenhead: Open University Press.

Rumsey, N., Bull, R. and Gahagan, D. (1986) A Preliminary Study of the Potential Social Skills for Improving the Quality of Social Interaction for the Facially Disfigured. *Social Behaviour* 1: 143–145.

Sander, L. (1988) The Event-Structure of Regulation in the Neonate-Caregiver System as a Biological Background for Early Organisation of Psychic Structure. In A. Goldberg (ed.) *Frontiers and Self Psychology*. Hillsdale, NJ: Analytic Press.

Sanders, C. and Vail, D. (2008) *Customising the Body: The Art and Culture of Tattooing*. Philadelphia, PA: Temple University Press.

Sandler, J. (1994) Phantasy, Defence and the Representational World. *Infant Mental Health* 15: 26–35.

Sartre, J-P. (1943) *Being and Nothingness*. London: Methuen.

Sarwer, D. (2006) Psychological Assessment of Cosmetic Surgery Patients. In D. Sarwer, T. Pruzinsky, T. Cash, R. Goldwyn, et al. (eds) *Psychological Aspects of Reconstructive and Cosmetic Plastic Surgery*. Philadelphia, PA: Lippincott, Williams & Wilkins.

Sarwer, D., Wadden, T., Pertschuk, M. and Whitaker, L. (1998) Body Image

Dissatisfaction and Body Dysmorphic Disorder in 100 Cosmetic Surgery Patients. *Plastic and Reconstructive Surgery* 101(6): 1644–1649.

Sarwer, D., Zanville, H., LaRossa, D., Bartlett, S., et al. (2004) Mental Health Histories and Psychiatric Medication Usage among Persons who Sought Cosmetic Surgery. *Plastic and Reconstructive Surgery* 114: 1927–1933.

Sarwer, D., Pruzinsky, T., Cash, T., Goldwyn, R., et al. (eds) (2006) *Psychological Aspects of Reconstructive and Cosmetic Plastic Surgery*. New York: Lippincott, Williams & Walkins.

Schacter, D. (1987) Implicit Memory: History and Current Status. *Journal of Experimental Psychology* 13: 501–518.

Schafer, R. (1960) The Loving and Beloved Superego in Freud's Structural Theory. *Psychoanalytic Study of the Child* 15: 163–188.

Schilder, P. (1950) *The Image and Appearance of the Human Body*. New York: International Universities Press.

Searles, H. (1963) The Place of Neutral Analyst-Responses in Psychotherapy with the Schizophrenic Patient. In H. Searles, *Collected Papers on Schizophrenia and Related Subjects*. London: Hogarth.

Seeger, J. (1993) Charting Ancient Waters with the Titans of Tribal. *Skin and Ink* October: 4–13.

Segal, H. (1952) A Psychoanalytical Approach to Aesthetics. *International Journal of Psychoanalysis* 33: 196–207.

Sennett, R. (1977) *The Fall of Public Man*. Cambridge: Cambridge University Press.

Shaviro, S. (1993) *The Cinematic Body*. Minneapolis, MN: University of Minnesota Press.

Shelley, M. (1818) *Frankenstein*. London: Penguin Classics.

Shelley, M. (1831) Author's Introduction to the First Novel Edition. In M. Shelley (1818) *Frankenstein*. London: Penguin Classics.

Sigman, A. (2009) Well Connected? The Biological Implications of Social Networking. *Biologists* 56(1): 14–20.

Silverman, K. (1986) Fragments of a Fashionable Discourse. In T. Modleski (ed.) *Studies in Entertainment*. Bloomington, IN: Indiana University Press.

Silverman, K. (1996) *The Threshold of the Visible World*. New York: Routledge.

Smolak, L. (2004) Body Image in Children and Adolescents: Where Do We Go from Here? *Body Image: An International Journal of Research* 1: 15–28.

Sodre, I. (2002) Certainty and Doubt: Transparency and Opacity of the Object. *Bulletin of the British Psychoanalytical Society* 38: 1–8.

Spark, M. (1988) *Mary Shelley*. London: Constable.

Spitz, R. (1961) Some Early Prototypes of Ego Defences. *Journal of the American Psychoanalytic Association* 9: 626–651.

Spitz, R. (1965) *The First Year of Life*. New York: International Universities Press.

Stanton, M., Wallstrom, J. and Levine, S. (1987) Maternal Contact Inhibits Pituitary-Adrenal Activity in Pre-weanling Rats. *Developmental Psychobiology* 20: 131–145.

St Clair, W. (1989) *The Godwins and the Shelleys: The Biography of a Family*. London: Faber & Faber.

Steiner, J. (1993) *Psychic Retreats*. London: Routledge.

Steiner, J. (2004) Gaze, Dominance and Humiliation in the Schreber Case. *International Journal of Psychoanalysis* 85: 269–284.

Steiner, J. (2006) Seeing and Being Seen: Narcissistic Pride and Narcissistic Humiliation. *International Journal of Psychoanalysis* 87: 939–951.

Steiner, J. (2008) The Repetition Compulsion, Envy, and the Death Instinct. In P.
Roth and A. Lemma (eds) *Envy and Gratitude Revisited.* London Karnac.

Stelarc (2009) Stelarc website. Available at www.stelarc.va.com.au (accessed 20
September 2009).

Stern, D. (1985) *The Interpersonal World of the Infant: A View from Psychoanalysis
and Developmental Psychology.* New York: Basic Books.

Stimmel, D. (2004) The Cause is Worse: Re-Meeting Jocasta. *International Journal
of Psychoanalysis* 85: 1175–1189.

Stoller, R. (1979) Fathers of Transsexual Children. *Journal of the American Psychoanalytical Association* 27: 837–866.

Sweetman, P. (2000) Anchoring the (Postmodern) Self? Body Modification, Fashion
and Identity. In M. Featherstone (ed.) *Body Modification.* London: Sage.

Tantleff-Dunn, S. and Thompson, K. (1998) Body Image and Appearance Related
Feedback: Recall, Judgement, and Affective Response. *Journal of Social and
Clinical Psychology* 17(3): 319–340.

Taylor, S. and Brown, J. (1994) Positive Illusions and Well-Being Revisited: Separating Fact from Fiction. *Psychological Bulletin* 116: 21–27.

Thompson, J. and Van Den Berg, P. (2002) Measuring Body Image Attitudes
among Adolescents and Adults. In T. Cash and T. Pruzinsky (eds) *Body Image: A
Handbook of Theory, Research and Clinical Practice.* London: Guilford.

Thompson, J., Heinberg, C., Altabe, J. and Tantleff-Dunn, S. (1999) *Exacting
Beauty: Theory, Assessment and Treatment of Body Image Disturbance.*
Washington, DC: American Psychological Association.

Turner, B. (2000) The Possibility of Primitiveness: Towards a Sociology of Body
Marks in Cool Societies. In M. Featherstone (ed.) *Body Modification.* London:
Sage.

Ulnik, J. (2007) *Skin in Psychoanalysis.* London: Karnac.

Vale, B. and Juno, A. (1990) Art Controversy is about Freedom of Expression. *San
Francisco Chronicle* 23 March.

Van Gennep, A. (1960) *The Rites of Passage.* Chicago, IL: University of Chicago
Press.

Veale, D. (2000) Outcome of Cosmetic Surgery and 'DIY' Surgery in Patients with
Body Dysmorphic Disorder. *Psychiatric Bulletin* 24: 218–221.

Veale, D. and Riley, S. (2001) Mirror, Mirror on the Wall, Who is the Ugliest of
Them All? The Psychopathology of Mirror-Gazing in Body Dysmorphic
Disorder. *Behaviour, Research and Therapy* 39: 1381–1393.

Veale, D., Boocock, A., Gournay, K. and Dryden, W. (1996) Body Dysmorphic
Disorder: A Survey of Fifty Cases. *British Journal of Psychiatry* 169: 196–201.

Verlaine, P. (1962) Mon rêve familier. In P. Verlaine, *Oeuvres Poétiques Complètes.*
Paris: Gallimard.

Waddell, M. (2007) Only Connect – The Links between Early and Later Life: In R.
Davenhill (ed.) *Looking into Later Life: The Psychoanalytic Approach to
Depression and Dementia in Old Age.* London: Karnac.

Wardle, J., Bindra, R., Fairclough, B. and Westcombe, A. (1993) Culture and Body
Image: Body Perception and Weight Concern in Young Asian and Caucasian

British Women. *Journal of Community and Applied Social Psychology* 3(3): 173–181.

Wardle, R. (ed.) (1966) *Godwin and Mary: Letters of William Godwin and Mary Wollstonecraft.* Lawrence, KS: University of Kansas Press.

Weiss, S. (1990) Parental Touching: Correlates of a Child Body Concept and Body Sentiment. In K. Barnard and T. Brazelton (eds) *Touch: The Foundation of Experience.* Madison, CT: International Universities Press.

Williams, G. (1997) *Foreign Bodies and Internal Landscapes.* London: Karnac.

Winnicott, D.W. (1945) Primitive Emotional Development. *International Journal of Psychoanalysis* 26: 137–143.

Winnicott, D.W. (1965) *The Maturational Processes and the Facilitating Environment.* New York: International Universities Press.

Winnicott, D.W. (1966) Psycho-Somatic Illness in its Positive and Negative Aspects. *International Journal of Psychoanalysis* 47: 510–516.

Winnicott, D.W. (1967) Mirror Role of Mother and Family in Child Development. In D.W. Winnicott, *Playing and Reality.* London: Tavistock.

Winnicott, D.W. (1972) Basis for Self in the Body. *International Journal of Child Psychotherapy* 1: 7–16.

Wojcik, D. (1985) *Punk and Neotribal Body Art.* Jackson, MS: University Press of Mississippi.

Wright, K. (1991) *Vision and Separation.* London: Free Association Books.

Yeats, W.B. (1865) Before the World was Made. In W.B. Yeats (1931) *A Woman Young and Old in the Collected Poems of W.B. Yeats.* London: Wordsworth.

Zugazagoitia, J. (2004) Orlan: The Embodiment of Totality? In R. Durand and E. Heartney (eds) *Orlan: Carnal Art.* Paris: Flammarion.

Index

abandonment 47, 48, 120, 163,
    179n10
abjection 95–6, 97, 101, 102, 166
abuse 1, 102, 156, 160, 163

'adhesive identification' 161–2
adolescence 6, 11, 22, 175; body
    dysmorphia 77; body imaginings 69,
    70; separation 93; taking control
    154–5; tattoos during 4, 17, 21, 70,
    154, 155
'aesthetic conflict' 39
ageing 131, 146, 176, 180n7
agoraphobia 93
amputation 61–2
anorexia 94, 114, 181n4; see also eating
    disorders
anxiety 83, 94, 101, 163; attachment 72;
    confusional 70; genital 69; maternal
    98; paranoid 80, 82, 128, 136, 142–4;
    persecutory 143; psychotic 103
Anzieu, Didier 65–6, 160, 161–2, 174
appearance anxiety 78
artistic works 23; Cronenberg's films 96,
    103–11, 116, 183n6; Orlan 121–5,
    183n5; Stelarc 125–8, 148
attachment 31, 66, 72

Bagwa people 16, 184n2
Bakhtin, M. 50–1, 166
Baudrillard, Jean 113
BDD see Body Dysmorphic Disorder
beauty 3, 15, 49–52, 74; cross-cultural
    studies 179n7; envy 117; media
    pressure 17–19; of mother 39–40;
    Orlan's work 125; pursuit of 131,
    137, 146; tyranny of 52–5, 131
beauty industry 14, 134

Becker, E. 174
Bell, D. 180n7
Bick, Esther 160–1
Birksted-Breen, D. 114
Blum, V. 180n5
body dissatisfaction 17–19, 21, 179n7
body; imaginings 61–73; mind-body
    dualism 11–12, 28, 176; mirror
    image 58–9, 60, 76
body dysmorphia 73, 74–7, 83–4;
    clinical examples 84–91; envy 117;
    satisfaction with surgery 182n6;
    thick and thin skinned 81–3, 84
Body Dysmorphic Disorder (BDD) 3,
    59, 61, 76–7, 83–4, 86—91, 136, 165,
    181n4; clinical examples 84–91; by
    proxy 54; satisfaction with surgery
    182n6; tattoos 165
body image 61, 62, 63, 75
body image disturbance 18–19, 60–1,
    70, 75
Bordo, S. 18
Botox 12, 131, 134, 137, 139
Brain, R. 16–17
branding 168, 170
Brazelton, T. 72
breast 39, 40, 65, 94; cosmetic surgery
    118–21, 136, 142–4; envy of the
    115–16
Bronstein, Catalina 11, 95, 178n1
The Brood (Cronenberg) 105–6
Brooks, P. 76

Cameroon 16, 184n2
children: body dissatisfaction 18; body-
    self development 63–71; mirror
    stage 58, 59–60; see also mother-
    infant relationship

claustrophobia 93, 142, 162
common skin 161–2
confusional anxiety 70
containment 160–1
control 78, 152, 154–5, 175, 185n3
Core Complex 93–4
cosmetic surgery 12, 24, 80, 81, 131–47;
    body dysmorphia 75, 77, 182n6;
    breast augmentation 118–21, 136,
    142–4; brief history of 132–4;
    clinical examples 98, 99–100, 101,
    103; computer simulations 174;
    makeover shows 13; Orlan 123–4,
    125; perfect match phantasy 79;
    preoccupation with 82; as 'prop to
    disintegrating personalities' 16–17;
    Seconds 129–30; self-made phantasy
    5, 30, 112, 113; skin modification
    comparison 164; tyranny of beauty
    54
cosmetics 16
Cosmopolitan 17
Cramer, B. 72
Crash (Cronenberg) 109–10
Creed, B. 180n1
Cronenberg, David 23, 96, 102, 103–11,
    116, 183n6
culture 4, 15–17, 18; body ideals 178n7;
    skin markings 149–51

Damasio, A. 62
Davis, K. 112
Dead Ringers (Cronenberg) 108–9
death 44, 45, 146, 175
Deleuze, Gilles 176–7
DeMello, M. 159, 160
dependency 2, 7–8, 29, 92, 113, 115,
    175
depression 78, 138
depressive position 146
Descartes, René 49–50
desirability 2, 3, 28–9, 35, 54, 56
desire 26–7, 29, 31–4, 40–1, 56; gender
    differences 33; Lacan 27, 28, 97;
    perfect match phantasy 34–9; the
    uncanny 102
Diderot, Denis 50
disfiguration 3
distorting-mirror-mother 79–81
Douglas, Mary 151
dreams 9–10, 89, 100–1, 106, 140–2, 143
drug abuse 1, 166

Durand, R. 122
dyadic body 7, 173

eating disorders 21, 61; see also anorexia
ego 10, 180n2; mirror image 58–60;
    'skin ego' 65–6, 161–2; see also self
Elliott, C. 133
Ely, David 129
envelope of suffering 162, 166
envy: Frankenstein 43, 45; maternal
    body 95, 114–18; self-made
    phantasy 5, 30, 113, 125
Erlich, S. 97
Ewald, F. 12
Extreme Makeover (TV show) 13

fantasies see phantasies
father 73, 97, 141, 144; absent 6–7,
    181n12; relationship with daughter
    33
Favazza, A. 5–6, 132, 150
Featherstone, M. 14
Feldman, M. 138
feminism 18–19, 131
Flanders, Sarah 11
flesh hangings 153
The Fly (Cronenberg) 107–8, 116
Fonagy, Peter 9, 11
Frank, A. 7
Frankenstein (Shelley) 42–7, 49, 52,
    75–6, 116
Fraser, K. 13
Freud, Sigmund: body, desire and
    sexuality 26; drives 10–11; ego 10;
    mother-infant relationship 32;
    mourning 175–6; narcissism 29;
    penis envy 117; 'repudiation of
    femininity' 115; the uncanny 101–2;
    use of the couch 178n2

Gaddini, E. 65, 117
gaze 3, 6, 27; Frankenstein 43, 45–6, 47;
    Lacan 28; mother's 31, 35, 38–9, 40,
    47, 56–8, 60; patient's 55;
    persecutory 61, 84; skin markings
    170–1; therapeutic relationship 8–9;
    see also vision
gender 23–4; body dissatisfaction 17;
    gendered body 19; genital anxieties
    69; mother-infant relationship 33;
    see also men; women
genitals 69, 70, 181n4

Giddens, A. 14, 173, 185n3
Gilman, S. 137
Glasser, M. 93–4
Gliori, D. 74
Godwin, William 47, 48–9
good-enough mother 30, 33, 57, 60, 84,
    96–7
Green, A. 10–11, 63, 78
Greenacre, P. 65, 67, 69
Grosz, E. 39
Guignard, S. 115, 174
guilt 131, 134, 137, 176, 180n7

Hagman, G. 52
Haiken, E. 132–3
Hamlet (Shakespeare) 32
Harlow, H. 65
hate 2, 3, 80; body dysmorphia 82;
    clinical examples 138, 139;
    Frankenstein 43; towards therapist
    83
horror: Cronenberg's films 104, 110,
    111; *Frankenstein* 43, 44; male birth
    myth 116, 180n1
humiliation 83

'ideal ego' 83
idealisation 29, 80, 140
identification 29–30, 63, 82, 117;
    'adhesive' 161–2; destructive 108;
    omnipotent object 12, 80; skin
    markings 170, 171; superego 84,
    90–1; *see also* projective
    identification
identity 4, 15; adolescence 155;
    alienation 58; body imaginings 69;
    Orlan 121; re-ordering of identity
    narratives 14; rites of passage 151;
    sexual 93; *see also* self
imitation 117
Ince, K. 123, 124
infant-mother relationship *see* mother-
    infant relationship
Internet 174
intimacy 7–8, 93, 157, 174
introjection 10, 15, 58; body imaginings
    63, 71, 175; Klein 95

Juno, A. 158

Kilborne, B. 78
Klein, Melanie 94–5, 96–7, 115–17

Korner, A. 181n7
Kristeva, Julia 23; abjection 95–6, 97,
    101–2, 166; maternal body 98, 102;
    the semiotic 28, 179n3, 182n3;
    'semiotic chora' 179n2

Lacan, J. 23, 76; desire 27, 28, 97; ego
    180n2; on *Hamlet* 32; 'lack' concept
    179n1, 179n4; mirror stage 58–60,
    95; the Real 180n1; specularity 15;
    the symbolic 182n3
Laplanche, J. 180n11
Laufer, Egle 11, 93
Laufer, Moses 11, 70, 93
Lemche, E. 181n9
Lentini, P. 153
Leonardo da Vinci 50
libido 31
loss 114–15, 128; denial of 170;
    Frankenstein 43, 46; mourning 176;
    pursuit of beauty 131, 134, 137;
    Shelley 48, 49

Main, M. 72
Mair, Avril 134
makeover shows 12–14, 22, 34–9, 117,
    179n10
masochism 151, 184n4
Matte Blanco, I. 40, 50
McDougall, Joyce 81
media pressure 14, 17–19, 91
Meltzer, D. 39, 40, 70, 78, 80, 103
memory 71–2
men: body dissatisfaction 17; male body
    17; *see also* gender
Mifflin, M. 148
Milner, M. 40
mind-body dualism 11–12, 28, 176
mirrors 56–61, 76; distorting-mirror-
    mother 79–81; Lacan's mirror stage
    58–60, 95; one-way-mirror-mother
    40, 77–9, 81; you-and-me-mirror-
    mother 80–1
Modern Primitives movement 153
monadic body 7–8, 173
Money-Kyrle, R. 113, 183n1
Moon, Julia 160
mother: abject 96, 97, 101; affective state
    67; beauty of 39–40; body
    imaginings 71, 72; desire 29, 31–4,
    56; distorting-mirror-mother 79–81;
    emotional unavailability 118–19;

envy of maternal body 114–18; *Frankenstein* 46–7, 49; good-enough 30, 33, 57, 60, 84, 96–7; grievance towards 146–7; idealised 146; maternal body 94–5, 97–8, 102, 106, 112, 114–18, 120–1; mirror role 29, 56–61, 77; neglectful 163; one-way-mirror-mother 40, 77–9, 81; Orlan 124; perfect match phantasy 34–9; as primary caregiver 24; psychic dependency 2; reclaiming phantasy 94; self-made phantasy 112, 113; separation from 3, 92–3, 97–8, 101, 114–15; symbiotic relationship with 7; tyranny of beauty 53–4; you-and-me-mirror-mother 80–1

mother-infant relationship 2, 6, 115; 'adhesive identification' 161–2; body-self development 63–71; containing object 160–1; desire 31–3; Klein 94–5, 96–7; mother-as-mirror 56–61, 77; object of desire 26–7

motor development 67–8

mourning 175–6

Musafar, Fakir 153

Myers, J. 158

narcissism 12, 25, 29, 86; body dysmorphia 76, 81, 82; defensive 60; destructive 183n1; *Frankenstein* 45; narcissistic envelope 162

neuromatrix theory 65

object of desire 26–7, 30, 31, 33–4, 39, 137, 181n4

Oedipus complex 31, 33, 83

Oliver, K. 97–8

Olivier, C. 179n7

omnipotence 12, 29, 114, 140, 172, 174

one-way-mirror-mother 77–9, 81

oral phase 95

Orbach, Susie 185n4

Orlan 23, 121–5, 183n5

Pacteau, F. 32, 50

pain 122–3, 151, 156, 157, 158; phantom limb 61–2; *see also* psychic pain

paranoia 45, 59, 82, 85

parental couple 113, 114, 139

Paris Psychosomatic School 11

Parry, Albert 184n4

phantasies 5, 11, 21, 31, 95, 178n1;

artistic works 23; body imaginings 63, 71; cosmetic surgery 137–8; distorting-mirror-mother 80; mother's 67, 72; omnipotent 140, 172, 174; skin markings 170–1; *see also* perfect match phantasy; reclaiming phantasy; self-made phantasy

photography 28

'physical transvestism' 117

piercings 151–2; caring for wounds 158–9; pain 156, 158; punk culture 165; taking control 154–5

Pirandello, L. 29

Pitts-Taylor, V. 178n4

postmodern body 18, 185n3

primitivism 153

projection 9, 10, 15; body dysmorphia 82; body imaginings 63, 71, 175; distorting-mirror-mother 79–80; *Frankenstein* 43, 46; Klein 95

projective identification 54, 81, 86; claustrophobia 93; *Frankenstein* 45, 46; 'physical transvestism' 117

Proust, M. 39–40

'psychic armour' 159

psychic dependency 2, 92

psychic pain 6, 12, 14, 19, 164, 176

'psychic retreat' 8, 11–12, 30, 131

psychosis 3, 34, 76, 104

puberty 69, 94, 176

punk culture 164–5, 169

Rabid (Cronenberg) 104

Raphael-Leff, J. 71, 72

reality TV shows 12–14, 22, 34–9, 117

reclaiming phantasy 5, 93, 94, 114; Orlan's work 125; skin markings 159–64, 170

rejection 43, 45–6, 47–8, 49, 76, 142

reparation 146

Resnik, S. 117

Rey, Henry 11, 93

Rickman, J. 51, 146

Rilke, R.M. 129

rites of passage 150–1, 158

ritual: abjection 102; Modern Primitives movement 153; primitive body modification practices 16; rites of passage 150–1; self-mutilation 5–6; Western beauty rituals 16–17

Rosenfeld, H. 81, 130, 183n1

sadism 21, 116–17
Sander, L. 66
Sartre, J.-P. 27–8, 40
scarification 16, 20, 150, 153; African
    groups 184n2; 'kiss of fire' 167, 168,
    170; pain 156
Schilder, P. 7, 15, 31, 62, 63, 181n10
Seconds (film) 129–31
Segal, H. 146
self: body-self development 63–71;
    idealised 83; integration of body-self
    6–7; mind-body dualism 11–12;
    mirror image 58–9, 61; narcissistic
    130; object of desire 26–7; one-way-
    mirror-mother 77–9; perfect match
    phantasy 5, 30; purification of the
    102; reclaiming phantasy 5, 159;
    secure sense of 173; self-made
    phantasy 5, 39; skin markings 151,
    152, 158, 161; ugliness as part of
    108; *see also* ego; identity
self-esteem 68, 133, 134
self-harm 4–5, 20, 76, 77
self-healing 6, 16
self-made phantasy 5, 30, 39, 112–14,
    131; clinical examples 141, 144;
    cosmetic surgery 137–8; Orlan's
    work 121, 125; paranoid anxiety
    144; 'perversion of loss' 49; skin
    markings 158, 170
self-mutilation 5–6, 165
self-regulation 66
self-stimulation 37
the semiotic 28, 179n3, 182n3
separation 3, 31, 92–3, 97–8, 175;
    abjection 101; *Dead Ringers* 109;
    denial of 170; distorting-mirror-
    mother 80; idealisation of 163; loss
    and 114–15; you-and-me-mirror-
    mother 80
sexuality 26, 32, 178n3
shame 30, 68
Shaviro, S. 104–5
Shelley, Mary 42–9, 74, 75–6, 180n3
Shivers (Cronenberg) 104–5
Sigman, A. 185n5
skin 148; common 161–2; containing
    function 160–1; Stelarc's work 126,
    127, 148
'skin ego' 65–6, 161–2
social status 150, 184n2
socio-cultural context 12–15, 19, 131

somatic delusion 80
specularity 15, 27–8
spirituality 4, 151, 152, 157
Spitz, R. 181n5
splitting 80, 82
Steiner, J. 115, 182n5
Stelarc 23, 125–8, 148, 183n6
Stimmel, D. 31
subcultures 17, 152, 159, 184n7
suicide 21, 77, 114, 136
superego 77, 83–4, 86, 90–1, 131
the symbolic 182n3
symmetry 50, 51

Tagliacozzi, Gaspare 132
Target, Mary 9, 11
tattoos 1–2, 4, 148, 172–3, 184n1;
    adolescence 4, 17, 21, 70, 154, 155;
    ancient peoples 15; caring for
    wounds 158–9; creativity 156–7;
    cross-cultural perspectives 16,
    149–51; deviance 184n4; facial 167,
    173; as mark of difference 164, 165;
    pain 156, 157; prevalence of 151–2;
    psychic meanings 9; reclaiming
    phantasy 159–64; as second skin
    161; taking control 154–5; visual
    violence 164–6
technology 173–5
television makeover shows 12–14, 22,
    34–9, 117, 179n10
Thompson, J. 18
touch 6, 43, 64, 67, 181n7; close physical
    contact 72; impact on self 31;
    importance of 65–6; maternal
    versus paternal 181n8; yearning for
    36–7
Turner, B. 151

ugliness 3, 50, 51–2, 55, 74; body
    dysmorphia 75, 76–7, 85; destructive
    impulses 146; distorting-mirror-
    mother 79, 80; *Frankenstein* 43,
    45–6; as part of the self 108;
    patient's anxiety 83
Ulnik, J. 161
the uncanny 102
uncertainty 40, 77, 78

Vale, B. 158
Van Gennep, A. 150–1
Veale, David 83–4

Verlaine, Paul 31
violence 21, 80; *Frankenstein* 43; history
    of physical/sexual 160; visual 164–6;
    see also abuse
virtual reality 174
vision 57, 64, 66, 67; *see also* gaze

Waddell, M. 146
Winnicott, Donald 60, 96
Wollstonecraft, Mary 47

womb envy 117
women: body dissatisfaction 17, 18;
    cosmetic surgery 12, 131; tattoos
    159; *see also* gender
Wright, K. 57–8

Yeats, W.B. 25
you-and-me-mirror-mother 80–1

Zimmerman, R. 65